Berlitz®

Eastern Europe

phrase book & dictionary

Berlitz Publishing
New York   London   Singapore

Contacting the Editors
Every effort has been made to provide accurate information in this publication, but changes are inevitable. The publisher cannot be responsible for any resulting loss, inconvenience or injury. We would appreciate it if readers would call our attention to any errors or outdated information. We also welcome your suggestions; if you come across a relevant expression not in our phrase book, please contact us at: **comments@berlitzpublishing.com**

All Rights Reserved
© 2015 Berlitz Publishing/APA Publications (UK) Ltd.
Berlitz Trademark Reg. U.S. Patent Office and other countries. Marca Registrada. Used under license from Berlitz Investment Corporation.

First Printing: 2015
Printed in China

Senior Commissioning Editor: Kate Drynan
Translation: updated by Alingua
Simplified phonetics: updated by Wordbank
Cover & Interior Design: Beverley Speight
Production Manager: Vicky Mullins
Picture Researcher: Beverley Speight interior; Tom Smyth cover
Cover Photo: all Micah Sarut except Richard Scofield green Russian building; iStockphoto coins, babuska dolls and red building

Interior Photos: all iStockphoto except red heart and Krakow monument Corrie Wingate; Rod Purcell Old Town Square Prague

Contents

How to use this Book

> Sometimes you see two alternatives separated by a slash. Choose the one that's right for your situation.

ESSENTIAL

I'm on vacation [holiday]/business.	**Jam me pushime/udhëtim pune.** *Yam meh poosheemeh/oodhehteem pooneh*
I'm going to...	**Po shkoj né...** *Poh shkoy neh...*
I'm staying at the...Hotel.	**Po qëndroj në Hotelin...** *Poh shkoy neh...*

> Words you may see are shown in YOU MAY SEE boxes.

YOU MAY SEE...

pagesa për hyrjen	cover charge
cmimi fiks	fixed price
specialitetet	specials

> Any of the words or phrases listed can be plugged into the sentence below.

Tickets

A...ticket.	**Një biletë...** *Nyeh bee-let-ëh...*
one-way	**njëdrejtimëshe** *nyedreyteemsheh*
return trip	**vajtje-ardhje** *vaytyeh-ardhye*
first class	**klasi i parë** *klaseeh ee pahreh*

Albanian phrases appear in purple.

Read the simplified pronunciation as if it were English. For more on pronunciation, see page 8.

Accepting & Rejecting

I'll come by at... **Do të vij në orën...** *Doh teh veey neh ohren*

I'm busy. **Jam i zënë *m*/e zënë *f***
Yam ee zehneh/eh zehneh.

For Social Media, see page 15.

Related phrases can be found by going to the page number indicated.

When different gender forms apply, the masculine form is followed by *m*; feminine by *f*

In an emergency, dial:
129 for the police
128 for the fire brigade
127 for an ambulance.

Information boxes contain relevant country, culture and language tips.

Expressions you may hear are shown in You May Hear boxes.

YOU MAY HEAR...

Plotësoni formularin. Fill out this form.
Plohtehsohnee formoolahreen

Color-coded side bars identify each section of the book.

Albanian

Essentials

Good morning.	**Mirëmëngjes.** *meermemjyehs*
Good afternoon.	**Mirëdita.** *meerdeetah*
Good night.	**Natën e mirë.** *nahtehn eh meer*
Good-bye.	**Mirupafshim.** *meeroopahfsheem*
Yes/No/Okay.	**Po/Jo.** *poh/yoh*
Excuse me!	**Më falni!** *(formal)*/**Më fal!** *(informal)*
(to get attention)	*meh fahlnee/meh fahl*
Excuse me.	**Më falni.** *meh fahl-nee*
(to get past)	
I'm sorry.	**Më falni.** *meh fahl-nee*
(when distrubing sb)	
I'm sorry. (apology)	**Më vjen keq.** *meh vyen kech*
I'd like…	**Do të doja…** *Doh teh doyah*
How much?	**Sa?** *sah*
And/or.	**Dhe/ose.** *Dheh/oseh*
Please.	**Të lutem.** *teh lootehm*
Thank you.	**Faleminderit.** *fahlehmeendehreet*
You're welcome.	**Ju lutem./Asgjë.** *Yoo lootehm*
Where is/are…?	**Ku është/janë…?** *koo ehshteh/yahn*
I'm going to…	**Po shkoj në…** *poh shkoy neh*
My name is…	**Unë quhem…** *oon chyoohehm…*
Please speak slowly.	**Ju lutem, flisni më ngadalë.**
	Yoo lootem, flees-neeh meh ngadahleh
Can you repeat that?	**A mund ta përsërisni atë që thatë?** *Ah moon tah pehr-*
	seh-reesneeh ahteh chyeh thahteh?
I don't understand.	**Nuk kuptoj.** *nook kooptoy*
Do you speak English?	**Flisni anglisht?** *fleesnee ahngleesht*
I don't speak	**Nuk flas (shumë)** *nook flahs (shoom)*
(much) Albanian.	**shqip.** *shchyeep*
Where's the restroom	**Ku është banjoja [tualeti]?** *koo ehshteh banyoya/*
[toilet]?	*too-ah-letty*
Help!	**Ndihmë!** *ndeehmeh*

You'll find the pronunciation of the Albanian letters and words written in gray after each sentence to guide you. Simply pronounce these as if they were English. As you hear the language being spoken, you will quickly become accustomed to the local pronunciation and dialect.

Numbers

0	**zero** *zehroh*
1	**një** *nyeh*
2	**dy** *duy*
3	**tre** *treh*
4	**katër** *kahter*
5	**pesë** *pehseh*
6	**gjashtë** *jâsht*
7	**shtatë** *shtaht*
8	**tetë** *teht*
9	**nëntë** *nehnteh*
10	**dhjetë** *dhyet*
11	**njëmbëdhjetë** *nyehmbehdhyet*
12	**dymbëdhjetë** *duy mbehdhyehteh*
13	**trembëdhjetë** *trehmbehdhyehteh*
14	**katërmbëdhjetë** *kahtermbehdhyehteh*
15	**pesëmbëdhjetë** *pehsehmbehdhyehteh*
16	**gjashtëmbëdhjetë** *jyahshtehmbehdhyehteh*
17	**shtatëmbëdhjetë** *shtahtehmbehdhyehteh*
18	**tetëmbëdhjetë** *tehtehmbehdhyehteh*
19	**nëntëmbëdhjetë** *nentehmbehdhyehteh*
20	**njëzetë** *nyehzeht*
21	**njëzetë një** *nyehzeht eh nye*
30	**tridhjetë** *treedhyeht*
40	**dyzetë** *duyzeht*
50	**pesëdhjetë** *pehsehdhyeht*
60	**gjashtëdhjetë** *jyahshtehdhyeht*
70	**shtatëdhjetë** *shtahtehdhyeht*
80	**tetëdhjetë** *tehtehdhyeht*

90	**nëntëdhjetë** *nentehdhyeht*
100	**njëqind** *nyeh chyeend*
101	**njëqind e një** *nyeh chyeend eh nyeh*
200	**dyqind** *duy chyeend*
500	**pesëqind** *pehseh chyeend*
1,000	**një mijë** *nyemeey*
10,000	**dhjetë mijë** *dhyet meey*
1,000,000	**një milion** *nyeh mee-lyon*

Time

What time is it?	**Sa është ora?** *Sah ehshteh orah?*
It's midday.	**Është mesditë.** *Ehshteh mess-deeteh*
Five past three.	**Tre e pesë minuta.** *Treh ej pehseh mee-noo-tah*
A quarter to ten.	**Dhjetë pa një çerek.** *Dhyet pa nyeh cherek*
5:30 a.m./p.m.	**Pesë e tridhjetë (në mëngjes)/Shtatëmbëdhjetë e tridhjetë (pasdite).** *Pehseh eh treedhyeteh (neh menjyes)/ shtahtehmbehdhyehteh eh treedhyeteh (pasdeeteh).*

Days

Monday	**e henë** *eh hehneh*
Tuesday	**e martë** *eh mahrteh*
Wednesday	**e mërkurë** *eh merkoor*
Thursday	**e enjte** *eh ehnyteh*
Friday	**e premte** *eh prehmteh*
Saturday	**e shtunë** *eh shtoon*
Sunday	**e dielë** *eh dyel*

Dates

yesterday	**dje** *dye*
today	**sot** *soht*
tomorrow	**nesër** *nehser*
day	**ditë** *deeteh*
week	**javë** *ya-veh*
month	**muaj** *moo-ay*
year	**vit** *veet*
Happy New Year!	**Gëzuar Vitin e Ri!** *Geh-zoo-ar Vee-teen eh Ree!*
Happy Birthday!	**Gëzuar ditëlindjen!** *Geh-zoo-ar deeteh leen-dyen!*

Months

January	**janar** *yahnahr*
February	**shkurt** *shkoort*
March	**mars** *mahrs*
April	**prill** *preell*
May	**maj** *may*
June	**qershor** *chyehrshohr*
July	**korrik** *kohrreek*
August	**gusht** *goosht*
September	**shtator** *shtahtohr*
October	**tetor** *tehtohr*
November	**nëntor** *nehntohr*
December	**dhjetor** *dhyetohr*

Arrival & Departure

I'm on vacation [holiday]/business.	**Jam me pushime/udhëtim pune.** *Yam meh poosheemeh/oodhehteem pooneh*
I'm going to…	**Po shkoj në…** *Poh shkoy neh…*
I'm staying at the… Hotel.	**Po qëndroj në Hotelin…** *Poh shkoy neh hoteleen…*

Money

Where's…?	**Ku është…?** *Koo ehshteh…?*
the ATM	**bankomati** *bahnko-matee*
the bank	**banka** *bankah*
the currency exchange office	**zyra e këmbimit valutor** *zoorah eh kembeemeet valootohr*
When does the bank open/close?	**Në ç'orë hapet/mbyllet banka?** *Neh chore hapet/mboollet bankah*
I'd like to change dollars/pounds sterling/euros into lek.	**Dua të këmbej disa dollarë/stërlina/euro në lekë.** *dooah teh shkehmbey deesah dohllahr/sterleenah/euro neh lehk*
I'd like to cash traveler's cheques.	**Do të doja të këmbej një çek udhëtimi me para në dorë.** *Doh teh doya teh kumbay nyeh chekh oodhehteemee meh parah neh doreh*

| Can I pay in cash? | **A mund të paguaj me para në dorë?** *Ah moon-teh pagoo-ay meh parah neh doreh* |
| Can I pay by (credit) card? | **A mund të paguaj më kartë krediti?** *Ah moon-teh pagoo-ay meh karteh kredeeteeh* |

For Numbers, see page 8.

Getting Around

How do I get to town?	**Si mund të shkoj në qytet?** *ee moon-teh shkoy neh kjytet?*
Where's…?	**Ku është…?** *koo ehshteh*
the airport	**aeroporti** *aerohportee*
the train station	**stacioni i trenave** *statseeohnee ee trenahveh*
the bus station	**stacioni i autobusëve** *statseeohnee ee aootoh-boozeh-veh*
the subway [underground] station	**stacioni i metrosë** *statseeohnee ee metroh-seh*
Is it far from here?	**A është larg prej këtu?** *Ah ehshteh largh prey kehtooh*
Where do I buy a ticket?	**Ku mund të blej një biletë?** *Koo moon-teh bley nye bee-leteh*
A one-way/return-trip ticket to…	**Një biletë njëdrejtimëshe/vajtje-ardhje për në…** *Nye bee-leteh nye-dreyteemsheh/vaytyeh-ardhye pehr neh*
How much?	**Sa kushton?** *Sah kooshtohn?*
Which gate/line?	**Cila platformë/linjë?** *Tsilah platformeh/leenyeh*
Which platform?	**Cila platformë?** *Tsilah platformeh*
Where can I get a taxi?	**Ku mund të gjej një taksi?** *Koo moon-teh jey nyeh tahksee*
Take me to this address.	**Ju lutem, më çoni tek kjo adresë.** *Yoo loohtehm meh chohnee tekh kyo adreseh*
To…Airport, please.	**Për në…aeroport, ju lutem.** *Pehr neh aerohport yoo loohtehm*
I'm in a rush.	**Po nxitoj.** *Poh ndzee-toy.*
Can I have a map?	**A mund të më jepni një hartë?** *Ah moon-teh meh yepnee nyeh harteh*

Tickets

For today/tomorrow.	**Për sot/nesër.** *Pehr soht/nehser.*
A…ticket.	**Një biletë….** *Nyeh bee-leteh*
one-way	**njëdrejtimëshe** *nyedreyteemsheh*

YOU MAY SEE...

The Albanian currency is the **lek**, which is divided into 100 **cents**.
Coins: 1, 5, 10, 20, 50 and 100
Bills: 200, 500, 1000, 2000, 5000

return trip	**vajtje-ardhje**	vaytyeh-ardhye
first class	**klasi i parë**	klaseeh ee pahreh
I have an e-ticket.	**Kam një biletë elektronike.**	Kahm nyeh bee-leteh elektroneekeh
How long is the trip?	**Sa zgjat udhëtimi?**	Sah zjyaht oodhehteemee?
Is it a direct train?	**A është ky tren direkt?**	Ah ehshteh kuy trehn deerekt
Is this the bus to...?	**A është ky autobusi për në...?**	Ah ehshteh kuy aootoh-boozee pehr neh...?
Can you tell me when to get off?	**A mund të më thoni se kur duhet të zbres?**	Ah moon-teh meh thohnee seh koor doohet teh zehbres
I'd like to...	**Do të doja të...**	Doh teh doya teh...
my reservation.	**rezervimin tim.**	rezerveemeen teem.
cancel	**anulloj**	anooloy
change	**ndryshoj**	ndrooshoy
confirm	**konfirmoj**	konfeermoy

For Time, see page 9.

Car Hire

Where's the car hire?	**Ku mund të marr një makinë me qira?**	Koo moon-teh marh nyeh makeeneh meh chyirah?
I'd like...	**Do të doja...**	Doh teh doya
a cheap/small car	**një veturë të lirë/të vogël**	nyeh vetoor teh leereh/teh voghel
an automatic/ a manual	**automatike/manuale**	aootohmateekeh/mahnooaleh
air conditioning	**ajër i kondicionuar**	ayehr ee konditsyonooahr
a car seat	**një sedilje veture**	nyeh sehdeelyeh vetooreh
How much...?	**Sa kushton...?**	Sah kooshtohn
per day/week	**për një ditë/javë**	pehr nyeh deeteh/yaveh
Are there any discounts?	**A ka ndonjë ulje çmimi?**	Ah kah ndonyeh oolyeh chmeemee?

YOU MAY HEAR…

Ec drejt. *Ets drejt.*		straight ahead
në të majtë *neh teh mayteh*		left
në të djathtë *neh teh dyathteh*		right
rreth qoshes *reth chyoshes*		around the corner
përballë *pehr balleh*		opposite
prapa *prapah*		behind
ngjitur *nyeetoor*		next to
pas *pahs*		after
veri/jug *vereeh/yoogh*		north/south
lindje/perëndim *leendyeh/pehrendeem*		east/west
në semafor *neh sehmafohr*		at the traffic light
në kryqëzim *neh kroochyeh-zeem*		at the intersection

Places to Stay

Can you recommend a hotel?	**A mund të më rekomandoni ndonjë hotel?** *Ah moon-teh meh rekohmandoneeh ndonyeh hotel?*
I made a reservation.	**Kam bërë një rezervim.** *Kahm behreh nyeh rezerveem*
My name is…	**Quhem…** *Chyoohem…*
Do you have a room…?	**A keni dhomë…?** *Ah kenee dhomeh?*
for one/two	**për një/dy person(a)** *pehr nyeh/duy person/personah*
with a bathroom	**me banjë** *meh banyeh*
with air conditioning	**me ajër të kondicionuar** *me ayehr teh konditsyonooahr*
For…	**Për…** *Pehr*
tonight	**sonte** *sonteh*
two nights	**dy nete** *duy neteh*
one week	**një javë** *nye yaveh*
How much?	**Sa kushton?** *Sah kooshton?*
Is there anything cheaper?	**A ka diçka më të lirë?** *Ah kah deechkah meh teh leereh?*
When's checkout?	**Kur është koha për të dalë?** *Koor ehshteh kohah pehr teh dahleh*

13

Can I leave this in the safe?	**A mund ta lë këtë në kasafortë?** *Ah moon-tah leh keteh neh kahsahforteh*
Can I leave my bags?	**A mund të lë çantat e mia?** *Ah moon-teh leh chantat eh mee-ah?*
Can I have my bill/ a receipt?	**A mund të më jepni faturën, ju lutem?** *Ah moon-teh meh yepnee fahtoorehn yoo loohtehm*
I'll pay in cash/ by credit card.	**Do të paguaj me para në dorë/me kartë krediti.** *Doh teh pagoo-ay meh parah neh dohreh/meh karteh kredeeteeh*

Communications

Where's an internet cafe?	**Ku mund të gjej një internet kafe?** *Koo moon-teh jey nyeh eenternet kahfeh?*
Can I access the internet/ check my email?	**A mund të hyj në Internet/të lexoj e-mailet e mia?** *Ah moon-teh huy neh eenternet teh ledzoy eemeylet eh mee-ah?*
How much per half hour/hour?	**Sa kushton një gjysmë ore/një orë?** *Sah kooshtohn nyeh juysmeh ohreh/nyeh ohreh?*
How do I connect/log on?	**Si mund të lidhem/kyçem?** *See moon-teh leedhem/kuychem*
A phone card, please.	**Një kartë telefonike, ju lutem.** *Nyeh karteh telefoneekeh yoo loohtehm.*
Can I have your phone number?	**A mund të më japësh numrin tënd?** *Ah moon-teh meh yapehsh noomreen tehnd?*
Here's my number/ email.	**Ky është numri im/e-maili im.** *Kuy ehshteh noomree eem/eemeylee eem.*
Call me/text me.	**Më telefono/më shkruaj mesazh.** *Meh telefonoh/meh shkrooay mesahzh*
I'll text you.	**Do të të shkruaj mesazh.** *Doh teh teh shkrooay mesahzh*
Email me.	**Më shkruaj e-mail.** *Meh shkrooay eemeyl*
Hello. This is...	**Mirëdita. Unë jam...** *Mirehdeetah. Ooneh yam...*
Can I speak to...?	**A mund të flas me...?** *Ah moon-teh flahs meh...?*
Can you repeat that?	**A mund ta përsëritësh atë që the?** *Ah moon-tah pehr-sehr-eetesh ateh cheh theh?*
I'll call back later.	**Do të të telefonoj më vonë.** *Doh teh teh telefonoy meh voneh*
Bye.	**Mirupafshim.** *Meeroopahfsheem*

Where's the post office?	**Ku është posta?** *koo ehshteh pohstah*
I'd like to send this to…	**Dua të dërgoj këtë në…** *Dooah teh dergoy keteh neh…*
Can I…?	**A mund të…?** *Ah moon-teh…?*
access the internet	**hyj në Internet** *huy neh eenternet?*
check my email	**lexoj e-mailet** *ledzoy eemaylet*
print	**printoj** *preentoy*
plug in/charge my laptop/iPhone/iPad/BlackBerry?	**vë në prizë/karikoj laptopin/ajfohneen/ajpadeen/blekhbereen** *veh neh preezeh/kareekoy laptohpeen/iPhoneen/iPadeen/Blackberreen*
access Skype?	**hyj në Skype?** *huy neh Skype?*
What is the WiFi password?	**Si është fjalëkalimi për WiFi-n?** *See ehshteh fyaleh-kaleemee pehr WiFi?*
Is the WiFi free?	**A është WiFi falas?** *Ah ehshteh WiFi fahlas?*
Do you have bluetooth?	**A keni bluetooth?** *Ah kenee Bluetooth?*
Do you have a scanner?	**A keni skaner?** *Ah kenee skanner?*

Social Media

Are you on Facebook/Twitter?	**A ke Facebook/Twitter?** *Ah keh Facebook/Twitter*
What's your username?	**Si është emri yt i përdoruesit?** *See ehshteh emree*
I'll add you as a friend.	**Do të të shtoj si shok.** *Doh teh teh shtoy see shokh.*
I'll follow you on Twitter.	**Do të të ndjek në Twitter.** *Doh teh teh ndyek neh Twitter.*
Are you following…?	**A po ndjek…?** *Ah poh ndyek?*
I'll put the pictures on Facebook/Twitter.	**Do t'i publikoj fotografitë në Facebook/Twitter.** *Doh tee pooblikoy fohtografeeteh neh Facebook/Twitter.*
I'll tag you in the pictures.	**Do të të etiketoj në fotografitë.** *Doh teh teh eteeketoy neh fohtografeeteh.*

Conversation

Hello!/Hi!	**Përshëndetje! /Ç'kemi!** *Pehrshehndetye! Chkemee!*
How are you?	**Si jeni?** *see yehnee*
Fine thanks.	**Mirë faleminderit.** *meer fahlehmeendehreet*
And you?	**Po ju?** *poh yoo*
Excuse me!	**Më falni!** *Meh fahlnee!*
Do you speak English?	**Flisni anglisht?** *fleesnee ahngleesht*
What's your name?	**Si ju quajnë?** *see yoo chyooayn*

My name is...	**Unë quhem...** *oon chyoohehm*
Nice to meet you.	**Gëzohem që ju njoh.** *Gehzohem cheh yoo nyoh*
Where are you from?	**Nga vini?** *ngah veenee*
I'm from the U.K./U.S.	**Unë jam nga Britania/USA.** *oon yahm ngah breetahneeah/oohsah*
What do you do for a living?	**Çfarë punë bëni?** *Chfareh puneh behnee?*
I work for...	**Po punoj për...** *Poh poonoy pehar...*
I'm a student.	**Jam student** *m/* **studente** *f. Yam stoodent/stoodenteh*
I'm retired.	**Jam pensionist** *m/* **pensioniste** *f.* *Yam pehnsyoneest/pehnsyoneesteh*

Romance

Would you like to go out for a drink/dinner?	**A keni dëshirë të shkojmë për kafe/drekë?** *Ah kenee dehsheereh teh shkoymeh pehr kafeh/drekeh?*
What are your plans for tonight/tomorrow?	**Çfarë planesh keni për sonte/nesër?** *Chfareh planesh kenee pehr sonte/nehsr*
Can I have your (phone) number?	**A mund të më jepni numrin tuaj të telefonit?** *Ah moon-teh meh yepnee noomreen too-ay teh telefohneet*
Can I join you?	**A mund t'ju shoqëroj?** *Ah moon-tyoo shochyeroy?*
Can I buy you a drink?	**A mund t'ju blej diçka për të pirë?** *Ah moon-tyoo bley dichkah pehr teh peer?*
I love you.	**Të dua.** *Teh dooah*

Accepting & Rejecting

I'd love to.	**Me gjithë qejf.** *Meh jeetheh kjeyf.*
Where should we meet?	**Ku mund të takohemi?** *Koo moon-teh takohemee?*
I'll meet you at the bar/your hotel.	**Do të të takoj në lokal/në hotelin tënd.** *Doh teh teh takoy neh lokal/neh hoteleen tehnd.*
I'll come by at...	**Do të vij në orën...** *Doh teh veey neh ohren*
I'm busy.	**Jam i zënë** *m/* **e zënë** *f. Yam ee zehneh/eh zehneh*
I'm not interested.	**Nuk jam i interesuar** *m* /**e interesuar** *f.* *Nook yam ee eentehresooahr/eh eentehresooahr*
Leave me alone.	**Më lini të qetë.** *Meh leenee teh chyehteh*
Stop bothering me!	**Mos më shqetëso më!** *Mohs meh shchyetehsoh meh!*

Food & Drink

Eating Out

Can you recommend	**A mund të më rekomandoni?** *Ah moon-teh meh rekohmandohneeh?*
a good restaurant/bar?	**një restorant/bar të mirë?** *Nyeh restohrant/bar teh mireh?*
Is there a traditional/	**A ka këtu afër ndonjë restorant tradicional/të lirë?**
an inexpensive	*Ah kah kehtooh ndonyeh restohrant tradeetsyonal/teh leereh*
restaurant nearby?	**restorante këtu pranë?** *restohranteh kehtooh praneh?*
A table for…, please.	**Një tavolinë për…, ju lutem.**
	Nye tavoleeneh pehr…yoo loohtehm
Can we sit…?	**A mund të ulemi…?** *Ah moon-teh oolemeeh…?*
here/there	**këtu/atje** *kehtooh/atyeh*
outside	**jashtë** *yashteh*
in a non-smoking area	**në një zonë pa duhan** *neh nye zohneh pah doo-han*
I'm waiting for someone.	**Po pres dikë.** *Poh press dike.*
Where are the toilets?	**Ku janë banjot (tualetet)?**
	Koo yaneh banyot (too-ah-lettet)
The menu, please.	**një menu, ju lutem.** *nye menooh, yoo loohtehm*
What do you recommend?	**Çfarë mund të na rekomandoni?** *Chfareh moon-teh nah rekohmandohneeh*
I'd like…	**Dua…** *dooah*
Some more…, please.	**Pak më shumë…, ju lutem.**
	Pahk meh shoomeh yoo loohtehm
Enjoy your meal!	**Ju bëftë mirë!** *Yoo behfteh meereh!*
The check [bill], please.	**Faturën, ju lutem.** *Fahtoorehn yoo loohtehm*

YOU MAY SEE…

pagesa për hyrjen *pagesah pehr huyryen*	cover charge
çmimi fiks *chmeemee feeks*	fixed price
menuja/specialiteti i ditës *menoohyah/spetsyalitetee ee deetehs*	menu (of the day)
shërbimi (nuk) është i përfshirë *sherbeemee (nook) ehshteh ee pehrfsheer*	service (not) included
specialitetet *spetsyalitetet*	specials

| Is service included? | **A është shërbimi i përfshirë në çmim?** *Ah ehshteh sherbeemee ee pehrfsheer neh chmeem?* |
| Can I pay by credit card/ have a receipt? | **A mund të paguaj me kartë krediti/a mund të më jepni faturën?** *Ah moon-teh pagoo-ay meh karteh kredeeteh/ah moon-teh meh yepnee fahtoorehn?* |

Breakfast

bukë/gjalpë *bookeh/jyahlpeh*	bread/butter
paraushqim i ftohtë *parahooshchyeem ee ftohteh*	cold cuts
djathë *dyatheh*	cheese
vezë… *vehzeh…*	…egg
e zjerë shumë/e zjerë pak *eh zyer shoomeh/ eh zyer pahk*	hard/soft boiled
vezë (të skuqura) *veze (teh skoochyoorah)*	fried
e fërguar, vezë petull *eh fer-goo-ar*	scrambled
reçel *rehchehl*	jam
omëletë *ohm-leteh*	omelette
tostë/bukë e thekur *toast/bookeh eh thekoor*	toast
kos *kohs*	yogurt

Appetizers

byrek me djathë *bûrehk meh dyatheh*	cheese pie
djathë i fërguar *dyatheh ee fergooahr*	fried cheese
supë barishte *soopeh bahreeshteh*	vegetable soup
supë magjericë *soopeh mahjyehreets*	chicken giblets soup
tarator *tahrahtohr*	yoghurt salad
ullij të mbushur *oolleey teh mbooshoor*	stuffed olives

Meat

mish lope *meesh lohpeh*	beef
mish qengji *meesh ch'ehnjyee*	lamb
mish derri/viçi *meesh dehrree/veechee*	pork/veal
pula/patë *poolah/reekah*	chicken/duck
çomlek me *chohmlehk meh*	stew
qepë *chyehpeh*	veal with onion
japrakë me mish *yaprahk meh meesh*	vine leaf stuffed with meat and rice

qofte *chyohfteh*	meatballs
tasqebap *tahschyehbahb*	kebab
tavë Elbasani	lamb and yoghurt casserole
tahveh ehlbahsahnee	from Elbasani

YOU MAY HEAR...

e pabërë *eh pahberreh*	underdone (rare)
e mesme *eh mehsmeh*	medium
e pjekur tamam *eh pyekoor tahmahm*	well-done

Fish & Seafood

fileto peshku *feelehtoh pehshkoo*	fish fillet
karkaleca të zier	boiled prawns
kahrkahlehtsah teh zeeehr	
koce e zgarës *kohtseh eh zgahreh*	grilled place
ngjalë e skuqur *nyahleh eh skoochyoor*	fried eel
peshk i pjekur *pehshk ee pyekoor*	roast fish
tavë me peshk *tahveh meh pehshk*	fish casserole

Vegetables

fasule *fahsooleh*	beans
lakër *lahker*	cabbage
presh *prehsh*	leeks
këpurdhë *kerpoordheh*	mushroom
qepë *chyehpeh*	onion
patate *pahtahteh*	potatoes
domate *dohmahteh*	tomato
lakër e mbushur *lahkeh eh mbooshoor*	stuffed cabbage
patëllxhane të mbushura *pahtehlljahneh teh mbooshoorah*	stuffed aubergines
spinuq me vezë e qumësht *eh chyoomehsht*	spinach with eggs and milk

Sauces & Condiments

Kripë *kreepeh*		Salt
Piper *peepehr*		Pepper
Mustardë *Moostardeh*		Mustard
Keçap *Kech-ahp*		Ketchup

Fruit & Dessert

mollë *mohlleh*		apple
banane *bahnahneh*		banana
limon *leemohn*		lemon
portokall *pohrtohkahll*		orange
kumbull *koombooll*		plum
luleshtrydhe *loolehshtrydheh*		strawberries
akullore *ahkoollohreh*		ice-cream
sheqerpare *shehchyehrpahreh*		syrup cake
shëndetlie *shemdehtlye*		honey cake
sultiash *soolteeahsh*		milk rice

Drinks

The wine list/drink menu, please.	**A mund të më sillni listën e verërave/e pijeve alkoolike, ju lutem.** *Ah moon-teh meh seellneeh leestehn eh vehreraveh/eh peeyeveh alkoholeekeh, yoo loohtehm.*
What do you recommend?	**Çfarë mund të na rekomandoni?** *Chfareh moon-teh meh rekohmandoneeh?*
I'd like a bottle/glass of red/white wine.	**Ju lutem, një shishe/gotë verë të kuqe/të bardhë.** *Yoo loohtehm, nyeh sheesheh/gohteh vehreh teh koochye/teh bardheh*
The house wine, please.	**Verë shtëpie, ju lutem.** *Vehreh shtehpeeyeh, yoo loohtehm*
Another bottle/glass, please.	**Edhe një shishe/gotë tjetër, ju lutem.** *Edheh nye sheesheh/gohteh tyetehr, yoo loohtehm*
I'd like a local beer.	**Ju lutem, birrë vendi.** *Yoo loohtehm beereh vendesh.*
Can I buy you a drink?	**A mund të të blej diçka për të pirë?** *Ah moon-teh teh bley dichkah pehr teh peer?*
Cheers!	**Gëzuar!** *Geh-zoo-ar*
A coffee/tea, please.	**Kafe/çaj, ju lutem.** *kahfeh/chay yoo loohtehm*
Black.	**E zezë (kafe)/I zi (çaj)** *Eh zeze (kahfeh)/ee zeeh (chay)*

With...	**me...** *meh...*
milk	**qumësht** *chyoomesh*
sugar	**sheqer** *shechyehr*
artificial sweetener	**sheqer artificial** *shechyehr arteefeetsyahl*
A..., please.	**Një..., ju lutem.** *Nye teh loohtehm*
juice	**lëng frutash** *lemg frootahsh*
soda [soft drink]	**soda [pije joalkoolike]** *sodah (peeyeh yohalkoholeekeh)*
(sparkling/still) water	**ujë (me gaz/pa gaz)** *ooyeh (meh gahz/pah gahz)*

Leisure Time

Sightseeing

Where's the tourist information office?	**Ku është zyra turistike?** *koo ehshteh zuyrah tooreesteekeh*
What are the main sights?	**Cilat janë monumentet kryesore?** *Tsihlat jahneh mohnoomentet kruyesoreh*
Do you offer tours in English?	**A ofroni vizitë me shoqërues në gjuhën angleze?** *Ah ofrohneeh veezeeteh meh sho-chye-roo-es neh jyehehn ahnglezeh?*
Can I have a map/guide?	**Ju lutem, a mund të jepni një hartë/udhërrëfyes?** *Yoo loohtehm, ah moon-teh yepnee nye harteh/oodheh-rrehfuyes?*

YOU MAY SEE...

| **e hapur/e mbyllur** *eh hapoor/eh mbuylloor* | open/closed |
| **hyrje/dalje** *huyrye/dalye* | entrance/exit |

Shopping

Where's the market/mall?	**Ku është tregu/qendra tregtare?** *Koo ehshteh trehgooh/chyendrah trehg-tareh*
I'm just looking.	**Vetëm po shikoj.** *Vetehm poh sheekoy*
Can you help me?	**A mund të më ndihmoni?** *Ah moon-teh meh ndeehmonee?*
I'm being helped.	**Po më ndihmon dikush tani.** *Poh meh ndeehmon deekoosh taneeh*

How much?	**Sa kushton?** *Sah kooshtohn?*
That one, please.	**Atë, ju lutem.** *Ateh, yoo loohtehm*
I'd like…	**Do të doja…** *Doh teh doyah*
That's all.	**Kaq, faleminderit.** *Kach, fahlehmeendehreet*
Where can I pay?	**Ku mund të paguaj?** *Koo moon-teh pagoo-ay*
I'll pay in cash/ by credit card.	**Do të paguaj me para në dorë/me kartë krediti.** *Doh teh pagoo-ay meh parah neh doreh/ meh karteh kredeeteeh*
A receipt, please.	**Faturën, ju lutem.** *Fahtoorehn yoo loohtehm*

Sport & Leisure

When's the game?	**Kur zhvillohet ndeshja?** *Koo zhveellohet ndeshya?*
Where's…?	**Ku është…?** *Koo ehshteh…?*
the beach	**plazhi** *plahzhee*
the park	**parku** *parkooh*
the pool	**pishina** *peesheenah*
Is it safe to swim here?	**A është e sigurtë të notoj këtu?** *Ah ehshteh eh seegoort teh nohtoy kehtooh?*
Can I hire clubs?	**A mund të marr shkop me qira?** *Ah moon-teh mahrr shkoph meh chyrah?*
How much per hour/ day?	**Sa kushton për një orë/ditë?** *Sah kooshtohn pehr nye ohreh/deeteh?*
How far is it to…?	**Sa larg është prej këtu në…?** *Sah largh ehshteh prey kehtooh neh…?*
Show me on the map, please.	**Më tregoni në hartë, ju lutem.** *Meh tregoneeh neh harteh, yoo loohtehm*

Going Out

What's there to do at night?	**Çfarë mund të bëjmë atje në mbrëmje?** *Chfareh moon-teh beymeh ahtye neh mbrehmye?*
Do you have a program of events?	**A keni një program të ngjarjeve?** *Ah keneeh nye program teh ngyaryeveh?*
What's playing tonight?	**Çfarë ka në repertor sonte?** *Chfareh kah neh repertohr sonteh?*
Where's…?	**Ku është…?** *Koo ehshteh…?*
the downtown area	**zona e qendrës së qytetit** *zohnah eh chyendrehs seh kjytetit*
the bar	**bari (lokali)** *bahreeh/lokaleeh*

| the dance club | **lokal për vallëzim** *lokahl pehr vahllehzeem* |
| Is this area safe at night? | **A është kjo zonë e sigurtë gjatë natës?** *Ah ehshteh kyo zohneh eh seegoort jyateh nahtes* |

Baby Essentials

Do you have…?	**A keni…?** *Ah keneeh?*
a baby bottle	**shishe për fëmijë** *sheesheh pehr fehmeeyeh*
baby food	**ushqim për fëmijë** *ooshchyeem pehr fehmeeyeh*
baby wipes	**letra të lagura për fëmijë** *lehtrah teh laghoorah pehr fehmeeyeh*
a car seat	**sedilje makine për fëmijë** *sehdeelyeh pehr fehmeeyeh*
a children's menu/ portion	**menu/porcion për fëmijë** *menooh/portsyohn pehr fehmeeyeh*
a child's seat/ highchair	**karrige/karrige e lartë për fëmijë** *kahrreegeh/kahrreegeh eh larteh pehr fehmeeyeh*
a crib/cot	**djep/shtrat fëmijësh** *pehr fehmeeyeh*
diapers [nappies]	**pelena** *pelehnah*
formula	**recetë** *retseteh*
a pacifier [dummy]	**biberon** *beeberohn*
a playpen	**boks (për fëmijë)** *boks pehr fehmeeyeh*
a stroller [pushchair]	**karrocë për fëmijë** *kahrrotseh pehr fehmeeyeh*
Can I breastfeed the baby here?	**A mund të ushqej fëmijën tim me gji këtu?** *Ah moon-tah ooshchyey fehmeeyen tihm meh jyi kehtooh?*
Where can I breastfeed/ change the baby?	**Ku mund të ushqej fëmijën me gji/ndërroj pelenën e fëmijës?** *Koo moon-tah ooshchyey fehmeeyen meh jyi/ndehrroy pelehnen e fehmeeyes*

For Eating Out, see page 17.

Disabled Travelers

Is there…?	**A ka këtu…?** *Ah kah kehtooh…?*
access for the disabled	**hyrje për persona me aftësi të kufizuara** *huyrye pehr personah meh aftehseeh teh koofeezooarah*
a wheelchair ramp	**platformë për karrocë invalidi** *platformeh pehr kahrrotseh eenvaleedeeh*
a disabled-accessible toilet	**banjo për persona me aftësi të kufizuara** *banyoh pehr personah meh aftehseeh teh koofeezooarah*

I need...	**Kam nevojë për...** *Kahm nevoyeh pehr...*
assistance	**ndihmë** *ndeehmeh*
an elevator [a lift]	**ashensor** *ahshensohr*
a ground-floor room	**dhomë në katin përdhe** *dhohmeh neh kahteen pehrdhe*
Please speak louder.	**Ju lutem, flisni me zë më të lartë.**
	yoo loohtehm fleesneeh meh zeh meh teh larteh

Health & Emergencies

Emergencies

Help!	**Ndihmë!** *ndeehmeh*
Go away!	**Largohu!** *Largo-hoo*
Stop, thief!	**Kapeni hajdutin!** *kahpehnee haydooteen*
Get a doctor!	**Thirrni mjekun!** *Theerrneeh myekoon*
Fire!	**Zjarr!** *Zyarr*
I'm lost.	**Kam humbur.** *kahm hoomboor*
Can you help me?	**A mund të më ndihmoni?** *A moon-teh meh ndeehmonee?*
Call the police!	**Thirrni policinë!** *theerrneeh pohleetseen*
Where's the police station?	**Ku është stacioni i policisë?** *Koo ehshteh statsyonee ee pohleetseeseh*
My child is missing.	**Fëmija im është zhdukur.** *Fehmeeyah eem ehshteh zhdookoor*

YOU MAY HEAR...

Plotësoni formularin.	Fill out this form.
Plohtehsohnee formoolahreen	
Kartën e identitetit tuaj, ju lutem.	Your ID, please.
Kahrten eh eeden-teete-teet yoo loohtehm	
Kur/Ku ka ndodhur kjo?	When/Where did it happen?
Koor/koo kah ndodhoor kyo?	
Si duket ai/ajo? *See dooket aee/ayoh?*	What does he/she look like?

In an emergency, dial:
129 for the police
128 for the fire brigade
127 for an ambulance

Health

I'm sick.	**Jam sëmurë.** *yahm sehmoor*
I need an English-speaking doctor.	**Kam nevojë për një mjek që flet anglisht.** *Kahm nevoyeh pehr deekeh cheh flet ahngleesht*
It hurts here.	**Më dhëmb këtu.** *Meh dhemb kehtooh.*
Where's the pharmacy?	**Ku është farmacia?** *Koo ehshteh farmatseeah?*
I'm (...months) pregnant.	**Jam (...muaj) shtatëzënë.** *Yam (...muay) shtatzehneh.*
I'm on...	**Marr...** *Mahrr*
I'm allergic to antibiotics/penicillin.	**Jam alergjik ndaj antibiotik/Penicilinë.** *Yam ahlerjyeek nday anteebyoteek/pehneetseeleen*

Dictionary

a **një**
acetaminophen [paracetamol] **paracetamol**
adaptor **përshtatës**
aid worker **punonjës i ndihmës së parë**
and **dhe**
antiseptic cream **krem antiseptik**
aspirin **aspirinë**
baby **bebe**
a backpack **çantë shpine**
bad **keq**
bag **çantë**
Band-Aid [plasters] **leukoplast**
bandages **fasho**

battleground **fushë beteje**
bee **bletë**
beige **bezh**
bikini **bikini**
bird **zog**
black **i zi** *m*, **e zezë** *f*
bland (food) **i lehtë** *m*, **e lehtë** *f*
blue **blu**
bottle opener **hapëse shishesh**
bowl **tas**
boy **djalë**
boyfriend **i dashur**
bra **sytjena**
brown **kafe**

Dictionary

26

camera **kamerë/aparat fotografik**

can opener **hapëse**

cat **mace matseh**

castle **kështjella/kala**

charger **karikues**

cigarettes **cigare**

cold **i ftohtë**

comb *n* **krehër**

computer **kompjuter**

condoms **prezervativ**

contact lens solution **lente kontakti**

corkscrew **tapënxjerrëse**

cup **filxhan**

dangerous **i rrezikshëm**

deodorant **deodorant**

diabetic **diabetik**

dog **qen**

doll **kukull**

fly *n* **mizë**

fork **pirun**

girl **vajzë**

girlfriend **e dashur**

glass **gotë**

good **i mirë** *m*, **e mirë** *f*, *(adj)*

gray **gri**

great **i madh***m*, **e madhe** *f*

green **jeshile**

a hairbrush **krehër**

hairspray **spray për flokë**

horse **kalë**

hot **i nxehtë**

husband **burrë/bashkëshort**

ibuprofen **ibuprofen**

ice **akull**

icy **i akullt**

injection **injeksion**

I'd like… **Do të doja…**

insect repellent **ilaç kundër insekteve**

jeans **pantallona/xhinsa**

(steak) knife **thikë (për biftek)**

lactose intolerant **jotolerues ndaj laktozës**

large **i madh**

lighter **çakmak**

lion **luan**

lotion [moisturizing cream] **locion [krem hidratues]**

love **dashuri**

matches **shkrepse**

medium **mesatar**

monkey **majmun**

museum **muzeum**

my **im** *m*, **ime** *f*

a nail file **limë për thonj**

napkin **shami dore**

nurse **infermier** *m*, **infermiere** *f*

or **ose**

orange **portokalli** (color)/**portokall** (fruit)

park **park**

partner **partner**

pen **stilolaps**

pink **rozë**

plate **pjatë**

purple **lejla**

pyjamas **pizhame**

rain **shiu**

a raincoat **xhaketë shiu**

a (disposable) razor **brisk (me një përdorim)**

razor blades **brisk rroje**

red **e kuqe**

safari **safari**

salty **i kripur** *m*, **e kripur** *f*

a sauna **saunë**

sandals **sandale**

sanitary napkins [pads] **lines**

scissors **gërshërë**

shampoo/conditioner **shampoo/krem për flokët**

shoes **këpucë**

small **i vogël** *m*, **e vogël** *f*

snake **gjarpër**

sneakers **këpucë sporti**

snow **borë**

soap **sapun**

socks **çorape**

spicy **pikant** *m*, **pikante** *f*

spider **merimangë**

spoon **lugë**

a sweater **triko**

stamp(s) **pull/ë(a) poste**

suitcase **valixhe**

sun **diell**

sunglasses **syze dielli**

sunscreen **krem dielli**

a sweatshirt **bluzë**

a swimsuit **rroba banje**

a T-shirt **bluzë (me mëngë të shkurtra)**

tampons **tampona**

terrible *adj* **i tmerrshëm** *m*, **e tmerrshme** *f*

tie **kravatë/kollare**

tissues **facoleta**

toilet paper **letër higjenike**

toothbrush **furçë dhëmbësh**

toothpaste **pastë dhëmbësh**

tough (meat) **(mish) i fortë**

toy **lodër**

underwear **të brendshme**

vegetarian **vegjetarian**

vegan **vegan**

white **e bardhë**

with **me**

wife **gruaja/bashkëshortja**

without **pa**

yellow **e verdhë**

your **yt** *m*, **jote** *f*

zoo **kopështi zoologjik**

Bulgarian

Hello/Hi.	**Здравейте/Здравей** zdruh-_vey_-teh/zdruh-_vey_
Good morning.	**Добро утро.** dob-_ro_ _oot_-ro
Good afternoon.	**Добър ден.** _do_-buhr _den_
Good night.	**Лека нощ** _leh_-kuh _nosht_
Good-bye.	**Довиждане.** do-_vizh_-duh-neh
Yes/No/Okay.	**Да/Не/Добре** da/neh/dob-_reh_
Excuse me! (to get attention)	**Извинете!** iz-vi-_neh_-teh
Excuse me. (to get past)	**Извинете.** iz-vi-_neh_-teh
I'm sorry.	**Съжалявам.** suh-zuh-_lya_-vuhm
I'd like...	**Искам да...** _is_-kuhm duh
How much?	**Колко струва?** _kol_-ko stroo-va
And/or.	**И/или.** i/i-_li_
Please.	**Извинете.** iz-vi-_neh_-teh
Thank you.	**Благодаря.** bluh-go-duh-_rya_
You're welcome.	**Пак заповядай/няма защо** pak zuh-po-_vya_-dye
Where is/are...?	**Къде е/са...?** kuh-_deh_ eh/sa
I'm going to... (place)	**Отивам да...** o-_ti_-vam duh
I'm going to... (plan to do sth)	**Аз ще...** as shteh
My name is	**...Казвам се** ..._kaz_-vuhm seh
Please speak slowly.	**Моля, говорете по-бавно.** mol-yuh go-vo-_reh_-teh po _bav_-no
Can you repeat that?	**Може ли да повторите това?** _mo_-zhe li duh pov-_to_-ri-teh to-_va_
I don't understand.	**Не разбирам.** neh ruhz-_bir_-uhm
Do you speak English?	**Говорите ли английски?** go-_vo_-ri-teh li ang-_lee_-ski
I don't speak (much) Bulgarian.	**Аз не говоря (много) български.** Az neh go-_vor_-ya (_mno_-go) _buhl_-guhr-ski
Where's the restroom [toilet]?	**Къде е тоалетната?** kuh-_deh_ eh to-uh-_let_-nuh-tuh
Help!	**ПОМОЩ** _po_-mosht

You'll find the pronunciation of the Bulgarian letters and words written in gray after each sentence to guide you. Simply pronounce these as if they were English, noting that any underlines indicate an additional emphasis or stress or a lengthening of a vowel sound. As you hear the language being spoken, you will quickly become accustomed to the local pronunciation and dialect.

Numbers

0	**нула** _noo_·luh
1	**едно** ed·_no_
2	**две** dveh
3	**три** tree
4	**четири** _cheh_·ti·ri
5	**пет** pet
6	**шест** shehst
7	**седем** _seh_·dehm
8	**осем** _o_·sehm
9	**девет** _deh_·veht
10	**десет** _deh_·seht
11	**единадесет** eh·di·_na_·deh·set
12	**дванадесет** dvuh·_na_·deh·set
13	**тринадесет** tree·_na_·deh·set
14	**четиринадесет** cheh·ti·ri·_na_·de·set
15	**петнадесет** pet·_na_·deh·set
16	**шестнадесет** shehst·_na_·deh·set
17	**седемнадесет** seh·dehm·_na_·deh·set
18	**оемнадесет** o·sehm·_na_·deh·set
19	**деветнадесет** deh·veht·_na_·deh·set
20	**двадесет** _dva_·deh·set
21	**двадесет и едно** dva·deh·seht i ed·_no_
30	**тридесет** _tree_·deh·set
40	**четиридесет** cheh·ti·_ri_·deh·set
50	**петдесет** pet·deh·_set_
60	**шестдесет** shehst·deh·_set_
70	**седемдесет** seh·dehm·deh·_set_

80	**осемдесет** o·sehm·deh·_set_
90	**деветдесет** deh·veht·deh·_set_
100	**сто** sto
101	**сто и едно** sto i ed·_no_
200	**двеста** _dveh_·stuh
500	**петстотин** _pet_·sto·tin
1,000	**хиляда** khil·_ya_·duh
10,000	**десет хиляди** _deh_·set _khil_·yuh·di
1,000,000	**един милион** eh·_din_ mi·li·_on_

Time

What time is it?	**Колко е часът?** _kol_·ko eh cha·_suht_
It's midday.	**Сега е обяд.** seh·_ga_ eh ob·_yad_
Five past three.	**Три часа и пет минути.** tree cha·_sa_ i pet mi·_noo_·ti
A quarter to ten.	**Десет без петнадесет.** _de_·set bes pet·_na_·de·set
5:30 a.m./p.m.	**5:30/17:30 преди обяд/след обяд** pet i po·lo·_vi_·na soot·rin·_ta_/sled ob·_yad_

Days

Monday	**понеделник** po·neh·_dehl_·nik
Tuesday	**вторник** _ftor_·nik
Wednesday	**сряда** _srya_·duh
Thursday	**четвъртък** cheht·_vuhr_·tuhk
Friday	**петък** _pet_·uhk
Saturday	**събота** _suh_·bo·tuh
Sunday	**неделя** neh·_dehl_·ya

Dates

yesterday	**вчера** _fcheh_·ra
today	**днес** dnehs
tomorrow	**утре** _oot_·reh
day	**ден** den
week	**седмица** _sed_·mi·tsuh
month	**месец** _meh_·sets
year	**година** go·_di_·na
Happy New Year!	**Честита Нова Година!** ches·_ti_·ta _no_·va go·_di_·na
Happy Birthday!	**Честит Рожден Ден!** chest·_tit_ rozh·_den_ den

Months

January	**януари**	*ya•noo•a•ri*
February	**февруари**	*fehv•roo•a•ri*
March	**март**	*mart*
April	**април**	*up•ril*
May	**май**	*my*
June	**юни**	*yoo•ni*
July	**юли**	*yoo•li*
August	**август**	*av•goost*
September	**септември**	*sehpt•ehm•vri*
October	**октомври**	*ok•tom•vri*
November	**ноември**	*no•ehm•vri*
December	**декември**	*dehk•ehm•vri*

Arrival & Departure

I'm on vacation [holiday]/business.	**Тук съм на почивка/по работа.** *took suhm na po•chiv•kuh*
I'm going to...	**Отивам на...** *o•ti•vuhm na*
I'm staying at the... Hotel.	**Аз съм в хотел...** *a•suhm f...kho•tel*

Money

Where's...?	**Къдее...?** *kuh•deh eh*
the ATM	**банкомат** *buhn•ko•mat*
the bank	**банка** *ban•kuh*
the currency exchange office	**бюро за обмяна на валута/валутното бюро** *byu•ro za ob•mya•nuh nuh vuh•loo•tuh/vuh•loot•no•to byu•ro*
When does the bank open/close?	**В колко часа отваря/затваря банката?** *f kol•ko cha•sa ot•va•ryuh/zuht•va•ryuh ban•cut•uh*
I want to change some dollars/pounds/euros into lev.	**Искам да обменя долари/лири/евро в левове.** *is•kam duh ob•men•ya do•la•ri/li•ri/ev•ro v leh•vo•veh*
I'd like to cash traveler's cheques.	**Искам да осребря пътнически чекове.** *is•kuhm duh os•reb•rya puht•ni•ches•ki chek•ov•eh*
Can I pay in cash?	**Може ли да платя в брой?** *mo•zhe li duh plat•ya f broy*

YOU MAY SEE...

The Bulgarian currency is the **lev, (лв.)**, which is divided into 100 **stokinki (стотинки)**.
Coins: 1,2, 5, 10, 20, 50 **stokinka; лв1**
Bills: **лв2**, 5, 10, 20, 50, 100

Can I pay by (credit) card?	**Може ли да платя с (кредитна) карта?** _mo_•zhe li duh plat•_ya_ s (_kre_•dit•nuh) _kar_•tuh

For Numbers, see page 30.

Getting Around

How do I get to town?	**Как да стигна до града?** _kak_ duh _stig_•nuh do gruh•_da_
Where's...?	**Къде е/са...?** kuh•_deh_ eh/sa
the airport	**летище** le•_tish_•teh•to
the train station	**жп гара** zheh peh _ga_•ruh•tuh
the bus station	**автогара** _af_•to _ga_•ra•tuh
the subway [underground] station	**спирка на метрото** spir•kuh•tuh nuh met•_ro_•to
Is it far from here?	**Далеч ли е от тук?** da•_lech_ li eh ot took
Where do I buy a ticket?	**Къде мога да купя билет?** kuh•_deh_ _mo_•ga duh _koop_•ya bill•_eht_
A one-way/return-trip ticket to...	**Еднопосочен/двупосочен билет за...** ed•no•po•_so_•chen/dvoo•po•_so_•chen bill•_eht_
How much?	**Колко струва?** _kol_•ko _stroo_•vuh
Which gate/line?	**Кой изход/коя линия?** coy _is_•hod/ko•_ya_ li•ni•yuh
Which platform?	**Кой коловоз?** coy ko•lo•_vos_
Where can I get a taxi?	**Къде мога да хвана такси?** kuh•_de_ _mo_•ga duh _khva_•nuh tuck•_si_
Take me to this address.	**Откарайте ме на този адрес.** ot•_ka_•rhy•teh meh na _to_•zi udd•_ress_
To...Airport, please.	**На летище..., моля.** na le•_tish_•te...mol•yuh
I'm in a rush.	**Бързам.** _buhr_•zuhm
Can I have a map?	**Може ли да получа карта?** _mo_•zhe li da po•_loo_•chuh _kar_•ta

Tickets

When's…to Sofia?	**Кога е…за София?** ko·ga eh Sofyia za
the (first) bus	**автобуса/първия автобус** af·to·boo·suh/puhr·vi·yuh af·to·boos
the (next) flight	**полета/следващия полет** po·leh·tuh/sled·vash·ti·yuh po·let
the (last) train	**влака/последния влак** vla·kuh/pos·led·ni·yuh vlak
One/Two ticket(s) please.	**Един билет/Два билета моля.** ed·in bill·et/dva bill·et·uh
For today/tomorrow.	**За днес/утре.** zuh dnes/zuh oot·reh
A…ticket.	**…билет.** bill·et
one-way	**еднопосочен** ed·no·po·so·chen
return trip	**отиване и връщане** o·ti·va·ne i vruh·shta·ne
first class	**първа класа** puhr·va klass·uh
I have an e-ticket.	**Имам електронен билет** im·am eh·lehk·tron·ehn bill·et
How long is the trip?	**Колко продължително е пътуването?** kol·ko pro·duhl·zhi·tel·no eh puh·too·va·neh·to
Is it a direct train?	**Това директен влак ли е?** to·vah di·rec·ten vlak li eh
Is this the bus to…?	**Това ли е автобусът за…?** to·va li e af·to·boos·uht zuh…
Can you tell me when to get off?	**Извинете, кога трябва да сляза?** iz·vi·neh·teh ko·ga tryab·vuh duh slya·zuh
I'd like to…	**Искам да…** is·kuhm duh…
my reservation.	**Моята резервация.** mo·ya·tuh reh·zehr·va·tsi·ya
cancel	**отменя** ot·men·ya
change	**променя** pro·men·ya
confirm	**потвърдя** pot·vuhr·dya

For Time, see page 31.

Car Hire

Where's the car hire?	**Къде мога да наема кола?** kuh·deh mo·guh duh na·e·ma ko·la
I'd like…	**Бих искал (m)/искала(f)** bikh is·khal/is·khal·uh…
a cheap/small car	**евтина/малка кола** ef·tin·uh/mal·kuh ko·la
an automatic/ a manual	**автоматична/ръчна** af·to·muh·tich·nuh/ruhch·nuh
air-conditioning	**климатик** kli·muh·tick
a car seat	**столче за кола** stol·cheh zuh ko·la

How much...?	**Колко струва...?** _kol_•ko stru•va
per day/week	**на ден/седмица** nuh den/_sed_•mi•tsuh
Are there any discounts?	**Има ли някакви отстъпки?** _imuh_ li _nya_•kuhk•vi ot•_stuhp_•ki

YOU MAY HEAR...

право напред _pra_•vo nuh•_pred_	straight ahead
отляво ot•_lya_•vo	left
отдясно ot•_dyas_•no	right
зад ъгъла zat _uh_•guh•luh	around the corner
срещу sresh•_too_	opposite
зад zat	behind
до do	next to
след slet	after
север/юг _seh_•vehr/yook	north/south
изток/запад _is_•took/_za_•puht	east/west
на сфетофара nuh sfe•to•_fa_•ruh	at the traffic light
на кръстовището nuh kruhs•_to_•vish•teh•to	at the intersection

Places to Stay

Can you recommend a hotel?	**Можете ли да ми препоръчате хотел?** _mo_•zheh•teh li da mi preh•po•_ruh_•cha•teh kho•_tel_
I made a reservation.	**Направих резервация.** nap•_ra_•vikh re•zer•_va_•tsi•ya
My name is...	**Казвам се...** _kaz_•vam seh
Do you have a room...?	**Имате ли...стая?** _i_•ma•te li _sta_•ya
for one/two	**единична/двойна** ed•i•_nitch_•nuh/_dvoy_•nuh
with a bathroom	**с баня** s _ban_•yuh
with air-conditioning	**с климатик** s kli•muh•_tick_
For...	**За...** zuh
tonight	**тази вечер** _ta_•zi _veh_•cher
two nights	**две нощувки** dveh nosh•_toov_•ki
one week	**една седмица** ed•_na_ _sed_•mi•tsuh
How much?	**Колко струва?** _kol_•ko _stroo_•va
Is there anything cheaper?	**Имате ли нещо по-евтино?** _ima_•teh li _nesh_•to po _ef_•ti•no

When's checkout?	**Кога е напускането на стаята?**
	ko-*ga* eh na-*pus*-ka-neh-to nuh *sta*-ya-tuh
Can I leave this in the safe?	**Мога ли да оставя това в сейфа?**
	os-*ta*-vyuh to-*va* f *sey*-fuh
Can I leave my bags?	**Мога ли да си оставя багажа?**
	mo-guh li duh si os-*ta*-vyuh buh-*ga*-zhuh
Can I have my bill/ a receipt?	**Може ли да получа сметката/квитанцията?**
	mo-zhe li duh po-*loo*-chuh *smet*-kuh-tuh/kvi-*tan*-tsi-yuh-tuh
I'll pay in cash/by credit card.	**Ще платя в брой/с кредитна карта.**
	shte plat-*ya* v broy

Communications

Where's an internet cafe?	**Къде има интернет кафе?** kuh-*deh* i-muh in-ter-net ka-*feh*
Can I access the internet/check my email?	**Може ли да получа достъп до интернет/ да проверя имейла си?** *mo*-zhe li da po-*loo*-chuh
	dos-tuhp do in-ter-net
How much per half hour/hour?	**Колко струва половин час/един час?** *kol*-ko *stroo*-va
	po-lo-*vin* chas
How do I connect/log on?	**Как да се свържа/логна?** kak da seh *svuhr*-zhuh/*log*-nuh
A phone card, please.	**Карта за телефон, моля.** *kar*-ta zuh te-le-*fon* *mol*-ya
Can I have your phone number?	**Може ли да ми дадете телефонния си номер?**
	mo-zhe li da mi da-*deh*-teh te-le-*fon*-ni-ya si *no*-mer
Here's my number/ email.	**Това е моят телефонен номер/имейл.** to-*va* eh *mo*-yat
	te-le-*fo*-nen *no*-mer/i-meyl
Call me/text me.	**Обадете ми се/напишете ми.** o-buh-*deh*-te mi seh/
	na-pi-*sheh*-te mi
I'll text you.	**Ще Ви напиша.** shte vi na-*pi*-sha
Email me.	**Изпратете ми имейл.** is-pra-*teh*-teh mi i-meyl
Hello. This is…	**Здравейте. Тук е…** zdruh-*vey*-teh tuk eh…
Can I speak to…?	**Може ли да говоря с…?** *mo*-zheh li duh go-*vo*-rya s
Can you repeat that?	**Може ли да повторитетова?**
	mo-zhe li duh pov-*to*-ri-te to-va
I'll call back later.	**Ще се обадя по-късно.** shte se o-*ba*-dyuh po *kuhs*-no
Bye.	**Довиждане.** do-*vizh*-da-neh
Where's the post office?	**Къде е пощата?** kuh-deh eh po-*shtuh*-tuh
I'd like to send this to…	**Искам да изпратя това на…**
	is-*kuhm* duh is-*pra*-tyuh to-*va* nuh…

Can I...?	**Може ли...?** _mo_·zheh li
access the internet	**да получа достъп до интернет** duh po·_loo_·chuh _dos_·tuhp do in·ter·net
check my email	**да проверя имейла си** duh pro·veh·_rya_
print	**да разпечатам** duh ras·peh·_chat_·uhm
plug in/charge my laptop/iPhone/iPad/ BlackBerry?	**да включа/да заредя компютъра/iPhone/iPad/ BlackBerry?** duh _fklyoo_·chuh/duh za·red·_ya_ kom·_pyoo_·tuh·ruh/_ay_·fon·uh/ay·pad·uh/_blek_·beh·ri·to
access Skype?	**да получа достъп до Skype?** duh po·_loo_·chuh _dos_·tuhp do skayp
What is the WiFi password?	**Каква е паролата за WiFi?** kak·va eh pa·ro·la·tuh zuh _why_·fy·uh
Is the WiFi free?	**Безплатен ли е достъпа до WiFi?** bes·_pla_·ten li eh _dos_·tuh·puh do why·fy
Do you have bluetooth?	**Имате ли bluetooth?** i·ma·teh li _bloo_·toot
Do you have a scanner?	**Имате ли скенер?** i·ma·teh li _skeh_·nehr

Social Media

Are you on Facebook/ Twitter?	**Имате ли акаунт наFacebook/Twitter?** i·ma·teh li uh·_kaunt_ na _feys_·book/_twit_·uhr
What's your username?	**Какво е потребителското ти име?** kak·_vo_ e pot·re·_bit_·el·sko·to ti i·meh
I'll add you as a friend.	**Ще те добавя към своите приятели.** shte teh do·_ba_·vya kuhm _svo_·i·te pri·_ya_·teh·li
I'll follow you on Twitter.	**Ще те следвам на Twitter** shte te _sled_·vam na _twit_·uhr
Are you following...?	**Следваш ли...?** _sled_·vash li
I'll put the pictures on Facebook/Twitter.	**Ще заредя снимки на Facebook/Twitter.** shte za·reh·_dyuh_ _snim_·ki nuh _feys_·bok
I'll tag you in the pictures.	**Ще те маркирам на снимките.** shteh teh mar·_ki_·ruhm nuh _snim_·ki·teh

Conversation

Hello!/Hi!	**Здравейте/Здравей.** zdruh·_vey_·teh/zdruh·_vey_
How are you?	**Как сте?** kak steh
Fine, thanks.	**Благодаря,добре.** bla·god·a·_rya_ dob·_reh_
Excuse me!	**Извинете!** iz·vin·_eh_·teh
Do you speak English?	**Говорите ли английски?** go·_vo_·ri·teh li an·glee·ski

What's your name?	**Как се казвате?** _kak_ seh _kaz_•va•teh
My name is…	**Казвамсе…** _kaz_•vam seh
Nice to meet you.	**Приятно ми е да се запознаем.** pri•_yat_•no mi eh duh seh za•poz•_na_•ehm
Where are you from?	**Откъде сте?** ot•kuh•_deh_ steh
I'm from the U.K./U.S.	**Аз съм от…** _a_•suhm ot
What do you do for a living?	**Какво работите?** kak•_vo_ ruh•_bo_•ti•teh
I work for…	**Работя в…** ra•_bot_•ya f
I'm a student.	**Аз съм студент.** _a_•suhm stoo•_dent_
I'm retired.	**Аз съм песионер.** _a_•suhm pen•si•o•_nehr_

Romance

Would you like to go out for a drink/dinner?	**Бихте ли искали да излезете на едно питие/вечеря?** _bikh_•teh li is•ka•li duh iz•_lez_•neh•teh na ed•_no_ pi•ti•_eh_
What are your plans for tonight/tomorrow?	**Какви са плановете Ви за довечера/утре?** kak•_vi_ sa _pla_•no•ve•teh vi zuh do•_veh_•cheh•ruh/_oot_•reh
Can I have your (phone) number?	**Може ли да получа Вашия (телефонен) номер?** _mo_•zhe li da po•_loo_•chuh _va_•shi•yuh (te•le•_fo_•nen) _no_•mer
Can I join you?	**Може ли да се присъединя към Вас?** _mo_•zhe li duh seh pri•suh•eh•din•_ya_ kuhm _vas_
Can I buy you a drink?	**Може ли да Ви почерпя с питие?** _mo_•zheh li duh vi po•_chehr_•pyuh s pi•ti•_eh_
I love you.	**Обичам те.** o•_bich_•uhm teh

Accepting & Rejecting

I'd love to.	**С удоволствие.** s u•do•_vols_•tvieh
Where should we meet?	**Къде ще се срещнем?** kuh•_deh_ shteh seh _sresht_•nem
I'll meet you at the bar/your hotel.	**Ще се срещнем в бара/във Вашия хотел.** shteh seh _sresht_•nehm f _bar_•uh
I'll come by at…	**Ще дойда към…** shteh _doy_•duh kuhm…
I'm busy.	**Зает (m) съм./Заета (f) съм.** za•_eht_ suhm/za•_eht_•uh suhm
I'm not interested.	**Не ме интересува.** neh meh in•teh•reh•_soo_•vuh
Leave me alone.	**Оставете ме на мира.** os•tuh•_veh_•teh meh nuh _mi_•ruh
Stop bothering me!	**Спрете да ме притеснявате!** _spreh_•teh duh meh pri•tes•_nya_•vuh•teh

Food & Drink

Eating Out

Can you recommend a good restaurant/bar?	**Можете ли да препоръчате добър ресторант/бар?** *mo·zhe·teh li duh preh·poh·ruh·chat·eh do·buhr res·to·rant*
Is there a traditional/ an inexpensive restaurant nearby?	**Има ли традиционен/евтин ресторант наблизо?** *ima li tra·di·tsi·on·en/ef·tin res·to·rant nab·li·zo*
A table for…, please.	**Маса за…моля.** *ma·sa zuh…mol·yuh*
Can we sit…?	**Може ли да седнем…?** *mo·zheh li duh sed·nem…*
here/there	**тук/там** *took/tam*
outside	**навън** *na·vuhn*
in a non-smoking area	**в зоната за непушачи** *v zo·nuh·tuh zuh ne·poo·sha·chi*
I'm waiting for someone.	**Чакам на някого.** *cha·kuhm na nya·kogo*
Where are the toilets?	**Къде са тоалетните?** *kuh·deh sa to·a·let·ni·teh*
The menu, please.	**Менюто, моля.** *men·yoo·to mol·yuh*
What do you recommend?	**Какво ще препоръчате?** *kak·vo shteh pre·po·ruh·chat·eh*
I'd like…	**Бих искал (m)/искала (f)…** *bikh is·kal/bikh is·kal·uh*
Some more…, please.	**Още малко…моля.** *osh·teh mal·ko mol·yuh*
Enjoy your meal!	**Добър апетит!** *do·buhr a·peh·tit*
The check [bill], please.	**Сметката, ако обичате.** *smet·ka·tuh uh·ko o·bich·a·teh*
Is service included?	**Услугата включена ли е?** *oos·loo·gut·uh fklyoo·cheh·nuh li eh*
Can I pay by credit card/ have a receipt?	**Може ли да платя с кредитна карта/да получа сметката?** *mo·zheh li duh pla·tya s kreh·dit·nuh kar·tuh/duh po·loo·chuh smet·kuh·tuh*

Breakfast

Искам… *is·kuhm*	I'd like (an/some)…
бекон/шунка *beh·kon/shoon·kuh*	bacon/ham
хляб/масло *khlyab/mas·lo*	bread/butter
сирене *si·reh·neh*	cheese
яйце *yay·tseh*	egg
конфитюр *kon·fi·tyur*	jam
кифли *kif·li*	rolls
тост *tost*	toast
наденица *na·deh·ni·tsuh*	sausage
йогурт *yo·goort*	yogurt

Appetizers

луканка loo-_kan_-kuh	piquant flat sausage
лютеница _lyu_-teh-ni-tsuh	red peppers and tomato sauce
сиренепошопски _si_-reh-neh po _shop_-ski	white cheese baked in earthenware
тарамасалата tuh-ruh-_ma_ suh-_la_-tuh	taramasalata
таратор tuh-_ra_-tor	cold cucumber and yoghurt soup
шкембечорба shkehm-_beh_ chor-_ba_	thick tripe broth
шопскасалата _shop_-skuh suh-_la_-tuh	tomato, cucumber, cheese salad

Meat

говеждо go-_vehzh_-do	beef
агнешко _ag_-nehsh-ko	lamb
свинско/телешко _svin_-sko/_te_-leh-shko	pork/veal
пиле/патица _pi_-leh/_pa_-ti-tsuh	chicken/duck
кебап keh-_bap_	meat in a rich sauce
кюфте kyuf-_teh_	meat ball
мусака moo-suh-_ka_	mousaka
пържола puhr-_zho_-luh	grilled pork steak
сарми suhr-_mi_	stuffed vine leaves
свинско със зеле _svin_-sko suhs _zeh_-leh	pork and sauerkraut

Fish & Seafood

бяларибапане _bya_-luh _ri_-buh puh-_neh_	pike-perch in batter
миди с ориз _mi_-di s or-_is_	mussels with rice
пушенпаламуд _poo_-shen _pa_-luh-moot	smoked tuna
пърженацаца _puhr_-zheh-nuh _tsa_-tsuh	fried sprat
рибеначорба _ri_-beh-nuh chor-_ba_	fish broth

YOU MAY HEAR...

лекозапечено _leh_-ko zuh-_peh_-cheh-no	rare
средноопечено _srehd_-no o-_peh_-cheh-no	medium
добреопечено dob-_reh_ o-_peh_-cheh-no	well-done

Vegetables

боб *bop*	beans
зеле *zeh·leh*	cabbage
краставички *kras·tuh·vich·ki*	gherkin
праз *pras*	leek
гъби *guh·bi*	mushroom
лук *look*	onion
картофи *kuhr·to·fi*	potatoes
домати *do·ma·ti*	tomato
баница *ba·ni·tsuh*	cheese pastry
вегетариански гювеч *veh·geh·tuh·ri·an·ski gyu·vehch*	stewed vegetables
пълненипиперки с ориз *puhl·neh·ni pi·pehr·ki s or·is*	peppers stuffed with rice

Sauces & Condiments

Сол *sol*	Salt
Пипер *pi·pehr*	Pepper
Горчица *gor·chi·tsuh*	Mustard
Кетчуп *keht·choop*	Ketchup

Fruit & Dessert

ябълка *ya·buhl·kuh*	apple
лимон *li·mon*	lemon
портокал *por·to·kahl*	orange
слива *sli·vuh*	plum
ягоди *ya·go·di*	strawberries
катми *kuht·mi*	jam or cheese pancakes
сладолед *sluh·do·lehd*	ice-cream
торта *tor·tuh*	gateau

Drinks

The wine list/drink menu, please.	**Менюто с вината/питиетата, ако обичате.** *meh·nyu·to s vi·na·ta ako o·bi·chuh teh*
What do you recommend?	**Какво ще препоръчате?** *kuhk·vo shteh preh·po·ruh·chuh·teh*

I'd like a bottle/glass of red/white wine.	**Бих искал** (m)/**искала** (f) **бутилка/чаша червено/бяло вино.** bikh _is_·kuhl/_is_·kuhl·uh boo·_til_·kuh/_cha_·shuh chehr·_veh_·no _vi_·no
The house wine, please.	**До къщата на виното, моля.** do _kuh_·shtuh·tuh nuh _vi_·no·to _mo_·lya
Another bottle/glass, please.	**Още една бутилка/чаша, моля.** _o_·shteh ehd·_na_ boo·_til_·kuh _mo_·lya
I'd like a local beer.	**Бих искал** (m)/**искала** (f) **местна бира.** bih _is_·kuhl/_is_·kuhl·uh _mest_·nuh _bi_·ruh
Can I buy you a drink?	**Може ли да Ви почерпя с питие?** _mo_· zheh li duh vi po·_chehr_·pya
Cheers!	**Наздраве!** nuh·_zdra_·veh
A coffee/tea, please.	**Чай/кафе, моля** chay/kuh·_feh_ _mo_·lya
Black.	**безмляко** behz _mlya_·ko
With…	**с…** s…
milk	**мляко** _mlya_·ko
sugar	**захар** _za_·khuhr
artificial sweetener	**подсладител** pod·sluh·_di_·tel
A…, please.	**…, моля.** _mo_·lya
juice	**сок** sok
soda [soft drink]	**сода [безалкохолно]** _so_·duh
(sparkling/still) water	**газирана/негазирана вода** guh·_zi_·ruh·nuh vo·_da_

Leisure Time

Sightseeing

Where's the tourist information office?	**Къде е туристическото бюро?** kuh·_deh_ eh too·ris·_ti_·cheh·sko·to _byu_·ro
What are the main sights?	**Какви са основните забележителности?** kuhk·_vi_ suh os·_nov_·ni·te zuh·beh·leh·_zhi_·tel·nos·ti
Do you offer tours in English?	**Предлагате ли ескурзии на английски език?** pred·_la_·guh·teh li ehks·_koor_·zee·i nuh ang·_lee_·ski e·_zik_
Can I have a map/guide?	**Може ли да получа карта/пътеводител?** _mo_·zheh li duh po·_loo_·chuh _kar_·tuh/puht·e·vo·_di_·tel

YOU MAY SEE…

| отворено/затворено | ot·<u>vo</u>·reh·no/zat·<u>vo</u>·reh·no | open/closed |
| вход/изход | vkhod/<u>iz</u>·khod | entrance/exit |

Shopping

Where's the market/mall?	**Къде е магазинът/моля?**	kuh·<u>deh</u> eh muh·guh·<u>zin</u>·uht mo·lya
I'm just looking.	**Просто разглеждам.**	<u>pros</u>·to ruhz·<u>glehzh</u>·duhm
Can you help me?	**Бихте ли ми помогнали?**	<u>bikh</u>·teh li mi po·<u>mog</u>·nuh·li
I'm being helped.	**Помогнаха ми.**	po·<u>mog</u>·nuh·khuh mi
How much?	**Колко струва?**	<u>kol</u>·ko <u>stroo</u>·vuh
That one, please.	**Онова там, моля.**	o·no·<u>va</u> tam <u>mo</u>·lya
I'd like…	**Бих искал (m)/искала (f)…**	bikh <u>is</u>·kuhl/<u>is</u>·kuhl·uh
That's all.	**Това е всичко.**	to·<u>va</u> eh fsich·ko
Where can I pay?	**Къде мога да платя?**	kuh·<u>deh</u> <u>mo</u>·guh duh pluh·<u>tya</u>
I'll pay in cash/by credit card.	**Ще платя в брой/с кредитна карта.**	shteh pluh·<u>tya</u> f broy
A receipt, please.	**Сметката, моля.**	<u>smeht</u>·kuh·tuh <u>mo</u>·lya

Sport & Leisure

When's the game?	**Кога е играта?**	ko·<u>ga</u> eh ig·<u>ra</u>·tuh
Where's…?	**Къде е…?**	kuh·<u>deh</u> eh
the beach	**на плажа**	nuh <u>pla</u>·zhuh
the park	**в парка**	f <u>par</u>·kuh
the pool	**на басейна**	nuh buh·<u>sehy</u>·nuh
Is it safe to swim here?	**Тук безопасно ли е да се плува?**	Took behz·oo·<u>pas</u>·no li eh duh seh <u>ploo</u>·vuh
Can I hire clubs?	**Може ли да наема комплект за голф?**	<u>mo</u>·zheh li duh <u>na</u>·eh·muh kom·plehkt zuh golf
How much per hour/day?	**Колко струва на час/ден?**	<u>kol</u>·ko <u>stroo</u>·vuh nuh <u>chas</u>/den
How far is it to…?	**Колко далеч е до…?**	<u>kol</u>·ko duh·<u>lech</u> eh do
Show me on the map, please.	**Покажете ми на картата, моля.**	po·kuh·<u>zheh</u>·teh mi nuh <u>kar</u>·tuh·tuh

Going Out

What's there to do at night?	**Какво може да се прави тук през нощта?** *kuhk-vo mo-zheh duh seh pra-vi took prehz nosht-tuh*
Do you have a program of events?	**Имате ли програма на мероприятията?** *i-muh-teh li prog-ra-muh-tuh nuh meh-ro-pri-ya-ti-ya-tuh*
What's playing tonight?	**Какво ще се състои тази вечер?** *kuhk-vo shteh seh suhs-to-i ta-zi veh-chehr*
Where's…?	**Къде е…?** *kuh-deh eh*
the downtown area	**центъра на града** *tsen-tuh-ruh nuh gruh-da*
the bar	**бара** *ba-ruh*
the dance club	**денс клуб** *dens kloop*
Is this area safe at night?	**Този район безопасен ли е през нощта?** *to-zi ray-on bez-o-pas-ehn li eh*

Baby Essentials

Do you have…?	**Имате ли…?** *i-muh-teh li*
a baby bottle	**бебешка бутилка** *beh-beh-shkuh boo-til-kuh*
baby food	**бебешка храна** *beh-beh-shkuh khruh-na*
baby wipes	**бебешки кърпи** *beh-beh-shki kuhr-pi*
a car seat	**столче за кола** *stol-cheh zuh ko-la*
a children's menu/ portion	**меню/порции за деца** *meh-nyu/por-tsi-i zuh deh-tsa*
a child's seat/ highchair	**детска седалка/столче за хранене** *deht-skuh seh-dal-kuh/stol-cheh zuh hra-na*
a crib/cot	**детско креватче/кошара** *deht-sko kreh-vat-cheh/ko-sha-ruh*
diapers [nappies]	**памперси [пелени]** *pam-pehr-si/peh-leh-ni*
formula	**сухо мляко за бебета** *soo-ho mlya-ko zuh beh-beh-tuh*
a pacifier [dummy]	**биберон** *bi-beh-ron*
a playpen	**кошара за игра** *ko-sha-ruh zuh ig-ra*
a stroller [pushchair]	**детска количка** *deht-ska ko-lich-kuh*
Can I breastfeed the baby here?	**Мога ли да кърмя бебето тук?** *mo-guh li duh kuhr-mya beh-beh-to took*
Where can I breastfeed/ change the baby?	**Къде мога да накърмя/преповия бебето?** *kuh-deh mo-guh duh nuh-kuhr-mya/preh-po-vi-ya beh-beh-to*

Disabled Travelers

Is there…?	**Има ли…?** _i·ma li_
access for the disabled	**достъп за хора с увреждания** _dos·tuhp zuh ho·ruh s oov·rehzh·duh·ni·ya_
a wheelchair ramp	**рампа за инвалидни колички** _ram·puh zuh in·vuh·lid·ni ko·lich·ki_
a disabled-accessible toilet	**достъпна тоалетна за инвалиди** _dos·tuhp·nuh to·uh·let·nuh zuh in·vuh·lid·i_
I need…	**Имам нужда от…** _i·muhm noozh·duh ot_
assistance	**помощ** _po·mosht_
an elevator [a lift]	**асансьор** _uh·suhn·syor_
a ground-floor room	**стая на приземен етаж** _sta·ya nuh pri·zeh·mehn eh·tazh_
Please speak louder.	**Моля, говорете по-силно.** _Mo·lya go·vo·reh·teh po·sil·no_

Health & Emergencies

Emergencies

Help!	**ПОМОЩ** _po·mosht_
Go away!	**Махай се!** _ma·high seh_
Stop, thief!	**Спрете, крадец!** _spreh·teh kra·dehts_
Get a doctor!	**Извикайте лекар!** _iz·vi·kuhy·teh leh·kuhr_
Fire!	**Пожар!** _po·zhar_
I'm lost.	**Изгубих се.** _iz·goo·bikh seh_
Can you help me?	**Можете ли да ми помогнете?** _mo·zheh·teh li duh mi po·mog·neh·teh_
Call the police!	**Обадетесевполицията** _o·buh·deh·teh seh f po·li·tsi·ya·tuh_
Where's the police station?	**Къде е полицейския участък?** _Kuh·deh eh po·li·tsey·ski·ya oo·chas·tuhk_
My child is missing.	**Детето ми изчезна.** _Deh·teh·to mi is·chez·nuh_

In an emergency, dial: **112.** Alternatively dial:
150 for an ambulance, **166** for the police, **160** for the fire brigade

YOU MAY HEAR...

Моля, попълнете формуляра.
mol•yuh, pop•blynete for•mu•lah•rah

Fill out this form.

Моля, покажете вашите документи.
mol•yuh, poh•kah•shay•teh va•shee•tay docu•men•tee

Your ID, please.

Кога/Къде се случи това? *ko•ga/kuh•deh seh sloochi to•va?*

When/Where did it happen?

Как изглеждаше той/тя?
kak iz•gles•dah•shay toy/tya

What does he/she look like?

Health

I'm sick.	**Болен (Болна) съм** *bo•lehn (bol•nuh) suhm*	
I need an English-speaking doctor.	**Трябва ми е лекар, говорещ английски език.** *Tryab•vuh mi leh•kuhr go•vo•resht un•glee•ski*	
It hurts here.	**Тук ме боли.** *took meh bo•li*	
Where's the pharmacy?	**Къде е аптеката?** *kuh•deh eh up•teh•kuh•tuh*	
I'm (...months) pregnant.	**Аз съм бременна в...месец.** *as suhm breh•mehn•nuh v...meh•sehts*	
I'm on...	**Аз съм на...** *a•suhm nuh...*	
I'm allergic to	**Алергичен (m)/алергична (f) съм към** *Uh•ler•gi•chen/uh•ler•gich•nuh suhm kuhm*	
antibiotics/ penicillin.	**антибиотици** *uhn•ti•bi•o•ti•tsi* **Пеницилин** *peh•ni•tsi•lin*	

Dictionary

adaptor **адаптер**
American **американски /и i**
aspirin **аспирин**
baby **бебе**
bad **лошо**
bag **торбичка**
Band-Aid **лейкопласт [пластири]**

bee **пчела**
black **черен**
bland (food) **лека (храна)**
blue **синьо**
bottle opener **отварачка за бутилки**
boy **момче**
boyfriend **приятеля**

bra **сутиен**
brown **кафяво**
charger **зарядно устройство**
cold **студено**
condoms **презервативи**
contact lens solution **разтвор за контактни лещи**
dangerous **опасно**
diabetic **диабетик**
doll **кукла**
English **английски**
fork **вилица**
girl **момиче**
girlfriend **приятелката**
glass **чаша**
good **добър**
gray **сив**
green **зелено**
hairbrush **четка за коса**
hot **горещо**
husband **мъжа**
ibuprofen **ибупрофен**
icy **ледено**
insect repellent **препарат против насекоми**
jeans **дънки**
(steak) knife **стек (нож)**
lactose intolerant **непоносимост към лактоза**
large **голям**
lighter **запалка**
love v **обичам**
or **или**
orange **оранжево**
partner **партньор**
pen **химикалка**

pink **розово**
plate **чиния**
purple **пурпурен**
rain **дъжд**
a raincoat **дъждобран**
razor **самобръсначки**
red **червено**
salty **солено**
sanitary napkins **дамски превръзки**
scissors **ножици**
shampoo/conditioner **шампоан/балсам**
shoes **обувки**
skis **ски**
small **малък**
snow **сняг**
spoon **лъжица**
stamp(s) **марка(и)**
suitcase **куфарче**
sun **слънце**
sunglasses **слънчеви очила**
sunscreen **плажен крем**
a swimsuit **бански костюм**
tampons **тампони**
terrible *adj* **ужасен**
tissues **кърпички**
toilet paper **тоалетна хартия**
toothbrush **четка за зъби**
toothpaste **пастазазъби**
toy **играчка**
vegetarian **вегетарианец** *(m)*
   вегетарианка *(f)*
white **бяло**
with **с**
wife (my) **жена(ми)**
without **без**
yellow **жълто**

47

Croatian

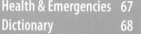

Essentials

Hello.	**Bog.** *bohg*
Goodbye.	**Doviđenja.** *doh•vih•jeh•nyah*
Yes.	**Da.** *dah*
No.	**Ne.** *neh*
O.K.	**O.K.** *oh•kehy*
Excuse me. (to get attention/get past)	**Oprostite.** *oh•proh•stih•teh*
I'm sorry.	**Žao mi je.** *zhah•oh mi yeh*
I'd like…	**Htio _m_ / Htjela _f_ bih…** *htih•oh/htyeh•lah bih…*
How much?	**Koliko?** *koh•lih•koh*
Where is…?	**Gdje je…?** *gdyeh yeh…*
Please.	**Molim Vas.** *moh•lihm vahs*
Thank you.	**Hvala.** *hvah•lah*
You're welcome.	**Molim.** *moh•lihm*
Please speak slowly.	**Molim Vas sporo govorite.** *moh•lihm vahs spoh•roh goh•voh•rih•teh*
Can you repeat that?	**Možete li ponoviti?** *moh•zheh•teh lih poh•noh•vih•tih*
I don't understand.	**Ne razumijem.** *neh rah•zoo•myehm*
Do you speak English?	**Govorite li engleski?** *goh•voh•rih•teh lih ehn•gleh•skih*
I don't speak Croatian.	**Ne govorim hrvatski.** *neh goh•voh•rihm hr•vah•tskih*
Where's the restroom [toilet]?	**Gdje je zahod?** *gdyeh yeh zah•hohd*
Help!	**Upomoć!** *oo•poh•moch*

49

You'll find the pronunciation of the Croatian letters and words written in gray after each sentence to guide you. Simply pronounce these as if they were English. As you hear the language being spoken, you will quickly become accustomed to the local pronunciation and dialect.

Numbers

0	**nula**	*noo·lah*
1	**jedan**	*yeh·dahn*
2	**dva**	*dvah*
3	**tri**	*trih*
4	**četiri**	*cheh·tih·rih*
5	**pet**	*peht*
6	**šest**	*shehst*
7	**sedam**	*seh·dahm*
8	**osam**	*oh·sahm*
9	**devet**	*deh·veht*
10	**deset**	*deh·seht*
11	**jedanaest**	*yeh·dah·nah·ehst*
12	**dvanaest**	*dvah·nah·ehst*
13	**trinaest**	*trih·nah·ehst*
14	**četrnaest**	*cheh·tr·nah·ehst*
15	**petnaest**	*peh·tnah·ehst*
16	**šestnaest**	*sheh·snah·ehst*
17	**sedamnaest**	*seh·dahm·nah·ehst*
18	**osamnaest**	*oh·sahm·nah·ehst*
19	**devetnaest**	*deh·veht·nah·ehst*
20	**dvadeset**	*dvah·deh·seht*
21	**dvadeset** jedan	*dvah·deh·seht yeh·dahn*
22	**dvadeset** dva	*dvah·deh·seht dvah*
30	**trideset**	*trih·deh·seht*
31	**trideset** jedan	*trih·deh·seht yeh·dahn*
40	**četrdeset**	*cheh ·tr·deh·seht*
50	**pedeset**	*peh·deh·seht*
60	**šestdeset**	*shehst·deh·seht*
70	**sedamdeset**	*seh·dahm·deh·seht*
80	**osamdeset**	*oh·sahm·deh·seht*
90	**devetdeset**	*deh·veh·deh·seht*
100	**sto**	*stoh*
101	**sto** jedan	*stoh yeh·dahn*
200	**dvjesto**	*dvyeh·stoh*
500	**petsto**	*peht·stoh*

1,000	**tisuću** *tih•soo•choo*
10,000	**deset tisuća** *deh•seht tih•soo•chah*
1,000,000	**milijun** *mih•lih•yoon*

Time

What time is it?	**Koliko je sati?** *koh•lih•koh yeh sah•tih*
It's noon [midday].	**Podne je.** *poh•dneh yeh*
At midnight.	**U ponoć.** *oo poh•nohch*
From one o'clock to two o'clock.	**Od jedan do dva sata.** *ohd yeh•dahn doh dvah sah•tah*
Five after [past] three.	**Tri i pet.** *trih ih peht*
A quarter to four.	**Petnaest do četiri.** *peht•nah•ehst doh cheh•tih•rih*
5:30 a.m./p.m.	**Peti trideset/sedamnaesti trideset.** *peh•tih trih•deh•seht/seh•dahm•nah•ehs•tih trih•deh•seht*

Days

Monday	**ponedjeljak** *poh•neh•dyeh•lyahk*
Tuesday	**utorak** *oo•toh•rahk*
Wednesday	**srijeda** *srih•yeh•dah*
Thursday	**četvrtak** *cheh•tvr•tahk*
Friday	**petak** *peh•tahk*
Saturday	**subota** *soo•boh•tah*
Sunday	**nedjelja** *neh•dyeh•lyah*

Dates

yesterday	**jučer** *yoo•chehr*
today	**danas** *dah•nahs*
tomorrow	**sutra** *soo•trah*
day	**dan** *dahn*
week	**tjedan** *tyeh•dahn*
month	**mjesec** *myeh•sehts*
year	**godina** *goh•dih•nah*

Months

January	**sječanj** *syeh•chahny*
February	**veljača** *veh•lyah•chah*
March	**ožujak** *oh•zhoo•yahk*

April	**travanj** *trah·vahny*
May	**svibanj** *svih·bahny*
June	**lipanj** *lih·pahny*
July	**srpanj** *sr·pahny*
August	**kolovoz** *koh·loh·vohz*
September	**rujan** *roo·yahn*
October	**listopad** *lih·stoh·pahd*
November	**studeni** *stoo·deh·nih*
December	**prosinac** *proh·sih·nahts*

Arrival & Departure

I'm here on vacation [holiday]/business.	**Na odmoru/poslu sam.** *nah ohd·moh·roo/poh·sloo sahm*
I'm going to…	**Idem u…** *ih·dehm oo…*
I'm staying at the…Hotel.	**Odsjeo m/Odsjela f sam u hotelu…** *ohd·syeh·oh/ohd·syeh·lah sahm oo hoh·teh·loo…*

Money

Where's…?	**Gdje je…?** *gdyeh yeh…*
the ATM	**bankomat** *bahn·koh·maht*
the bank	**banka** *bahn·kah*
the currency exchange office	**mjenjačnica** *myeh·nyah·chnih·tsah*
What time does the bank open/close?	**Kada se banka otvara/zatvara?** *kah·dah seh bahh·kah oh·tvah·rah/zah·tvah·rah*
I'd like to change some dollars/pounds into kuna.	**Htio m /Htjela f bih promijeniti dolare/funte u kune.** *htih·oh/htyeh·lah bih proh·mih·yeh·nih·tih doh·lah·reh/foon·teh oo koo·neh*

YOU MAY SEE…

The Croatian currency is the **kuna**, divided into **lipa**.
1 kuna = 100 lipa
Coins: 1, 2, 5, 10, 50 **lipa** and 1, 2, 5, 25 **kuna**
Bills: 5, 10, 20, 50, 100, 200, 500, 1000 **kuna**
The euro is also widely accepted.

I want to cash some traveler's checks [cheques].	**Htio** m/**Htjela** f **bih unovčiti putničke čekove.** *htih·oh/htyeh·lah bih oo·noh·vchih·tih poot·nih·chkeh cheh·koh·veh*

For Numbers, see page 50.

Getting Around

How do I get to town?	**Kako mogu stići do grada?** *kah·koh moh·goo stih·chih doh grah·dah*
Where's...?	**Gdje je...?** *gdyeh yeh...*
the airport	**zračna luka** *zrah·chnah loo·kah*
the train [railway] station	**željeznički kolodvor** *zheh·lyeh·znih·chkih koh·loh·dvohr*
the bus station	**autobusni kolodvor** *ah·oo·toh·boo·snih koh·loh·dvohr*
How far is it?	**Koliko je daleko?** *koh·lih·koh yeh dah·leh·koh*
Where do I buy a ticket?	**Gdje kupujem kartu?** *gdyeh koo·poo·yehm kahr·too*
A one-way/return-trip ticket to...	**Jednu kartu u jednom smjeru/povratnu do...** *yeh·dnoo kahr·too oo yeh·dnohm smyeh·roo/poh·vrah·tnoo doh...*
How much?	**Koliko?** *koh·lih·koh*
Is there a discount?	**Ima li popust?** *ih·mah lih poh·poost*
Which gate?	**Koji izlaz?** *koh·yih ihz·lahz*
Which line?	**Koja linija?** *koh·yah lee·nih·ya*
Which platform?	**Koji peron?** *koh·yih peh·rohn*
Where can I get a taxi?	**Gdje mogu uzeti taksi?** *gdyeh moh·goo oo·zeh·tih tah·ksee*
Take me to this address.	**Odvedite me do ove adrese.** *ohd·veh·dih·teh meh doh oh·veh ah·dreh·seh*
Where's the car rental [hire]?	**Gdje je rent-a-car?** *gdyeh yeh rehn·tah·kahr*
Can I have a map?	**Mogu li dobiti kartu?** *moh·goo lih doh·bih·tih kahr·too*

Tickets

When's...to Zagreb?	**Kada ima...za Zagreb?** *kah·dah ih·mah...zah zah·grehb*
(first) bus	**(prvi) autobus** *(pr·vee) ah·oo·toh·boos*
(next) flight	**(sljedeći) let** *(slyeh·deh·chih) leht*
(last) train	**(posljednji) vlak** *(poh·slyeh·dnyih) vlahk*
Is there...trip?	**Ima li...put?** *ih·mah lih...poot*
an earlier	**raniji** *rah·nih·yee*

a later	**kasniji** *kah·snih·yee*
an overnight	**noćni** *noh·chnih*
a cheaper	**jeftiniji** *yeh·ftih·nih·yee*
Where do I buy a ticket?	**Gdje mogu kupiti kartu?**
	gdyeh moh·goo koo·pih·tih kahr·too
One/two ticket(s),	**Jednu kartu/Dvije karte, molim Vas.** *yeh·dnoo kahr·too/*
please.	*dvih·yeh kahr·teh moh·lihm vahs*
For today/tomorrow.	**Za danas/sutra.** *zah dah·nahs/soo·trah*
A...ticket.	**Jednu kartu...** *yeh·dnoo kahr·too...*
one-way	**u jednom smjeru** *oo yeh·dnohm smyeh·roo*
round-trip [return]	**povratnu** *poh·vrah·tnoo*
first class	**za prvu klasu** *zah prvoo klah·soo*
business class	**za biznis klasu** *zah bihz·nihs klah·soo*
economy class	**za ekonomsku klasu** *zah eh·koh·nohm·skoo klah·soo*
one-day	**za jedan dan** *zah yeh·dahn dahn*
multiple-trip	**za višekratno putovanje** *zah vih·sheh·krah·tnoh*
	poo·toh·vah·nyeh
The express bus/train,	**Brzi autobus/vlak, molim Vas.** *br·zih ah·oo·toh·boos/*
please.	*vlahk moh·lihm vahs*
The local bus/train,	**Lokalni autobus/vlak, molim**
please.	*loh·kahl·nih ah·oo·toh·boo·s/vlah·kh, moh·lih·m*
How much?	**Koliko?** *koh·lih·koh*
Is there...discount?	**Ima li popust za...?** *ih·mah lih poh·poost zah...*
a child	**djecu** *dyeh·tsoo*
a student	**studente** *stoo·dehh·teh*
a senior citizen	**umirovljenike** *oo·mih·roh·vlyeh·nee·keh*
a tourist	**turiste** *too·rih·steh*
I have an e-ticket.	**Imam e-kartu.** *ih·mahm ee·kahr·too*
Can I buy a ticket on the	**Mogu li kupiti kartu u autobusu/vlaku?** *moh·goo lih*
bus/train?	*koo·pih·tih kahr·too oo ah·oo·toh·boo·soo/vlah·koo*
Do I have to stamp the	**Moram li ovjeriti kartu prije ukrcavanja?** *moh·rahm lih*
ticket before boarding?	*oh·vyeh·rih·tih kahr·too prih·yeh oo·kr·tsah·vah·nyah*
How long is this ticket	**Koliko važi ova karta?** *koh·lih·koh vah·zhih oh·vah kahr·tah*
valid?	
Can I return on the same	**Mogu li se vratiti s istom kartom?** *moh·goo lih seh*
ticket?	*vrah·tih·tih sih·stohm kahr·tohm*

I'd like to...	**Htio** *m* /**Htjela** *f* **bih... svoju rezervaciju.**
	htih•oh/htyeh•lah bih... svoh•yoo reh•zehr•vah•tsih•yoo
my reservation.	
cancel	**poništiti** *poh•nih•shtih•tih*
change	**promijeniti** *proh•mee•yeh•nih•tih*
confirm	**potvrditi** *poh•tvr•dih•tih*

For Days, see page 51.

Car Hire

Where's the car rental [hire]?	**Gdje je rent-a-car?** *gdyeh yeh rehn•tah•kahr*
I'd like...	**Htio** *m* /**Htjela** *f* **bih** *htih•oh/htyeh•lah bih...*
a cheap/small car	**jeftini/mali automobil** *yeh•ftih•nih/mah•lih ah•oo•toh•moh•bihl*
an automatic/ a manual	**automatik/automobil s ručnim mjenjačem** *ah•oo•toh•mah•tihk/ah•oo•toh•moh•bihl s roo•chnihm myeh•nyah•chehm*
a 2-/4-door	**s dvoja/četvora vrata** *s dvoh•yah/cheht•voh•rah vrah•tah*
air conditioning	**klima-uređaj** *klih•mah oo•reh•jahy*
a car seat	**sjedalo za djete** *syeh•dah•loh zah dyeh•teh*
How much...?	**Koliko je...?** *koh•lih•koh yeh...*
per day/week	**po danu/tjednu** *poh dah•noo/tyeh•dnoo*
for...days	**za...dana** *zah...dah•nah*
per kilometer	**po kilometru** *poh kih•loh•meh•troo*
for unlimited mileage	**za neograničenu kilometražu** *zah neh•oh•grah•nih•cheh•noo kih•loh•meh•trah•zhoo*
with insurance	**sa osiguranjem** *sah oh•sih•goo•rah•nyehm*
Are there any discounts?	**Ima li popust?** *ih•mah lih poh•poost*
Where's the parking meter?	**(Gdje je) automat za parkiranje?** *gdyeh yeh ah•oo•toh•mah•t zah pahr•kih•rah•nyeh*
Where's... the parking garage?	**(Gdje je...) garaža?** *gdyeh yeh...gah•rah•zhah*

YOU MAY HEAR...

pravo *prah·voh*	straight ahead
lijevo *lih·yeh·voh*	left
desno *deh·snoh*	right
na uglu *nah oo·gloo*	on the corner
iza ugla *ih·zah oo·glah*	around the corner
prekoputa *preh·koh·poo·tah*	opposite
iza *ih·zah*	behind
pored *poh·rehd*	next to
poslije *poh·slih·yeh*	after
sjever/jug *syeh·vehr/yoog*	north/south
istok/zapad *ih·stohk/zah·pahd*	east/west
na semaforu *nah seh·mah·foh·roo*	at the traffic light
na raskrižju *nah rah·skrih·zhyoo*	at the intersection

Places to Stay

Can you recommend a hotel?	**Možete li mi preporučiti hotel?** *moh·zheh·teh lih mih preh·poh·roo·chih·tih hoh·tehl*
I have a reservation.	**Imam rezervaciju.** *ih·mahm reh·zehr·vah·tsih·yoo*
My name is…	**Moje ime je…** *moh·yeh ih·meh yeh…*
Do you have a room…?	**Imate li sobu…?** *ih·mah·teh lih soh·boo…*
for one/two	**za jednu osobu/dvije osobe** *zah yeh·dnoo oh·soh·buh/dvih·yeh oh·soh·beh*
with a bathroom	**s kupaonicom** *s koo·pah·oh·nih·tsohm*
with air conditioning	**s klima-uređajem** *s klih·mah oo·reh·jah·yehm*
For…	**Za…** *zah…*
tonight	**večeras** *veh·cheh·rahs*
two nights	**dvije noći** *dvih·yeh noh·chih*
one week	**tjedan dana** *tyeh·dahn dah·nah*
How much?	**Koliko?** *koh·lih·koh*
Is there anything cheaper?	**Ima li nešto jeftinije?** *ih·mah lih neh·shtoh jeh·ftih·nih·yeh*

When's check-out?	**Kada moramo napustiti?** *kah·dah moh·rah·moh nah·poo·stih·tih*
Can I leave this in the safe?	**Mogu li ostaviti ovo u sefu?** *moh·goo lih oh·stah·vih·tih oh·voh oo seh·foo*
Can I leave my bags?	**Mogu li ostaviti torbe?** *moh·goo lih oh·stah·vih·tih tohr·beh*
Can I have my bill/ a receipt?	**Mogu li dobiti račun/priznanicu?** *moh·goo lih doh·bih·tih rah·choon/prih·znah·nih·tsoo*
I'll pay in cash/by credit card.	**Plaćam gotovinom/kreditnom karticom.** *plah·chahm goh·toh·vih·nohm/kreh·dih·tnohm kahr·tih·tsohm*

Communications

Where's an internet cafe?	**Gdje ima internet cafe?** *gdyeh ih·mah ihn·tehr·neht kah·feh*
Does it have wireless internet?	**Ima li bežični internet?** *ih·mah lih beh·zhih·chnih ihn·tehr·neht*
What is the WiFi password?	**Koja je lozinka za bežičnu mrežu?** *koh·yah yeh loh·zihn·kah zah beh·zhih·chnoo mreh·zhoo*
Is the WiFi free?	**Je li bežična mreža besplatna?** *yeh lih beh·zhih·chnah mreh·zhah behs·plaht·nah*
Do you have bluetooth?	**Imate li bluetooth?** *ih·mah·teh lih bloo·tooth*
How do I turn the computer on/off?	**Kako uključivam/gasim računar?** *kah·koh oo·klyoo·chih·vahm/gah·sihm rah·choo·nahr*
Can I…?	**Mogu li…?** *moh·goo lih…*
use any computer	**koristiti bilo koji računar** *koh·rih·stih·tih bih·loh koh·yih rah·choo·nahr*
access the internet	**pristupiti internetu** *prih·stoo·pih·tih ihn·tehr·neh·too*
check my email	**provjeriti e-mail** *proh·vyeh·rih·tih ee·mehyl*
print	**printati** *prihn·tah·tih*
plug in/charge my laptop/iPhone/iPad/ BlackBerry?	**uključiti/napuniti svoj laptop/iPhone/iPad?** *ook·lyoo·chih·tih/nah·puh·nih·tih svohy lap·top/i·phone/i·pad*
access Skype?	**Mogu li koristiti Skype?** *moh·goo lih koh·rih·stih·tee skype*
How much per hour/ half hour?	**Koliko košta po satu/pola sata?** *koh·lih·koh koh·shtah poh sah·too/poh·lah sah·tah*
How do I…?	**Kako se…?** *kah·koh seh…*
connect/disconnect	**konektiram/diskonektiram** *koh·neh·ktih·rahm/dis·koh·neh·ktih·rahm*

57

log on/off	**logiram/odlogiram** *loh-gih-rahm/od-loh-gih-rahm*
type this symbol	**tipka ovaj znak** *tihp-kah oh-vahy znahk*
What's your email?	**Koja je vaša e-mail adresa?** *koh-yah yeh vah-shah ee-mehyl ah-dreh-sah*
My email is...	**Moja e-mail adresa je...** *moh-yah ee-mehyl ah-dreh-sah yeh...*
Do you have a scanner?	**Imate li skener?** *ih-mah-teh lih skeh-nehr*

Social Media

Are you on Facebook/Twitter?	**Jesi li na Facebooku/Twitteru?** *yeh-sih lih nah fehys-boo-koo/twih-teh-roo*
What's your username?	**Koje ti je korisničko ime?** *koh-yeh tih yeh koh-rihs-nihch-koh ihmeh*
I'll add you as a friend.	**Dodat ću te za prijatelja.** *doh-daht choo teh zah prih-ya-teh-lya*
I'll follow you on Twitter.	**Slijedit ću te na Twitteru.** *slih-yeh-diht choo teh nah twih-teh-roo*
Are you following...?	**Slijediš li...?** *slih-yeh-dish lih*
I'll put the pictures on Facebook/Twitter.	**Stavit ću slike na Facebook/Twitter.** *stah-viht choo slih-keh nah fehys-book/twih-tehr*
I'll tag you in the pictures.	**Tagirat ću te na slikama.** *tah-gih-raht choo teh nah slih-kah-mah*

Conversation

Hello!	**Bog!** *bohg*
Hi!	**Zdravo!** *zdrah-voh*
How are you?	**Kako ste?** *kah-koh steh*
Fine, thanks.	**Dobro, hvala.** *doh-broh hvah-lah*
Excuse me!	**Oprostite!** *oh-proh-stih-teh*
Do you speak English?	**Govorite li engleski?** *goh-voh-rih-teh lih ehn-gleh-skih*
What's your name?	**Kako se zovete?** *kah-koh seh zoh-veh-teh*
My name is...	**Moje ime je...** *moh-yeh ih-meh yeh...*
Nice to meet you.	**Drago mi je.** *drah-goh mih yeh*
Where are you from?	**Odakle ste?** *oh-dah-kleh steh*
I'm from the U.S./U.K.	**Ja sam iz S.A.D.-a/Velike Britanije.** *yah sahm ihz ehs-ah-deh-ah/veh-lih-keh brih-tah-nih-yeh*

What do you do?	**Čime se bavite?** *chee·meh seh bah·vih·teh*
I work for...	**Radim za...** *rah·dihm zah...*
I'm a student.	**Studiram.** *stoo·dih·rahm*
I'm retired.	**U mirovini sam.** *oo mih·roh·vih·nih sahm*
Do you like...?	**Sviđa li Vam se...?** *svih·jah lih vahm seh...*
Goodbye.	**Doviđenja.** *doh·vih·jeh·nyah*
See you later.	**Vidimo se kasnije.** *vih·dih·moh seh kah·snih·yeh*

Romance

Would you like to go out for a drink/dinner?	**Želite li izaći na piće/večeru?** *zheh·lih·te lih ih·zah·chih nah pih·cheh/veh·cheh·roo*
What are your plans for tonight/tomorrow?	**Mogu li dobiti Vaš broj?** *moh·goo lih doh·bih·tih vahsh brohy*
Can I have your number?	**Mogu li dobiti Vaš broj?** *moh·goo lih doh·bih·tih vahsh brohy*
Can I join you?	**Mogu li Vam se pridružiti?** *moh·goo lih vahm seh prih·droo·zhih·tih*
Can I get you a drink?	**Mogu li Vas počastiti pićem?** *moh·goo lih vahs poh·chah·stih·tih pih·chehm*
I like you.	**Sviđaš mi se.** *svih·jahsh mih seh*
I love you.	**Volim te.** *voh·lihm teh*

Accepting & Rejecting

I'd love to.	**Rado.** *rah·doh*
Where should we meet?	**Gdje ćemo se sastati?** *gdyeh cheh·moh seh sah·stah·tih*
I'll meet you at the bar/your hotel.	**Naći ćemo se u baru/vašim hotelu.** *nah·chih cheh·moh seh oo bah·roo/vah·shihm hoh·teh·loo*
I'll come by at...	**Doći ću u...** *doh·chih choo oo...*
I'm busy.	**Zauzet m/Zauzeta f sam.** *zah·oo·zeht/zah·oo·zeh·tah sahm*
I'm not interested.	**Ne zanima me.** *neh zah·nih·mah meh*
Leave me alone.	**Ostavite me na miru.** *oh·stah·vih·teh meh nah mih·roo*
Stop bothering me!	**Prestanite mi dosađivati!** *preh·stah·nih·teh mih doh·sah·jih·vah·tih*

For Time, see page 51.

Food & Drink

Eating Out

Can you recommend a good restaurant/bar?	**Možete li preporučiti dobar restoran/bar?** *moh-zheh-teh lih preh-poh-roo-chih-tih doh-bahr reh-stoh-rahn/bahr*
Is there a traditional Croatian/an inexpensive restaurant nearby?	**Ima li blizu tradicionalni hrvatski/jeftin restoran?** *ih-mah lih blih-zoo trah-dih-tsih-oh-nahl-nih hr-vah-tskih/yehf-tihn reh-stoh-rahn*
A table for..., please.	**Stol za jednu osobu/dvoje, molim Vas.** *stohl zah yeh-dnoo oh-soh-boo/dvoh-yeh moh-lihm vahs*
Can we sit...?	**Možemo li sjesti...?** *moh-zheh-moh lih syeh-stih...*
here/there	**ovdje/tamo** *ohv-dyeh/tah-moh*
outside	**vani** *vah-nih*
in a non-smoking area	**u prostor za nepušače** *oo proh-stohr zah neh-poo-shah-cheh*
I'm waiting for someone.	**Čekam nekoga.** *cheh-kahm neh-koh-gah*
Where are the toilets?	**Gdje je zahod?** *gdyeh yeh zah-hohd*
A menu, please.	**Jelovnik, molim Vas.** *jeh-loh-vnihk moh-lihm vahs*
What do you recommend?	**Što preporučate?** *shtoh preh-poh-roo-chah-teh*
I'd like...	**Htio** *m***/Htjela** *f* **bih...** *htih-oh/htyeh-lah bih...*
Some more..., please.	**Još malo..., molim Vas.** *johsh mah-loh... moh-lihm vahs*
Enjoy your meal!	**Dobar tek!** *doh-bahr tehk*
The check [bill], please	**Račun, molim Vas.** *rah-choon moh-lihm vahs*
Is service included?	**Je li usluga uračunata u cijenu?** *yeh lih oo-sloo-gah oo-rah-choo-nah-tah oo cih-yeh-noo*
Can I pay by credit card/have a receipt?	**Mogu li platiti kreditnom karticom/dobiti račun?** *moh-goo lih plah-tih-tih kreh-diht-nohm kahr-tih-tsohm/doh-bih-tih rah-choon*
Thank you.	**Hvala Vam!** *hvah-lah vahm*

YOU MAY SEE...

(DNEVNI) MENI	menu (of the day)
USLUGA (NIJE) UKLJUČENA U CIJENU	service (not) included
DODATCI	specials

Breakfast

kruh *krooh*	bread
maslac *mah·slats*	butter
hladni naresci *hlah·dnih nah·rehs·tsih*	cold cuts [charcuterie]
...jaje *...yah·yeh*	...egg
tvrdo kuhano *tvr·doh koo·hah·noh*	hard-boiled
meko kuhano *meh·koh koo·hah·noh*	soft-boiled
na oko *nah oh·koh*	fried
kajgana *kahy·gah·nah*	scrambled
pekmez/marmelada *pehk·mehz/ mahr·meh·lah·dah*	jam/jelly
omlet *ohm·leht*	omelet
tost *tohst*	toast
jogurt *yoh·goort*	yogurt

Appetizers

kulen *koo·lehn*	sausage, spicy, flavored with paprika (Slavonia)
pohani sir *poh·hah·nih sihr*	cheese, fried in breadcrumbs
pršut i sir *pr·shoot ih sihr*	smoked ham and cheese
riblja pašteta *rih·blyah pah·shteh·tah*	fish pâté
rižot *rih·zhoht*	risotto
salata od hobotnice *sah·lah·ta ohd hoh·boh·tnih·tseh*	octopus salad
slani inćuni *slah·nih ihn·choo·nih*	salted anchovies

Meat

govedina *goh·veh·dih·nah*	beef
janjetina *jah·nyeh·tih·nah*	lamb
svinjetina *svih·nyeh·tih·nah*	pork
teletina *teh·leh·tih·nah*	veal
piletina *pih·leh·tih·nah*	chicken
patka *pah·tkah*	duck
čevapčići *cheh·vahp·chih·chih*	rolls of ground meat, grilled
jetrica *yeh·trih·tsah*	liver
kobasica *koh·bah·sih·tsah*	sausage
kunić *koo·nihch*	rabbit
odrezak *oh·dreh·zahk*	steak

pašticada *pah·shtih·tsah·dah*	stewed beef with proscuitto, in wine, lemon, rosemary
purica *poo·rih·tsah*	turkey
ražnjići *rahzh·nyih·chih*	meat kebabs
šunka *shoon·kah*	ham

Fish & Seafood

bakalar *bah·kah·lahr*	cod
brodet *broh·deht*	fish stew
haringa *hah·rihn·gah*	herring
hobotnica *hoh·boh·tnih·tsah*	octopus
iverak *ih·veh·rahk*	halibut
jastog *yah·stohg*	lobster
kamenica *kah·meh·nih·tsah*	oyster
kozice *koh·zih·tseh*	shrimp
lignje *lihg·nyeh*	squid
list *lihst*	sole
losos *loh·sohs*	salmon
lubin *loo·bihn*	sea bass
pastrva *pah·str·vah*	trout
rakovi *rah·koh·vih*	crab
sabljarka *sahb·lyahr·kah*	swordfish
školjke *shkohly·keh*	clam
tuna *too·nah*	tuna

Vegetables

grah *grahh*	beans
kupus *koo·poos*	cabbage
gljive *glyih·veh*	mushroom
luk *look*	onion
krumpir *kroom·pihr*	potato
rajčica *rahy·chih·tsah*	tomato
patlidžan *pah·tlih·jahn*	eggplant [aubergine]
špinat *shih·naht*	spinach
crvena/zelena paprika *cr·veh·nah/zeh·leh·nah pah·prih·kah*	red/green pepper
tikvica *tih·kvih·tsah*	zucchini [courgette]

Sauces & Condiments

sol *sohl*	salt
papar *pah·pahr*	pepper
senf *sehnf*	mustard
kečap *keh·chahp*	ketchup

Fruit & Dessert

jabuka *yah·boo·kah*	apple
banana *bah·nah·nah*	banana
limun *lih·moon*	lemon
naranča *nah·rahn·chah*	orange
šljiva *shlyih·vah*	plum
jagoda *yah·goh·dah*	strawberry
sladoled *slah·doh·lehd*	ice cream
palačinka... *pah·lah·chihn·kah...*	pancake...
sa čokoladom i orasima *sah choh·koh·lah·dohm ih oh·rah·sih·mah*	with chocolate and walnuts
sa džemom *sah jeh·mohm*	with jam
sa sladoledom *sah slah·doh·leh·dohm*	with ice cream

Drinks

The wine list/drink menu, please.	**Vinsku kartu/Kartu pića, molim Vas.** *veen·skoo kahr·too/ kahr·too pih·chah moh·lihm vahs*
What do you recommend?	**Što preporučate?** *shtoh preh·poh·roo·chah·teh*
I'd like a bottle/glass of red/white wine.	**Htio** *m*/**Htjela** *f* **bih bocu/čašu crnog/bijelog vina.** *htih·oh/htyeh·lah bih boh·tsoo/chah·shoo cr·nohg/ bih·yeh·lohg veeh·nah*
The house wine, please.	**Vino kuće, molim Vas.** *vee·noh koo·cheh moh·lihm vahs*
Another bottle/glass, please.	**Još jednu bocu/čašu, molim Vas.** *yohsh yeh·dnoo boh·tsoo/ chah·shoo moh·lihm vahs*
I'd like a local beer.	**Htio** *m*/**Htjela** *f* **bih lokalno pivo.** *htih·oh/htyeh·lah bih loh·kahl·noh pih·voh*
Can I buy you a drink?	**Mogu li Vas počastiti pićem?** *moh·goo lih vahs poh·chah·stih·tih pih·chehm*
Cheers!	**Živjeli!** *zhih·vyeh·lih*

A coffee/tea, please.	**Kavu/Čaj, molim Vas.** *kah•voo/chahy moh•lihm vahs*
With…	**Sa…** *sah…*
milk	**mlijekom** *mlih•yeh•kohm*
sugar	**šećerom** *sheh•cheh•rohm*
artificial sweetener	**umjetnim sladilom** *oo•myeh•tnihm slah•dih•lohm*
…, please.	**…, molim Vas.** *…moh•lihm vahs*
Juice	**Sok** *sohk*
Soda	**Gazirani sok** *gah•zih•rah•nih sohk*
(Sparkling/Still)	**(Mineralnu/Običnu) Vodu**
Water	*(mih•neh•rahl•noo/oh•bih•chnoo) voh•doo*
Is the water safe to drink?	**Je li voda pitka?** *lih voh•dah pih•tkah*

Leisure Time

Sightseeing

Where's the tourist information office?	**Gdje je turistički informativni ured?** *gdyeh yeh too•rih•stih•chkih ihn•fohr•mah•tih•vnih oo•rehd*
What are the main attractions?	**Koje su glavne znamenitosti?** *koh•yeh soo glah•vneh znah•meh•nih•toh•stih*
Do you have tours in English?	**Imate li ture na engleskom?** *ih•mah•teh lih too•reh nah ehn•gleh•skohm*
Can I have a map/ guide?	**Mogu li dobiti zemljopisnu kartu/vodič?** *moh•goo lih doh•bih•tih zeh•mlyoh•pih•snoo kahr•too/voh•dihch*

YOU MAY SEE…

OTVORENO/ZATVORENO	open/closed
KABINA ZA PRESVLAČENJE	fitting room
KASA	cashier
SAMO GOTOVINSKO PLAĆANJE	cash only
PRIMAMO KREDITNE KARTICE	credit cards accepted
UZLAZ/IZLAZ	entrance/exit
PAUZA ZA RUČAK	closed for lunch
RADNO VRIJEME	opening hours

Shopping

Where is the market/ mall [shopping centre]?	**Gdje je tržnica/trgovački centar?** *gdyeh yeh tr-zhnih-tsah/ tr-goh-vah-chkih tsehn-tahr*
I'm just looking.	**Samo razgledam.** *sah-moh rahz-gleh-dahm*
Can you help me?	**Možete li mi pomoći?** *moh-zheh-teh lih mih poh-moh-chih*
I'm being helped.	**Već sam uslužen** *m* **/uslužena** *f. vehch sahm oo-sloo-zhehn/oo-sloo-zheh-nah*
How much?	**Koliko?** *koh-lih-koh*
That one, please.	**To, molim Vas.** *toh moh-lihm vahs*
That's all.	**To je sve.** *toh yeh sveh*
Where can I pay?	**Gdje mogu platiti?** *gdyeh moh-goo plah-tih-tih*
I'll pay in cash/ by credit card.	**Plaćam gotovinom/kraditnom karticom.** *plah-chahm goh-toh-vih-nohm/kreh-diht-nohm kahr-tih-tsohm*
A receipt, please.	**Račun, molim Vas.** *rah-choon moh-lihm vahs*

Sport & Leisure

When's the game?	**Kada je utakmica?** *kah-dah yeh oo-tah-kmih-tsah*
Where's…?	**Gdje je…?** *gdyeh yeh…*
the beach	**plaža** *plah-zhah*
the park	**park** *pahrk*
the pool	**bazen** *bah-zehn*
Is it safe to swim here?	**Je li sigurno kupati se ovdje?** *yeh llih sih-goor-noh koo-pah-tih seh ohv-dyeh*
Can I rent [hire] golf clubs?	**Mogu li iznajmiti palice za golf?** *moh-goo lih ihz-nahy-mih-tih pah-lih-tseh zah gohlf*
How much per hour?	**Koliko košta po satu?** *koh-lih-koh koh-shtah poh sah-too*
How far is it to…?	**Koliko je daleko od…?** *koh-lih-koh yeh dah-leh-koh ohd…*
Show me on the map, please.	**Pokažite mi na karti, molim Vas.** *poh-kah-zhih-teh mih nah kahr-tih moh-lihm vahs*

Going Out

What's there to do at night?	**Kakav je noćni život?** *kah-kahv yeh noh-chnih zhih-voht*
Do you have a program of events?	**Imate li program događanja?** *ih-mah-teh lih proh-grahm doh-gah-jah-nyah*
What's playing tonight?	**Tko svira večeras?** *tkoh svih-rah veh-cheh-rahs*
Where's…?	**Gdje je…?** *gdyeh yeh…*

the downtown area	**centar grada** *tsehn·tahr grah·dah*
the bar	**bar** *bahr*
the dance club	**disko klub** *dih·skoh kloob*

Baby Essentials

Do you have...?	**Imate li...?** *ih·mah·teh lih...*
a baby bottle	**bočicu za bebe** *boh·chih·tsoo zah beh·beh*
baby food	**dječiju hranu** *dyeh·chih·yoo hrah·noo*
baby wipes	**vlažne maramice** *vlah·zhneh mah·rah·mih·tseh*
a car seat	**dječije sjedalo za auto**
	dyeh·chih·yeh syeh·dah·loh zah ah·oo·toh
a children's menu/	**dječiji meni/dječiju porciju** *dyeh·chih·yih meh·nih/*
portion	*dyeh·chih·yoo pohr·tsih·yoo*
a child's seat/	**sjedalo za dijete/stolicu za hranjenje djece**
a highchair	*syeh·dah·loh zah dyeh·teh/stoh·lih·tsoo zah*
	hrah·nyeh·nyeh dyeh·tseh
a crib/a cot	**dječiji krevetić/kolijevka** *dyeh·chih·yih kreh·veh·tihch/*
	koh·lih·yehv·kah
diapers [nappies]	**pelene** *peh·leh·neh*
formula [baby food]	**dječiju hranu** *dyeh·chih·yoo hrah·noo*
a pacifier [soother]	**dudu** *doo·doo*
a playpen	**hodalicu** *hoh·dah·lih·tsoo*
a stroller [pushchair]	**dječija kolica** *dyeh·chih·yah koh·lih·tsah*
Can I breastfeed the	**Mogu li dojiti dijete ovdje?** *moh·goo lih doh·yih·tih*
baby here?	*dih·yeh·teh ohv·dyeh*
Where can I	**Gdje mogu dojiti/presvući dijete?**
breastfeed/change	*gdyeh moh·goo doh·yih·tih/preh·svoo·chih dih·yeh·teh*
the baby?	

For Eating Out, see page 60.

Disabled Travelers

Is there...?	**Ima li...?** *ih·mah lih...*
access for the	**prilaz za hendikepirane** *prih·lahz zah*
disabled	*hehn·dih·keh·pih·rah·neh*
a wheelchair ramp	**ulaz za invalidska kolica** *oo·lahz zah ihn·vah·lihd·skah*
	koh·lih·tsah

a disabled-accessible toilet	**zahod za hendikepirane** *zah-hohd zah hehn-dih-keh-pih-rah-neh*
I need…	**Treba mi…** *treh-bah mih…*
assistance	**pomoć** *poh-mohch*
an elevator [a lift]	**lift** *lihft*
a ground-floor room	**soba na prizemlju** *soh-bah nah prih-zehm-lyoo*

Health & Emergencies

Emergencies

Help!	**Upomoć!** *oo-poh-mohch*
Go away!	**Odlazi!** *oh-dlah-zih*
Stop thief!	**Stop, lopov!** *stohp loh-pohv*
Get a doctor!	**Dovedite doktora!** *doh-veh-dih-teh doh-ktoh-rah*
Fire!	**Požar!** *poh-zhahr*
I'm lost.	**Izgubio** *m*/**Izgubila** *f* **sam se.** *ihz-goo-bih-oh/ ihz-goo-bih-lah sahm seh*
Can you help me?	**Možete li mi pomoći?** *moh-zheh-teh lih mih poh-moh-chih*
Call the police!	**Zovite policiju!** *zoh-vih-teh poh-lih-tsih-yoo*
Where's the police station?	**Gdje je policijska postaja?** *gdyeh yeh poh-lih-tsihy-skah poh-stah-yah*
My child is missing.	**Moje dijete je nestalo.** *moh-yeh dyeh-teh yeh neh-stah-loh*

YOU MAY HEAR…

Popunite ovaj obrazac.
poh-poo-nih-teh oh-vahy oh-brah-zahts

Fill out this form.

Vašu osobnu ispravu, molim *Vas. vah-shoo oh-soh-bnoo ihs-prah-voo moh-lihm vahs*

Your ID, please.

Kada/Gdje se to dogodilo?
kah-dah/gdyeh seh toh doh-goh-dih-loh

When/Where did it happen?

Kako je izgledao *m*/**izgledala** *f*?
kah-koh yeh ihz-gleh-dah-oh/ihz-gleh-dah-lah

What does he/ she look like?

In an emergency, dial: **112**
For the telephone directory, dial **988**.

Health

I'm sick [ill].	**Bolestan** *m* /**Bolesna** *f* **sam.**
	boh·leh·stahn/boh·leh·snah sahm
I need an English-speaking doctor.	**Treba mi doktor koji govori engleski.** *treh·bah mih*
	dohk·tohr koh·yih goh·voh·rih ehn·gleh·skih
It hurts here.	**Tu me boli.** *too meh boh·lih*
I have a stomachache.	**Boli me stomak.** *boh·lih meh stoh·mahk*
Where's the pharmacy [chemist]?	**Gdje je ljekarna?** *gdyeh yeh lyeh·kahr·nah*
I'm (...months) pregnant.	**Trudna sam (...mjeseci).**
	troo·dnah sam (...myeh·seh·tsih)
I'm on...	**Uzimam...** *oo·zih·mahm...*
I'm allergic to	**Alergičan** *m* /**Alergična** *f* **sam na** *ah·lehr·gih·chahn/*
	ah·lehr·gih·chnah sahm nah
antibiotics/penicillin.	**antibiotike/penicilin.** *ahn·tih·bih·oh·tih·keh/*
	peh·nih·tsih·lihn

68

Dictionary

adapter **adapter**
and **i**
aspirin **aspirin**
baby **beba**
bad **loš**
bag **torba**
bandage **zavoj**
battleground **borilište**
bikini **bikini**
bird **ptica**
bland **blijed**

bottle opener **otvarač za boce**
bowl **zdjela**
boy **dječak**
boyfriend **dečko**
bra **grudnjak**
camera **fotoaparat**
can opener **otvarač za konzerve**
castle **dvorac**
cold *adj* (weather) **hladno;** *n* **hunjavica**
comb **češalj**
computer **računar**

condom **prezervativ**
corkscrew **vadičep**
cup **šalica**
dangerous **opasan**
deodorant **dezodorans**
diabetic *n* **dijabetičar**
dog **pas**
doll **lutka**
fly *n* (insect) **muha;** *v* **letjeti**
fork **vilica**
girl **djevojka**
girlfriend **djevojka**
glass **čaša**
good **dobar**
great *adj* **velik;** *adv* **izvrsno**
hot **vruć**
husband **muž**
icy **leden**
injection **injekcija**
insect repellent **odbojan za insekte**
jeans **traperice**
knife **nož**
large **velik**
lighter *n* **upaljač**
love *n* **ljubav;** *v* **voljeti**
match *n* (light) **šibica;** (play) **utakmica**
medium **srednji**
museum **muzej**
my **moj**
nail file **turpija za nokte**
napkin **ubrus**
nurse **medicinska sestra**
or (either/or) **ili**
park *n* **park;** *v* **parkirati**
partner (romance, business) **partner**
pen **olovka**

plate **tanjur**
pyjamas [BE] **pidžama**
rain *n* **kiša**
raincoat **kišni mantil**
razor **brijač**
razor blade **britvica**
sandal **sandala**
sanitary napkin **higijenski uložak**
sauna **sauna**
scissors **škare**
shampoo **šampon**
shoe **cipela**
small **mali**
sneaker **tenisica**
snow **snijeg**
soap **sapun**
sock **čarapa**
spicy **začinjen**
spoon **žlica**
stamp (postal) **poštanska markica**
suitcase **kofer**
sunglasses **sunčane naočale**
sunscreen **krema za sunčanje**
sweater **džemper**
swimsuit **kupaći kostim**
tampon **tampon**
terrible **grozan**
tissue **maramica**
toilet paper **toaletni papir**
toothbrush **četkica za zube**
toothpaste **pasta za zube**
toy **igračka**
T-shirt **majica**
underpants [BE] **gaćice**
vegetarian *n* **vegetarijanac**
zoo **zoološki vrt**

Czech

Essentials

Hello./Hi.	**Dobrý den./Nazdar.** <u>dohb</u>·ree dehn/<u>nahz</u>·dahr
Good afternoon.	**Dobré odpoledne.** <u>dohb</u>·reh ohd·poh·lehd·neh
Good night.	**Dobrou noc.** <u>dohb</u>·roh nohts
Goodbye.	**Na shledanou.** nahs·hleh·dah·noh
Yes.	**Ano.** <u>ah</u>·noh
No.	**Ne.** Neh
OK.	**Dobře.** <u>dob</u>·rzheh
Excuse me! (to get attention)	**Promiňte!** proh·mihn'·teh
Sorry!	**Pardon!** <u>pahr</u>·dohn
I'd like...	**Chtěl m/Chtěla f bych...** khtyehl/<u>khtyeh</u>·lah bihkh...
How much?	**Kolik?** <u>koh</u>·lihk
Where is/are...?	**Kde je/jsou...?** gdeh yeh/<u>yeh</u>·soh...
Please.	**Prosím.** proh·<u>seem</u>
Thank you.	**Děkuji.** <u>dyeh</u>·koo·yih
You're welcome.	**Není zač.** <u>neh</u>·nee zahch
Please speak more slowly.	**Mluvte, prosím, pomalu.** <u>mloo</u>·vteh proh·<u>seem</u> <u>poh</u>·mah·loo
Could you repeat that?	**Můžete to zopakovat?** <u>moo</u>·zheh·teh toh <u>zoh</u>·pah·koh·vaht
I don't understand.	**Nerozumím.** <u>neh</u>·roh·zoo·meem
Do you speak English?	**Mluvíte anglicky?** <u>mloo</u>·vee·teh <u>ahn</u>·glihts·kih
I don't speak much Czech.	**Neumím moc česky.** <u>neh</u>·oo·meem mohts <u>chehs</u>·kih
Where are the restrooms [toilets]?	**Kde jsou záchody?** gdeh <u>yeh</u>·soh <u>zah</u>·khoh·dih
Help!	**Pomoc!** <u>poh</u>·mohts

You'll find the pronunciation of the Czech letters and words written in gray after each sentence to guide you. Simply pronounce these as if they were English, noting that any underlines and bolds indicate an additional emphasis or stress or a lengthening of a vowel sound. As you hear the language being spoken, you will quickly become accustomed to the local pronunciation and dialect.

Numbers

0	**nula**	_noo_·lah
1	**jedna**	_yehd_·nah
2	**dva**	dvah
3	**tři**	trzhih
4	**čtyři**	_chtih_·rzhih
5	**pět**	pyeht
6	**šest**	shehst
7	**sedm**	sehdm
8	**osm**	ohsm
9	**devět**	_deh_·vyeht
10	**deset**	_deh_·seht
11	**jedenáct**	_yeh_·deh·**nah**tst
12	**dvanáct**	_dvah_·**nah**tst
13	**třináct**	_trzhih_·**nah**tst
14	**čtrnáct**	chtrn**ah**tst
15	**patnáct**	_paht_·**nah**tst
16	**šestnáct**	_shehst_·**nah**tst
17	**sedmnáct**	_sehdm_·**nah**tst
18	**osmnáct**	_ohsm_·**nah**tst
19	**devatenáct**	_deh_·vah·teh·**nah**tst
20	**dvacet**	_dvah_·tseht
21	**dvacet jedna**	_dvah_·tseht yehd·nah
22	**dvacet dva**	_dvah_·tseht dvah
30	**třicet**	_trzhih_·tseht
31	**třicet jedna**	_trzhih_·tseht yehd·nah
40	**čtyřicet**	_chtih_·rzhih·tseht
50	**padesát**	_pah_·deh·**saht**
60	**šedesát**	_sheh_·deh·**saht**
70	**sedmdesát**	_sehdm_·deh·**saht**
80	**osmdesát**	_ohsm_·deh·**saht**
90	**devadesát**	_deh_·vah·deh·**saht**
100	**sto**	stoh
101	**sto jedna**	_stoh_ yehd·nah
200	**dvě stě**	_dvyeh_ styeh
500	**pět set**	_pyeht_ seht

1,000	**tisíc** _tih_·**see**ts
10,000	**deset tisíc** _deh_·seht tih·**see**ts
1,000,000	**milión** _mih_·lih·**ohn**

Time

What time is it?	**Kolik je hodin?** _koh_·lihk yeh _hoh_·dihn
It's noon [midday].	**Je dvanáct hodin poledne.** yeh _dvah_·**nah**tst _hoh_·dihn poh·**lehd**·neh
It's midnight.	**Je půlnoc.** yeh _pool_·nohts
From 9 o'clock to 5 o'clock.	**Od deváté do páté.** _ohd_·deh·**vah**·teh _doh_·**pah**·teh
twenty after [past] four	**za deset minut půl páté** _zah_·deh·seht _mih_·noot _pool_ **pah**·**teh**
a quarter to nine	**tři čtvrtě na devět** trzih _chtvur_·tyeh _nah_·deh·vyeht
5:30 a.m./p.m.	**půl šesté/sedmnáct třicet** pool _shehs_·teh/_sehdm_·**nah**tst _tzih_·tseht

Days

Monday	**pondělí** _pohn_·dyeh·**lee**
Tuesday	**úterý** _oo_·teh·**ree**
Wednesday	**středa** _strzheh_·dah
Thursday	**čtvrtek** chtfrtehk
Friday	**pátek** _pah_·tehk
Saturday	**sobota** _soh_·boh·tah
Sunday	**neděle** _neh_·dyeh·leh

Dates

yesterday	**včera** _fcheh_·rah
today	**dnes** dnehs
tomorrow	**zítra** _zeet_·rah
day	**den** dehn
week	**týden** _tee_·dehn
month	**měsíc** _myeh_·**see**ts
year	**rok** rohk
Happy Birthday!	**Všechno nejlepší k narozenínám!** _Vseh_·khnoh _ney_·lep·shee k _nah_·roh·zeh·nyih·nahm
Happy New Year!	**Šťastný nový rok!** _Shtya_·stnee _noh_·vee rock

Months

January	**leden** _leh_·dehn
February	**únor** _oo_·nohr
March	**březen** _brzheh_·zehn
April	**duben** _doo_·behn
May	**květen** _kfyeh_·tehn
June	**červen** _chehr_·vehn
July	**červenec** _chehr_·veh·nets
August	**srpen** srpehn
September	**září** _zah_·rzhee
October	**říjen** _rzhee_·yehn
November	**listopad** _lih_·stoh·paht
December	**prosinec** proh·sih·nehts

Arrival & Departure

I'm here on vacation [holiday]/business.	**Jsem zde na dovolené/služebně.** _ysehm zdeh nah_·doh·voh·leh·_neh_/_sloo_·zhehb·nyeh
I'm going to…	**Jedu do…** _Yeh_·doo doh…
I'm staying at the…Hotel.	**Ubytoval m/Ubytovala f jsem se v hotelu…** _oo_·bih·toh·vahl/_oo_·bih·toh·vah·lah ysehm se _fhoh_·teh·loo…

Money

Where's…?	**Kde je…?** gdeh yeh…
the ATM	**bankomat** _bahn_·koh·maht
the bank	**banka** _bahn_·kah
the currency exchange office	**směnárna** smyeh·_nahr_·nah
What time does the bank open/close?	**V kolik otvírají/zavírají banku?** _fkoh_·lihk _oht_·fee·rah·yee/_zah_·vee·rah·yee _bahn_·koo
I'd like to change dollars/pounds into crowns.	**Chtěl m/Chtěla f bych si vyměnit dolary/libry na koruny.** khtyehl/_khtyeh_·lah bihkh sih _vih_·myeh·niht _doh_·lah·rih/_lihb_·rih _nah_·koh·roo·nih
I'd like to cash some travelers checks [cheques].	**Chtěl m/Chtěla f bych si vyměnit cestovní šeky.** khtyehl/_khtyeh_·lah bihkh sih _vih_·myeh·niht _tsehs_·tohv·_nee sheh_·kih

For Numbers, see page 72.

YOU MAY SEE...

The monetary unit is the **Česká koruna, Kč** (Czech crown), plural **korun**, which is divided into 100 **haléřů, h.**
Coins: 10, 20 and 50 **h**; 1, 2, 5, 10 and 20 **Kč**
Notes: 20, 50, 100, 200, 500, 1000, 2000 and 5000 **Kč**

Getting Around

How do I get to town?	**Jak se odtud dostat do mešta?** _yahk seh ohd·tood dohs·taht doh meh·shtah_
Where's...?	**Kde je...?** _gdeh yeh..._
the airport	**letiště** _leh·tihsh·tyeh_
the train station	**nádraží** _nah·drah·zhee_
the bus station	**autobusové nádraží** _ow·toh·boo·soh·veh nah·drah·zhee_
the subway [underground] station	**stanice metra** _stah·nih·tseh meht·rah_
How far is it?	**Jak je to daleko?** _yahk yeh toh dah·leh·koh_
Where can I buy tickets?	**Kde si mohu koupit jízdenku?** _gdeh sih moh·hoo koh·piht yeez·dehn·koo_
A one-way [single] ticket.	**Jedním směrem.** _yehd·neem smyeh·rehm_
A round-trip [return] ticket.	**Zpáteční.** _spah·tehch·nee_
How much?	**Kolik?** _koh·lihk_
Are there any discounts?	**Jsou nějaké slevy?** _ysoh nyeh·yah·keh sleh·vih_
Which gate/platform?	**Který východ/nástupiště?** _kteh·ree vee·khohd/nahs·too·pihsh·tyeh_
Which line?	**Která linka?** _kteh·rah lihn·kah_
Where can I get a taxi?	**Kde najdu taxík?** _gdeh nahy·doo tah·kseek_
Please take me to this address.	**Dovezte mě laskavě na tuhle adresu.** _doh·vehs·teh myeh lahs·kah·vyeh nah too·hleh ahd·reh·soo_
A map please.	**Prosím mapu.** _proh·seem mah·poo_

Tickets

When's...to Prague?	**V kolik je...do Prahy?** _fkoh·lihk yeh...doh prah·hih_
the (first) bus	**(první) autobus** _(prvnee) ow·toh·boos_
the (next) flight	**(další) let** _(dahl·shee) leht_

the (last) train	**(poslední) vlak** _(pohs·lehd·nee)_ vlahk
Where can I buy train/plane tickets?	**Kde si mohu koupit jízdenku/letenku?** _gdeh sih moh·hoo koh·piht yeez·dehn·koo/leh·tehn·koo_
One/Two ticket(s) please.	**Prosím jednu jízdenku/dvě jízdenky.** _Proh·seem yed·nu yeez·den·koo_
For today/tomorrow.	**Na dnešek/zítřek.** nah _dneh·shehk/zee·trzhehk_
. . . plane/train ticket.	**Letenka/Jízdenka . . .** _leh·tehn·kah/yeez·dehn·kah . . ._
A one-way	**jedním směrem** _yehd·neem smyeh·rehm_
A return trip	**zpáteční** _spah·tehch·nee_
A first class	**do první** _doh·prvnee_
business class	**Třída business** Trzee·dah biz·niss klahs
An economy class	**ekonomické třídy** _eh·koh·noh·mihts·keh trzhee·dih_
How much?	**Kolik?** _koh·lihk_
Is there a discount for . . . ?	**Je sleva pro . . . ?** yeh _sleh·vah proh . . ._
children	**děti** _dyeh·tih_
students	**studenty** _stoo·dehn·tih_
senior citizens	**starší občany** _stahr·shee ohp·chah·nih_
tourists	**turisté** _too·riss·teh_
The express bus/ express train, please.	**Prosím jízdenku na dálkový autobus/rychlík.** _Proh·seem yeez·den·koo nah dahl·ko·vee ah·oo·toh·boos/rih·khleek_
The local bus/train, please.	**Prosím jízdenku na místní autobus/osobní vlak.** _Proh·seem yeez·den·koo nah meest·nyee ah·oo·toh·boos/ os·ob·nee vlahk_
I have an e-ticket.	**Mám elektronický lístek.** _mahm eh·lehk·troh·nihts·kee lees·tehk_
Can I buy a ticket on the bus/train?	**Mohu si koupit jízdenku v autobusu/ve vlaku?** _moh·hoo sih koh·piht yeez·dehn·koo fow·toh·boo·soo/veh vlah·koo_
Can I buy the ticket before boarding?	**Mohu si koupit jízdenku před nastoupením do autobusu/vlaku?** _moo·hoo sih koh·piht yeez·dehn·koo przed nas·toe·pe·nyeem doh ah·oo·toh·boo·soo/vlah·koo_
How long is this ticket valid?	**Jak dlouho platí jízdenka?** Yahk _dloe·hoh plah·tyee yeez·den·kah?_
Can I return on the same ticket?	**Platí stejná jízdenka i pro zpáteční jízdu?** _Plah·tyee stay·nah yeez·den·kah se proh spaa·tetch·nyee yeez·doo?_
I'd like to . . . my reservation.	**Chtěl** m/**Chtěla** f **bych . . . moji rezervaci.** _khtyehl/khtyeh·lah bihkh . . . moh·yih reh·zehr·vah·tsih_

cancel	**zrušit** _zroo_·shiht
change	**změnit** _zmyeh_·niht
confirm	**potvrdit** _pohtfr_·diht

For Time, see page 73.

Car Hire

Where can I rent a car?	**Kde si mohu půjčit auto?** _gdeh sih moh·hoo **pooy**·chiht ow·toh_
I'd like to rent...	**Chtěl** m/**Chtěla** f **bych si půjčit...** _khtyehl/khtyeh·lah bihkh sih **pooy**·chiht..._
a 2-/4-door car	**dvoudveřové/čtyřdveřové auto** _dvoh·dveh·rzhoh·**veh**/ chtihrzh·dveh·rzhoh·**veh** ow·toh_
an automatic	**auto s automatickou převodovkou** _ow·toh sow·toh·mah·tihts·koh przheh·voh·dohf·koh_
a manual car	**Automobil s manuální převodovkou** _Ah·owo·toh·moh·bil s mah·noo·aahl·nyee przeh·voh·doh·fkoe_
a car with air-conditioning	**auto s klimatizací** _ow·toh sklih·mah·tih·zah·tsee_
a car seat	**autosedačka** _ow·toh·seh·dahch·kah_
How much...?	**Kolik stojí...?** _koh·lihk stoh·yee..._
per day/week	**na den/týden** _nah dehn/**tee**·dehn_

YOU MAY HEAR...

přímo před vámi _przhee·moh przhehd **vah**·mih_	straight ahead
vlevo _vleh·voh_	on the left
vpravo _fprah·voh_	on the right
na rohu/za rohem _nah roh·hoo/zah roh·hehm_	on/around the corner
naproti... _nah·proh·tih_	opposite...
za... _zah..._	behind...
vedle... _vehd·leh..._	next to...
za _zah_	after
na sever/na jih _nah·seh·vehr/nah·yihh_	north/south
na východ/na západ _nah·vee·khohd/nah·zah·pahd_	east/west
na světlách _nah·sfyeht·lahkh_	at the traffic lights
na křižovatce _na krzhih·zhoh·vaht·tseh_	at the intersection

per kilometer	**za kilometr** _zah-kih-loh-mehtr_
for unlimited	**bez kilometrového limitu** _behs_
mileage	_kih-loh-meht-roh-veh-hoh lih-mih-tuh_
with insurance	**s pojištěním** _spoh-yihsh-tyeh-neem_
Are there any discounts?	**Máte speciální slevy?** _mah-teh speh-tsyahl-nee sleh-vih_

Places to Stay

Can you recommend a hotel?	**Který hotel byste mi doporučil?** _kteh-ree hoh-tehl bihs-teh mih doh-poh-roo-chihl_
I have a reservation.	**Objednal** _m_/**Objednala** _f_ **jsem si pokoj.** _ohb-yehd-nahl/ oh-byehd-nah-lah ysehm sih poh-kohy_
My name is...	**Jmenuji se...** _ymeh-noo-yih seh..._
Do you have a room...?	**Máte volný pokoj...?** _mah-teh vohl-ne poh-kohy..._
for one/two	**jednolůžkový/dvoulůžkový** _yeh-dnoh-loozh-koh-vee/ dvoh-loozh-koh-vee_
with a bathroom	**s koupelnou** _skoh-pehl-noh_
with air conditioning	**s klimatizací** _sklih-mah-tih-zah-tsee_
for tonight	**na jednu noc** _nah-yehd-noo nots_
for two nights	**na dvě noce** _nah-dvyeh noh-tseh_
for one week	**na týden** _nah-tee-dehn_
How much?	**Kolik?** _koh-lihk_
Do you have anything cheaper?	**Máte něco levnějšího?** _mah-teh nyeh-tsoh lehv-nyehy-shee-hoh_
When's check-out?	**V kolik hodin musíme uvolnit pokoj?** _fkoh-lihk hoh-dihn moo-see-meh oo-vohl-niht poh-kohy_
Can I leave this in the safe?	**Mohu tohle nechat v sejfu?** _moh-hoo toh-hleh neh-khaht fsehy-foo_
Can I leave my bags here?	**Mohu si zde nechat zavazadla?** _moh-hoo sih zdeh neh-khaht zah-vah-zah-dlah_
Can I have the bill/ a receipt?	**Mohu dostat stvrzenku/účet?** _moh-hoo dohs-taht stvrzehn-koo/oo-cheht_
I'll pay in cash/ by credit card.	**Zaplatím v hotovosti/kreditní kartou.** _zah-plah-teem fhoh-toh-vohs-tih/kreh-diht-nee kahr-toh_

Communications

| Where's an internet cafe? | **Kde je internetová kavárna?** _gdeh yeh ihn-tehr-neh-toh-vah kah-vahr-nah_ |

Does it have wireless internet?	**Je tady bezdrátový internet?** *yeh tah-dih behz-drah-toh-vee ihn-tehr-neht*	
What is the WiFi password?	**Jaké je heslo pro WiFi?** *Yah-keh yeh hes-loh proh Wih-Fih?*	
Is the WiFi free?	**Je WiFi zdarma?** *Yeh Wih-Fih zdah-rmah?*	
Do you have bluetooth?	**Máš bluetooth?** *Maash bluetooth?*	
How do I turn the computer on/off?	**Jak se zapíná/vypíná počítač?** *yahk seh zah-pee-nah/vih-pee-nah poh-chee-tahch*	
Can I...?	**Mohu...?** *moh-hoo...*	
access the internet here	**se odtud připojit na internet** *seh oht-tood przhih-poh-yiht nah-ihn-tehr-neht*	
check e-mail	**skontrolovat poštu** *skohn-troh-loh-vaht pohsh-too*	
print	**něco vytisknout** *nyeh-tsoh vih-tihs-knoht*	
use any computer	**používat počítač** *poh-oo-zhee-vaht poh-chee-tahch*	
plug in/charge my laptop/iPhone/iPad/BlackBerry?	**si připojit/nabít svůj notebook/iPhone/iPad?** *sih przih-poh-yit/nah-beet svooy notebook/iPhone/iPad?*	
How much per hour/half hour?	**Kolik stojí hodina/půl hodiny?** *koh-lihk stoh-yee hoh-dih-nah/pool hoh-dih-nih*	
How do I...?	**Jak se mohu...?** *yahk seh moh-hoo...*	
connect/disconnect	**připojit na síť/odpojit** *przhih-poh-yiht nah seet'/oht-poh-yeet*	
log on/off	**zalogovat/vylogovat** *zah-loh-goh-vaht/vih-loh-goh-vaht*	
type this symbol	**zapsat tento symbol** *zahp-saht tehn-toh sihm-bohl*	
What's your e-mail?	**Jakou máte emailovou adresu?** *yah-koh mah-teh eh-mehy-loh-voh ahd-reh-soo*	
My e-mail is...	**Moje emailová adresa je...** *moh-yeh eh-mehy-loh-vah ahd-reh-sah yeh...*	
Do you have a scanner?	**Máte skener?** *Maah-teh sken-nehr?*	

Social Media

Are you on Facebook/Twitter?	**Máš účet na Facebooku/Twitteru?** *Maash oo-tchet nah Face-boo-koo/Twi-tte-roo?*	
What's your username?	**Jaké je tvoje uživatelské jméno?** *Yah-keh yeh tvoh-yeh oo-zhih-vah-tell-skeh ye-meh-noh?*	
I'll add you as a friend.	**Přidám si tě do přátel.** *Przih-daahm sih tyeh doh przaah-tell*	

I'll follow you on Twitter. **Začnu tě sledovat na Twitteru.** *Zatch·noo tyeh sleh·doh·vaht nah Twi·tte·roo*

Are you following...? **Sledujete...?** *Sleh·doo·yeh·teh*

I'll put the pictures on Facebook/Twitter. **Dám fotky na Facebook/Twitter.** *Daam fot·kih nah Facebook*

I'll tag you in the pictures. **Označím tě na fotkách.** *Oz·nah·tcheem tyeh nah fot·kaahk*

Conversation

Hello./Hi!	**Dobrý den./Nazdar!**	<u>dohb</u>·ree dehn/<u>nahz</u>·dahr
How are you?	**Jak se máte?**	yahk seh <u>mah</u>·teh
Fine, thanks.	**Dobře, děkuji.**	<u>dohb</u>·rzeh <u>dyeh</u>·koo·yih
Excuse me!	**Promiňte!**	proh·mihn'·teh
Do you speak English?	**Mluvíte anglicky?**	<u>mloo</u>·vee·teh <u>ahn</u>·glihts·kih
What's your name?	**Jak se jmenujete?**	yahk seh <u>ymeh</u>·noo·yeh·teh
My name is...	**Jmenuji se...**	<u>ymeh</u>·noo·yih seh...
Pleased to meet you.	**Těší mě.**	<u>tyeh</u>·shee myeh
Where are you from?	**Odkud jste?**	<u>oht</u>·koot ysteh
I'm from the U.S./the U.K.	**Jsem ze Spojených Státú/z Velké Británie.**	ysehm <u>zeh</u>·spoh·yeh·neekh <u>stah</u>·too/<u>sfehl</u>·keh brih·<u>tah</u>·nyeh
What do you do?	**Čím jste?**	cheem ysteh
I work for...	**Pracuji pro...**	<u>prah</u>·tsoo·yih proh...
I'm a student.	**Jsem student** *m*/**studentka** *f*.	ysehm <u>stoo</u>·dehnt/<u>stoo</u>·dehnt·kah
I'm retired.	**Jsem v důchodu.**	ysehm <u>vdoo</u>·khoh·doo
Do you like...?	**Chcete...?**	<u>khtseh</u>·teh...
Goodbye.	**Na shledanou.**	<u>nahs</u>·hleh·dah·noh
See you later.	**Na viděnou.**	<u>nah</u>·vih·dyeh·noh

Romance

Would you like to go out for a drink/meal?	**Nešli bychom si dát drink/jídlo?**	<u>nesh</u>·lih <u>bih</u>·khohm sih daht drihnk/<u>jeed</u>·loh
What are your plans for tonight/tomorrow?	**Jaké máte plány na dnešní večer/zítřek?**	<u>yah</u>·keh <u>mah</u>·teh <u>plah</u>·nih nah <u>dnehsh</u>·nee <u>veh</u>·chehr/<u>zeet</u>·rzhehk
Can I have your number?	**Dáte mi Vaše telefonní číslo?**	<u>dah</u>·teh mih <u>vah</u>·sheh teh·leh·fohn·nee <u>chees</u>·loh
Can I join you?	**Můžu se přisednout?**	<u>moo</u>·hoo seh przhih·sehd·noht

Can I buy you a drink?	**Mohu Vám objednat něco k pití?** _moh_·hoo **vahm**
	ohb·yehd·naht _nyeh_·tsoh _kpih_·**tee**
I like you.	**Mám tě rád** m **/ráda** f. **mahm** tyeh **rahd**/_rah_·dah
I love you.	**Miluji tě.** _mih_·loo·yih tyeh

Accepting & Rejecting

Thank you. I'd love to.	**Děkuji. Velice rád** m/ráda f. _dyeh_·koo·yih _veh_·lih·tseh **raht**/_rah_·dah
Where shall we meet?	**Kde se setkáme?** _gdeh_ seh _seht_·**kah**·meh
I'll meet you at the bar/ your hotel.	**Sejdeme se v baru/ve vašem hotelu.** _sehy_·deh·meh seh _fbah_·roo/_veh_·vah·shehm _hoh_·teh·loo
I'll come by at...	**Přijdu v...** _przhihy_·doo v...
What's your address?	**Kde bydlíte?** _gdeh_ _bihd_·**lee**·teh
I'm busy.	**Jsem zaneprázdněný** m **/zaneprázdněná** f. _ysehm_ _zah_·nehp·**rahzd**·nyeh·**nee**/_zah_·nehp·**rahzd**·nyeh·**nah**
I'm not interested.	**Nemám zájem.** _neh_·**mahm** _zah_·yehm
Leave me alone, please.	**Nechte mí, prosím.** _nekh_·teh **mee** _proh_·**seem**
Stop bothering me!	**Ne otravujte mně!** neh _oht_·rah·vooy·teh mnyeh

Food & Drink

Eating Out

Can you recommend a good restaurant/bar?	**Můžete mi doporučit dobrou restauraci/bar?** _moo_·zheh·teh mih _doh_·poh·roo·chiht _doh_·broh _rehs_·tow·rah·tsih/**bahr**
Is there a traditional Czech/an inexpensive restaurant near here?	**Je tu někde nablízku tradiční česká/levná restaurace?** yeh too _nyek_·deh _nahb_·**lees**·koo _trah_·dihch·nee chehs·kah/_lehv_·nah rehs·tow·rah·tseh
A table for..., please.	**Stůl pro..., prosím.** stool proh... _proh_·**seem**
Could we sit...?	**Mohli bychom si sednout...?** _moh_·hlih _bih_·khohm sih _sehd_·noht...
here/there	**tady/tam** _tah_·dih/tahm
outside	**venku** _vehn_·koo
in a non-smoking area	**v části pro nekuřáky** _fchahs_·tih proh _neh_·koo·rzh**ah**·kih
I'm waiting for someone.	**Čekám někoho.** _cheh_·**kahm** nyeh·koh·hoh

Where are the restrooms [toilets]?	**Kde jsou záchody?** *gdeh ysoh <u>zah</u>·khoh·dih*
A menu, please.	**Jídelní lístek, prosím.** <u>*yee*</u>·*dehl·nee lees·tehk <u>proh</u>·seem*
What do you recommend?	**Co nám můžete doporučit?** *tsoh nahm <u>moo</u>·zheh·the doh·poh·roo·chiht*
I'd like...	**Chtěl m/Chtěla f bych...** *khtyehl/khtyeh·lah bikh...*
Some more..., please.	**Ještě trochu..., prosím.** *yehsh·tyeh troh·khoo... <u>proh</u>·seem*
Enjoy your meal.	**Nechte si chutnat.** <u>*nehkh*</u>·*teh sih <u>khoot</u>·naht*
The check [bill], please.	**Účet, prosím.** <u>*oo*</u>·*cheht <u>proh</u>·seem*
Is service included?	**Je v tom zahrnutá obsluha?** *yeh ftohm <u>zah</u>·hrnoo·t<u>ah</u> ohp·sloo·hah*
Can I pay by credit card?	**Mohu zaplatit kreditní kartou?** <u>*moh*</u>·*hoo <u>zah</u>·plah·tiht <u>kreh</u>·diht·nee <u>kahr</u>·toh*
Can I have a receipt?	**Mohu dostat stvrzenku?** <u>*moh*</u>·*hoo <u>dohs</u>·taht <u>stvrzehn</u>·koo*
Thank you.	**Děkuji.** <u>*dyeh*</u>·*koo·yih*

YOU MAY SEE...

JÍDELNÍ LÍSTEK	menu
NABÍDKA DNE	menu of the day
KUVERT A SERVIS (NENÍ) V CENĚ JÍDLA	cover charge and service (not) included in price
OBSLUHA NENÍ/JE ZAJIŠTĚNA	service (not) included
SPECIÁLNÍ PŘÍLOHY	specials

Breakfast

chléb *khlehb*	bread
máslo <u>*mah*</u>·*sloh*	butter
...vejce ...<u>*vehy*</u>·*tseh*	...egg
míchaná <u>*mee*</u>·*khah·nah*	scrambled
smažená <u>*smah*</u>·*zheh·nah*	fried
vařená <u>*vah*</u>·*rzheh·nah*	boiled
džem *dzhehm*	jam
topinka <u>*toh*</u>·*pihn·kah*	toast
jogurt <u>*yoh*</u>·*goort*	yogurt

džus *dzhoos*	juice
kukuřičné vločky <u>koo</u>·koo·rzhihch·**neh** <u>vlohch</u>·kih	cornflakes
med *meht*	honey

Appetizers

křenová rolka <u>krzheh</u>·noh·**vah** <u>rohl</u>·kah	ham and horseradish roll
ruská vejce <u>roos</u>·kah <u>vehy</u>·tseh	egg with mayonnaise
salám s okurkou <u>sah</u>·**lahm** <u>soh</u>·koor·koh	salami with pickles
šunka s okurkou <u>shoon</u>·kah <u>soh</u>·koor·koh	ham with pickles
šunka v aspiku <u>shoon</u>·kah <u>vahs</u>·pih·koo	ham in aspic
tlačenka s cibulí <u>tlah</u>·chehn·kah <u>stsih</u>·boo·**lee**	rolled pork with onion
tresčí játra s cíbulkou <u>trehs</u>·chee <u>yah</u>·trah <u>stsee</u>·bool·koh	cod liver with onion
uzený jazyk <u>oo</u>·zeh·nee <u>yah</u>·zihk	smoked tongue
zavináče <u>zah</u>·vih·**nah**·cheh	pickled herring [rollmops]

Meat

hovězí <u>hoh</u>·vyeh·**zee**	beef
jehněčí <u>yeh</u>·hnyeh·**chee**	lamb
vepřové <u>vehp</u>·rzhoh·**veh**	pork
telecí <u>teh</u>·leh·**tsee**	veal
kuře <u>koo</u>·rzheh	chicken
kachna <u>kahkh</u>·nah	duck
bažant <u>bah</u>·zhahnt	pheasant
biftek <u>bihf</u>·tehk	steak
guláš <u>goo</u>·**lah**sh	goulash
husa <u>hoo</u>·sah	goose
klobása <u>kloh</u>·**bah**·sah	sausage
králík <u>krah</u>·leek	rabbit
krůta <u>krooh</u>·tah	turkey
párka <u>pahr</u>·kah	type of thick sausage
slanina <u>slah</u>·nih·nah	bacon
šunka <u>shoon</u>·kah	ham
zajíc <u>zah</u>·**yee**ts	hare
zvěřina <u>zvyeh</u>·rzhih·nah	game

Fish & Seafood

candát _tsahn_·**d**_aht_	pike perch
garnát _gahr_·_naht_	shrimp [prawn]
humr _hoomr_	lobster
chobotnice _khoh_·_boht_·_nih_·_tseh_	octopus
kapr... _kahpr..._	carp...
smažený _smah_·_zheh_·_nee_	fried in bread crumbs
na černo _nah_·_chehr_·_noh_	in a thick sauce of vegetables, dark beer and prunes
na česneku _nah_·_chehs_·_neh_·_koo_	grilled with butter and garlic
kaviár _kah_·_vyahr_	caviar
krab _krahb_	crab
losos _loh_·_sohs_	salmon
mořský jazyk _mohrzh_·_skee_ _yah_·_zihk_	sole
platýz _plah_·_tees_	plaice
pstruh na másle _pstrooh nah_ _mah_·_sleh_	trout fried in butter
rybí filé _rih_·_bee_ _fih_·_leh_	fish fillet
slaneček _slah_·_neh_·_chehk_	herring
štika _shtih_·_kah_	pike
treska _trehs_·_kah_	cod
tuňák _too_·_n'ahk_	tuna
ústřice _oo_·_strzhih_·_tseh_	oyster

84

Vegetables

fazolové lusky _fah_·_zoh_·_loh_·_veh_ _loos_·_kih_	green beans
zelí _zeh_·_lee_	cabbage
pórek _poh_·_rehk_	leek
houba _hoh_·_bah_	mushroom
žampiony _zhahm_·_pyoh_·_nih_	mushrooms
cibule _tsih_·_boo_·_leh_	onion
brambor _brahm_·_bohr_	potato
rajče _rahy_·_cheh_	tomato
paprika _pahp_·_rih_·_kah_	pepper
červená řepa _chehr_·_veh_·_nah_ _rzheh_·_pah_	beet [beetroot]

Sauces & Condiments

sůl *sool*	salt
pepř *pehprzh*	pepper
hořčice *horz·chi·tse*	mustard
kečup *keh·tshoop*	ketchup

Fruit & Dessert

jablko *yah·blkoh*	apple
banán *bah·nahn*	banana
pomeranč *poh·meh·rahnch*	orange
švestka *shfehst·kah*	plum
jahoda *yah·hoh·dah*	strawberry
zmrzlina *zmrzlih·nah*	ice cream
jablečný závin *yahb·lehch·nee zah·vihn*	apple strudel
makový koláč *mah·koh·vee koh·lahch*	poppy seed cake
medovník *meh·dohv·neek*	honey cake
ovocný koláč *oh·vohts·nee koh·lahch*	fruit cake

Drinks

May I see the wine list/drink menu, please?	**Smím prosit vínný lístek/nápojový lístek?** *smeem proh·siht veen·nee lees·tehk/nah·poh·yoh·vee lees·tehk*
What do you recommend?	**Co mi můžete doporoučit?** *tsoh mih moo·zheh·teh doh·poh·roh·chiht*
I'd like a bottle/glass of red/white wine.	**Chtěl** *m***/Chtěla** *f* **bych láhev/pohár červeného/bílého vína.** *khtyehl/khteh·lah bihkh lah·hef/poh·hahr chehr·veh·neh·hoh/bee·leh·hoh vee·nah*
The house wine, please.	**Stolní víno, prosím.** *stohl·nee vee·noh proh·seem*
Another bottle/glass, please.	**Ještě jednu láhev/pohár, prosím.** *yeh·shtyeh yehd·noo lah·hef/poh·hahr proh·seem*
I'd like a local beer.	**Chtěl** *m***/Chtěla** *f* **bych místní pivo.** *khtyehl/khtyeh·lah bihkh meest·nee pih·voh*
Can I buy you a drink?	**Mohu vám objednat něco k pití?** *moh·hoo vahm ohb·yehd·naht nyeh·tsoh kpih·tee*
Cheers!	**Na zdraví!** *nah·zdrah·vee*
A coffee/tea, please.	**Kávu/Čaj, prosím.** *kah·voo/chahy proh·seem*
A..., please.	**...prosím.** *...proh·seem*

juice	**Džus** *dzhoos*
soda	**Sodou** <u>*soh*</u>*•doh*
(sparkling/still) water	**Vodu (s bublinkami/bez bublinek)** <u>*voh*</u>*•doo (*<u>*zboob*</u>*•lihn•kah•mih/*<u>*behz*</u>*•boob•lih•nehk)*
Is the tap water safe to drink?	**Může se pít kohoutková voda?** <u>*moo*</u>*•zheh seh peet* *koh•hoht•koh•***vah** <u>*voh*</u>*•dah*

Leisure Time

Sightseeing

Where's the tourist information office?	**Kde je turistická kancelář?** *gdeh yeh* <u>*too*</u>*•rihs•tihts•k***ah** *kahn•tseh•***lah**rzh
What are the main points of interest?	**Co tady stojí za prohlédnutí?** *tsoh* **tah**•dih *stoh•yee* *zah* *proh*•hl**ehd**•noo•tee
Are there tours in English?	**Jsou prohlídky s anglickým průvodcem?** *ysoh* *proh*•hl**ee**t•kih *sahn*•glihts•k**eem** <u>*proo*</u>*•voht•tsehm*
Could I have a map/guide?	**Můžete mi dát mapu/průvodce?** <u>*moo*</u>*•zheh•teh* *mih d***ah**t *mah*•poo/<u>*proo*</u>*•vohd•tseh*

> **YOU MAY SEE...**
>
> | | |
> |---|---|
> | **OTEVŘENO/ZAVŘENO** | open/closed |
> | **VÝCHOD** | exit |

Shopping

Where is the market/ mall?	**Kde je tržnice/nákupní centrum?** *gdeh yeh* <u>*trzhnih*</u>*•tseh/* <u>*nah*</u>*•koop•nee* <u>*tsehnt*</u>*•room*
I'm just looking.	**Jenom se dívám.** <u>*yeh*</u>*•nohm seh* <u>*dee*</u>*•vahm*
Can you help me?	**Můžete mi pomoci?** <u>*moo*</u>*•zheh•teh mih* <u>*poh*</u>*•moh•tsih*
I'm being helped.	**Již mě obsluhují.** *yihzh myeh* <u>*ohp*</u>*•sloo•hoo•yee*
How much?	**Kolik?** <u>*koh*</u>*•lihk*
That one.	**Tamten.** <u>*tahm*</u>*•tehn*
That's all, thanks.	**To je všechno, děkuji.** *toh yeh* <u>*vsheh*</u>*•khnoh* <u>*dyeh*</u>*•koo•yih*
Where do I pay?	**Kde zaplatím?** *gdeh* <u>*zah*</u>*•plah•teem*

I'll pay in cash/	**Zaplatím v hotovosti/kreditní kartou.**
by credit card.	_zah_·plah·**tee**m _fhoh_·toh·voh·stih/_kreh_·diht·nee _kahr_·toh
A receipt, please.	**Stvrzenku, prosím.** _stvrzehn_·koo _proh_·**see**m

Sport & Leisure

Where's the game?	**Kde se tady hraje?** _gdeh seh _tah_·dih _hrah_·yeh
Where's…?	**Kde je…?** _gdeh yeh…_
the beach	**pláž** _plahzh_
the park	**park** _pahrk_
the pool	**bazén** _bah_·**zehn**
Is it safe to swim/	**Dá se tady bezpečně plavat/skákat do vody?** _dah seh_
dive here?	_tah_·dih _behs_·pehch·nyeh _plah_·vaht/_skah_·kaht _doh_·voh·dih
Can I rent [hire] golf	**Můžu si vypůjčit golfové hole?** _moo_·zhoo sih
clubs?	_vih_·**poo**y·chiht _gohl_·foh·**veh** _hoh_·leh
How much per hour?	**Kolik se platí za hodinu?** _koh_·lihk seh _plah_·**tee**
	zah·hoh·dih·noo
How far is it to…?	**Jak je to daleko do…?** _yahk_ yeh toh _dah_·leh·koh doh…
Can you show me on	**Můžete mi to ukázat na mapě?** _moo_·zheh·teh mih toh
the map?	_oo_·**kah**·zaht _nah_·mah·pyeh

Going Out

What is there to do	**Co se tady dá dělat večer?** _tsoh seh _tah_·dih _dah_
in the evenings?	_dyeh_·laht _veh_·chehr
Do you have a program	**Jaký je program?** _yah_·kee yeh _prohg_·rahm
of events?	
What's playing at the	**Co dnes večer hrají v kině?** _tsoh dnehs _veh_·chehr_
movies tonight?	_hrah_·yee _fkih_·nyeh
Where's…?	**Kde je…?** _gdeh yeh…_
the downtown area	**centrum** _tsehn_·troom
the bar	**bar** _bahr_
the dance club	**diskotéka** _dihs_·koh·**teh**·kah
Is there an admission	**Platí se tam vstupné?**
charge?	_plah_·**tee** seh tahm _vstoop_·**neh**

Baby Essentials

Do you have...?	**Máte...?** _mah_·teh...
a baby bottle	**dětskou láhev s dudlíkem** _dyeht_·skoh _lah_·hehf _sdood_·lee·kehm
baby wipes	**navlhčené ubrousky** _nahvl_·hcheh·neh _oo_·broh·skih
a car seat	**autosedačku** _ow_·toh·seh·dahch·koo
a children's menu/ portion	**jídelník pro děti/dětskou porci** _yee_·dehl·neek proh _dyeh_·tih/_dyeht_·skoh _pohr_·tsih
a child's seat/ highchair	**židli pro dítě/židličku** _zhih_·dlih proh _dee_·tyeh/ _zhih_·dlih·chkoo
a crib/cot	**kolébku/skládací postel** _koh_·lehp·koo/_sklah_·dah·tsee pohs·tehl
diapers [nappies]	**plenky** _plehn_·kih
formula	**dětskou směs** _dyeht_·skoh smyehs
a pacifier [dummy]	**dudlík** _dood_·leek
a playpen	**ohrádku** _oh_·hrahd·koo
a stroller [pushchair]	**kočárek** _koh_·chah·rehk
Can I breastfeed the baby here?	**Můžu zde kojit dítě?** _moo_·zhoo zdeh _koh_·yiht _dee_·tyeh
Where can I change the baby?	**Kde mohu přebalit dětí?** gdeh _moh_·hoo _przheh_·bah·liht _dyeh_·tee

For Eating Out, see page 81.

Disabled Travelers

Is there...?	**Je zde...?** yeh zdeh...
access for the disabled	**přístup pro tělesně postižené** _przhee_·stoop proh _tyeh_·lehs·nyeh _pohs_·tih·zheh·neh
a wheelchair ramp	**podjezd pro invalidní vozíky** _pohd_·yehzd proh _ihn_·vah·lihd·nee _voh_·zee·kih
a handicapped- [disabled-] accessible toilet	**toalety pro tělesně postižené** _toh_·ah·leh·tih proh _tyeh_·lehs·nyeh _pohs_·tih·zheh·neh
I need...	**Potřebuji...** _poh_·trzheh·boo·yih...
assistance	**pomoc** _poh_·mohts
an elevator [lift]	**výtah** _vee_·tah
a ground-floor room	**pokoj v přízemí** _poh_·kohy fprzee·zeh·mih

Health & Emergencies

Emergencies

Help!	**Pomoc!** _poh_•mohts
Go away!	**Jděte pryč!** _ydyeh_•teh prihch
Stop, thief!	**Zastavte zloděje!** _zahs_•tahf•teh _zloh_•dyeh•yeh
Get a doctor!	**Zavolejte lékaře!** _zah_•voh•lehy•teh _leh_•kah•rzheh
Fire!	**Hoří!** _hoh_•rzhee
I'm lost.	**Ztratil** m/**Ztratila** f **jsem se.** _strah_•tihl/_strah_•tih•lah ysehm seh
Can you help me?	**Můžete mi pomoci?** _moo_•zheh•teh mih _poh_•moh•tsih
Call the police!	**Zavolejte policii!** _zah_•voh•lehy•teh _poh_•lih•tsyih
Where's the police station?	**Kde je policejní stanice?** _gdeh_ yeh _poh_•lih•tsehy•nee _stah_•nih•tseh
My child is missing.	**Moje dítě se ztratilo.** _moh_•yeh _dee_•tyeh seh _strah_•tih•loh

YOU MAY HEAR...

Vyplňte prosím tento formulář.
vihpl•n'teh _proh_•**seem** tehn•toh _fohr_•moo•**lahr**z

Please fill out this form.

Doklad totožnosti, prosím. _dohk_•lahd
toh•tohzh•nohs•tih _proh_•**seem**

Your ID, please.

Kdy/Kde se to stalo? _gdih/gdeh_ seh toh _stah_•loh

When/Where did it happen?

Jak on vypadal m/**ona vypadala** f ?
yahk on _vih_•pah•dahl/_oh_•nah _vih_•pah•dah•lah

What does he/she look like?

Health

I'm sick [ill].	**Jsem nemocný** m/**nemocná** f. ysehm _neh_•mohts•**nee**/ _neh_•mohts•**nah**
I need an English-speaking doctor.	**Potřebuji lékaře, který mluví anglicky.** _poht_•rzheh•boo•yih _leh_•kah•rzheh _kteh_•ree _mloo_•vee _ahn_•glihts•kih
It hurts here.	**Tady to bolí.** _tah_•dih toh _boh_•lee
I have a stomachache.	**Bolí mí břicho.** _boh_•lee mee _brzhih_•khoh

Where's the nearest pharmacy [chemist's]?	**Kde je nejbližší lékárna?** gdeh yeh _nehy_·blihzh·shee _leh_·kahr·nah
I'm (… months) pregnant.	**Jsem v (… měsíci) těhotenství.** ysehm v (… _mnyeh_·sih·tsih) _tyeh_·hot·tenst·vee
I'm on…	**Užívám…** _oo_·zhih·vahm…
I'm allergic to antibiotics/penicillin.	**Jsem alergický na antibiotika/penicillin.** ysehm _ah_·lehr·gihts·kee nah _ahn_·tih·byoh·tih·kah/_peh_·nih·tsih·lihn

---

In an emergency, dial **150** for the fire brigade, **155** for an ambulance, or **158** for the police.

Dictionary

baby **dítě**	comb **hřeben**
backpack **ruksak**	computer **počítač**
bad **špatný**	condom **kondom**
bag **kabelka**	corkscrew **vývrtka**
bandage **obinadlo**	cup **šálek**
battle site **bitevní pole**	deodorant **deodorant**
bikini **bikiny**	diabetic **diabetik**
bird **pták**	doll **panenka**
blue **modrý**	fly (insect) **moucha**
bottle opener **otvírač na láhve**	fork **vidlička**
bowl **miska**	girl **děvče**
boy **chlapec**	girlfriend **milenka**
boyfriend **milenec**	glass (drinking) **sklenice**
bra **podprsenka**	good **dobrý**; (delicious) **výborný**
camera **fotoaparát**	gray **šedý**
can opener **otvírač na plechovky**	great **úžasný**
castle **hrad**	green **zelený**
cigarette **cigareta**	hairspray **lak na vlasy**
cold adj **studený**; (weather) **chladný**; n **chlad**	horse **kůň**

hot (temperature) **horký;** (weather) **horko**

husband **manžel**

ice **led**

icy **zledovatělý**

injection **injekce**

insect repellent **repelent proti hmyzu**

jeans **džíny**

knife **nůž**

large **velký**

lighter (cigarette) **zapalovač**

love **milovat**

matches **zápalky**

medium (size) **střední**

moisturizer (cream) **zvlhčující krém**

museum **muzeum**

napkin **ubrousek**

nurse **zdravotní sestra**

or **nebo**

orange (color) **oranžový**

park **park**

partner (male) **partner;** (female) **partnerka**

pen **pero**

pink **růžový**

plate **talíř**

rain n **déšť;** v **pršet**

raincoat **pláštěnka**

razor **holicí strojek**

sandals **sandály**

sanitary napkin **dámská vložka**

sauna **sauna**

scissors **nůžky**

shampoo **šampon**

shoe **bot**

small **malý**

sneakers **tenisky**

snow n **sníh;** v **sněžit**

soap **mýdlo**

socks **ponožky**

spicy **kořeněný**

spoon **lžíce**

stamp **známka**

sun **slunce**

sunglasses **sluneční brýle**

sweater **svetr**

sweatshirt **tričko**

swimsuit **dámské plavky**

tampon **tampón**

terrible **hrozný**

tie **kravata**

tissue **papírový kapesník**

toilet paper **toaletní papír**

toothbrush **kartáček na zuby**

toothpaste **zubní pasta**

tough (food) **tuhý**

toy **hračka**

underwear **spodní prádlo**

vegetarian **vegetariánský**

wife **manželka**

with **s**

without **bez**

zoo **zoo**

Estonian

Hello/Hi.	**Tere.** *tere*
Goodbye.	**Head aega.** *head aega*
Yes/No/Okay.	**Jaa (Jah)/Ei/okei** *yaa (yah)/ei/okey*
Excuse me! (to get attention)	**Vabandage!** *vabandage*
Excuse me. (to get past)	**Vabandage.** *vabandage*
I'm sorry.	**Vabandust!** *vabandusst*
I'd like…	**Ma sooviksin…** *ma sooviksin*
How much?	**Kui palju?** *kui palyu*
And/or.	**Ja/või** *ya/voei*
Please.	**Palun.** *palun*
Thank you.	**Tänan.** *taenan*
You're welcome.	**Võtke heaks!** *voetke heaks*
Where's…?	**Kus on…?** *kus on*
I'm going to…	**Ma lähen…** *ma leahen*
My name is…	**Minu nimi on…** *minu nimi on*
Please speak slowly.	**Palun rääkige aeglaselt.** *palun reaakige aeglaselt*
Can you repeat that?	**Kas saaksite seda korrata?** *kas saaksite seda korrata*
I don't understand.	**Ma ei saa aru.** *ma ei saaa aru*
Do you speak English?	**Kas te räägite inglise keelt?** *kas te reaagite inglise keeelt*
I don't speak (much) Estonian.	**Ma ei oska eesti keelt.** *ma ei oska eesti keeelt*
Where's the restroom [toilet]?	**Kus asub tualettruum?/Kus asub WC?** *kus asub tualetttruuum/kus asub vee tsee?*
Help!	**Appi!** *apppi*

You'll find the pronunciation of the Estonian letters and words written in gray after each sentence to guide you. Simply pronounce these as if they were English. As you hear the language being spoken, you will quickly become accustomed to the local pronunciation and dialect.
Estonian is in general quite easy to pronounce as most words are pronounced as they are written.

Numbers

0	**null** *nulll*	
1	**üks** *ewks*	
2	**kaks** *kaks*	
3	**kolm** *kolm*	
4	**neli** *neli*	
5	**viis** *viiis*	
6	**kuus** *kuuus*	
7	**seitse** *seitse*	
8	**kaheksa** *kaheksa*	
9	**üheksa** *ewheksa*	
10	**kümme** *kewmme*	
11	**üksteist** *ewksteist*	
12	**kaksteist** *kaksteist*	
13	**kolmteist** *kolmteist*	
14	**neliteist** *neliteist*	
15	**viisteist** *viiisteist*	
16	**kuusteist** *kuuusteist*	
17	**seitseteist** *seitseteist*	
18	**kaheksateist** *kaheksateist*	
19	**üheksateist** *ewheksateist*	
20	**kakskümmend** *kakskewmmend*	
21	**kakskümmend üks** *kakskewmmend ewks*	
30	**kolmkümmend** *kolmkewmmend*	
40	**nelikümmend** *nelikewmmend*	
50	**viiskümmend** *viiiskewmmend*	
60	**kuuskümmend** *kuuuskewmmend*	
70	**seitsekümmend** *seitsekewmmend*	
80	**kaheksakümmend** *kaheksakewmmend*	
90	**üheksakümmend** *ewheksakewmmend*	
100	**sada** *sada*	
101	**sadaüks** *sada ewks*	
200	**kakssada** *kaks sada*	
500	**viissada** *viiis sada*	
1,000	**tuhat** *tuhat*	
10,000	**kümme** *kewmme tuhat*	
1,000,000	**miljon** *millyon*	

Time

What time is it?	**Mis kell on?**	*miss kell on*
It's midday.	**Kaksteist päeval.**	*kaksteist paeeval*
Five past three.	**Kell on viis minutit kolm läbi.**	*kell on viiis minutit kolm laebi.*
A quarter to ten.	**Kolmveerand kümme.**	*kolmveeerand kewmme*
5:30 a.m./p.m.	**5:30/17:30 viiis kolmkewmmend/seitseteist kolmkewmmend.**	*viiis kolmkewmmend/seitseteist kolmkewmmend*

Days

Monday	**esmaspäev**	*esmaspaeev*
Tuesday	**teisipäev**	*teisipaeev*
Wednesday	**kolmapäev**	*kolmapaeev*
Thursday	**neljapäev**	*nelyapaeev*
Friday	**reede**	*reeede*
Saturday	**laupäev**	*laupaeev*
Sunday	**pühapäev**	*pewhapaeev*

Dates

yesterday	**eile**	*eile*
today	**täna**	*taena*
tomorrow	**homme**	*hommme*
day	**päev**	*paeev*
week	**nädal**	*naedal*
month	**kuu**	*kuu*
year	**aasta**	*aaasta*
Happy New Year!	**Head uut aastat!**	*Head uuut aaastat*
Happy Birthday!	**Palju õnne sünnipäevaks!**	*Palyu oenne sewnnipaeevaks*

Months

January	**jaanuar**	*yaaanuar*
February	**veebruar**	*veeebruar*
March	**märts**	*maerts*
April	**aprill**	*aprill*
May	**mai**	*mai*
June	**juuni**	*yuuni*
July	**juuli**	*yuuli*

August	**august** *august*
September	**september** *september*
October	**oktoober** *oktooober*
November	**november** *november*
December	**detsember** *detsember*

Arrival & Departure

I'm on vacation [holiday]/business.	**Ma olen puhkusel/komandeeringus.** *ma olen puhhkusel/komandeeringus*
I'm going to...	**Ma lähen...** *ma laehen*
I'm staying at the...Hotel.	**Ma peatun... hotellis.** *Ma peatun... hotellis*

Money

Where's...?	**Kus on...?** *kus on...*
the ATM	**sularahaautomaat** *sularaha automaat*
the bank	**pank** *pank*
the currency exchange office	**valuutavahetuspunkt** *valuuta vahetus punkt*
When does the bank open/close?	**Mis kell pank avatakse/suletakse?** *Miss kell pank avatakse/suletakse*
I'd like to change dollars/pounds sterling into euros.	**Ma soovin vahetada dollareid/naelu eurodeks.** *ma soovin vahetada dollareid/naelu eurodeks*
I'd like to cash traveler's cheques.	**Sooviksin reisitšekid rahaks vahetada.** *Sooviksin reisi tšekid rahaks vahetada*
Can I pay in cash?	**Kas ma saan maksta sularahas?** *Kas ma saaan makksta sularahas*
Can I pay by (credit) card?	**Kas ma saan maksta (krediit)kaardiga?** *Kas ma saaan makksta (krediiit) kaardiga*

For Numbers, see page 94.

YOU MAY SEE...

The Estonian currency is the **euro**, €, which is divided into 100 **cents**.
Coins: 1, 2, 5, 10, 20 and 50 **cents**; €1, 2
Bills: €5, 10, 20, 50, 100, 200 and 500

Getting Around

How do I get to town?	**Kuidas ma linna saan?**	*Kuidas ma linna saan*
Where's…?	**Kus on…?**	*Kus on…*
the airport	**lennujaam**	*lennu jaam*
the train station	**rongijaam**	*rongi jaam*
the bus station	**bussipeatus**	*bussi peatus*
the subway [underground] station	**metroojaam**	*metroo jaam*
Is it far from here?	**Kas see on siit kaugel?**	*Kas see on siit kaugel*
Where do I buy a ticket?	**Kust ma saan pileti osta?**	*Kust ma saan pileti ossta*
A one-way/return-trip ticket to…	**Üks ühe otsa/edasi-tagasi pilet…**	*ewks ewhe ottsa/ eddasi-tagasi pilett*
How much?	**Kui palju see maksab?**	*Kui pallyu see maksab*
Which gate/line?	**Missugune värav/liin?**	*Missugune vaerav/liin*
Which platform?	**Mis platvorm?**	*Mis platform*
Where can I get a taxi?	**Kust ma saan takso?**	*Kust ma saan takso*
Take me to this address.	**Viige mind sel aadressil.**	*viige mind sell aadressil*
To…Airport, please.	**Palun…lennujaama.**	*Palun…lennu jaama*
I'm in a rush.	**Mul on kiire.**	*Mul on kiire*
Can I have a map?	**Kas saaksin kaardi?**	*Kas saaksin kaardi*

Tickets

When's…to Talinn?	**Millal läheb…Tallinnasse?**	*Millal laeheb…Tallinnasse*
the (first) bus	**(esimene) buss**	*(esimene) buss*
the (next) flight	**(järgmine) lend**	*(jaergmine) lend*
the (last) train	**(viimane) rong**	*(viimane) rong*
One/Two ticket(s) please.	**Üks/kaks pilet(it), palun!**	*Ewks/kaks pilet(itt) palun*
For today/tomorrow.	**Tänaseks/homseks.**	*Taenaseks/hommseks*
A…ticket.	**Üks…pilet.**	*Ewks…pilet*
one-way	**üheotsa piletit**	*ewheotsa piletit*
return trip	**edasi-tagasi piletit**	*edasitagasi piletitt*
first class	**esimene klass**	*esimene klass*
I have an e-ticket.	**Mul on e-pilet.**	*Mul on ee-pilet*
How long is the trip?	**Kui kaua sõit kestab?**	*kui kaua seit kestab*
Is it a direct train?	**Kas see on otserong?**	*Kas see on otserong*
Is this the bus to…?	**Kas see buss sõidab…?**	*kas see buss seidab*

Can you tell me when to get off?	**Kas saaksite mulle öelda, millal pean maha minema?** *kas saaksite mulle uelda, millal pean maha minema*
I'd like to...	**Ma sooviksin oma broneeringu(t)...** *ma sooviksin*
my reservation.	*oma broneeringu(t)...*
cancel	**tühistada** *tewhistada*
change	**muuta** *muuuta*
confirm	**kinnitada** *kinnitada*

For Time, see page 95.

Car Hire

Where's the car hire?	**Kust saan auto rentida?** *kust saan auto rentida*
I'd like...	**Ma sooviksin...** *ma sooviksin...*
a cheap/small car	**odavat/väikest autot** *odavat/vaekest autot*
an automatic/ a manual	**automaat-/manuaalkäigukastiga** *automaat-/ manuaal kaeigukasstiga*
air conditioning	**kliimaseadmega** *kliimaseadmega*
a car seat	**lapse turvatooliga** *lapse turvatooliga*
How much...?	**Kui palju maksab...?** *kui pallyu see maksab*
per day/week	**üks päev/nädal** *ewks paeev/naedal*
Are there any discounts?	**Kas pakute hinnasoodustusi?** *kas pakute hinnasoodustusi*

98

YOU MAY HEAR...

Minge otse edasi. *Minge otse edasi*	straight ahead
vasakul *vasakul*	left
paremal *paremal*	right
ümber nurga *ewmber nurga*	around the corner
vastas *vastas*	opposite
taga *taga*	behind
kõrval *koerval*	next to
pärast *paerast*	after
põhjas/lõunas *pehjas/leunas*	north/south
idas/läänes *idas/laenes*	east/west
valgusfoori juures *valgusfoori yuures*	at the traffic light
ristmikul *ristmikul*	at the intersection

Places to Stay

Can you recommend a hotel?	**Kas oskate hotelli soovitada?** *kas oskate hotelli soovitada*
I made a reservation.	**Mul on broneering.** *mul on broneering*
My name is...	**Minu nimi on...** *minu nimi on*
Do you have a room...?	**Kas teil on tuba...?** *kas teil on tuba*
for one/two	**ühele/kahele** *ewhele/kahele*
with a bathroom	**vannitoaga** *vannitoaga*
with air conditioning	**kliimaseadmega** *kliimaseadmega*
For...	-
tonight	**Tänaseks ööks** *taenaseks uewks*
two nights	**Kaheks ööks** *kaheks uewks*
one week	**Üheks nädalaks** *ewheks naedalaks*
How much?	**Kui palju see maksab?** *kui palju see maksab*
Is there anything cheaper?	**Kas teil on pakkuda midagi odavamat?** *kas teil on pakkuda midagi odavamat*
When's checkout?	**Mis kell pean toast lahkuma?** *mis kell pean toast lahhkuma*
Can I leave this in the safe?	**Kas ma saan selle seifi jätta?** *kas ma saan selle seiffi jätta*
Can I leave my bags?	**Kas ma saan oma pagasi pagasihoidu jätta?** *kas ma saan oma pagasi pagasihoydu jaetta*
Can I have my bill/ a receipt?	**Palun arvet/tšekki!** *palun arvet/tšekki*
I'll pay in cash/by credit card.	**Maksan sularahas/krediitkaardiga.** *Maksan sularahas/krediitkaardiga*

Communications

Where's an internet cafe?	**Kus asub internetikohvik?** *kus asub interneti koffik*
Can I access the internet/ check my email?	**Kas ma saan internetti kasutada/oma e-posti vaadata?** *kas ma saan internetti kasutada/oma ee-posti vaadata*
How much per half hour/hour?	**Kui palju maksab pool tundi/tund?** *kui palyu maksab pool tundi/tunnd*
How do I connect/ log on?	**Kuidas saan internetiühenduse/sisse logida?** *kuidas saan internetiyhenduse/sisse logida*
A phone card, please.	**Palun ühe telefonikaardi!** *palun ewhe telefonikaardi*
Can I have your phone number?	**Kas annaksite mulle oma telefoninumbri?** *kas annaksite mulle oma telefoninummbri*

Here's my number/email.	**Siin on minu telefoninumber/e-posti aadress.** *siin on minu telefoninummber/ee-posti aadress*
Call me/text me.	**Helista mulle/saada mulle sõnum!** *helista mulle/saada mulle soenum*
I'll text you.	**Saadan teile sõnumi.** *saadan teile soenumi*
Email me.	**Saatke mulle e-kiri.** *saatke mulle ee-kiri*
Hello. This is…	**Tere! Kas…kuuleb?** *Tere! kas…kuuleb*
Can I speak to…?	**Kas ma saaksin rääkida…?** *Kas ma saaksin raeekida…?*
I'll call back later.	**Helistan hiljem tagasi.** *helistan hilyem tagasi*
Bye.	**Head aega!** *head aega*
Where's the post office?	**Kus asub postkontor?** *kus asub posstkontor*
I'd like to send this to…	**Sooviksin selle saata…** *sooviksin selle saata…*
Can I…?	**Kas ma võin…?** *kas ma voein…?*
access the internet	**internetti kasutada** *internetti kasutada*
check my email	**oma e-posti vaadata** *oma ee-posti vaadata*
print	**printida** *printida*
plug in/charge my laptop/iPhone/iPad/ BlackBerry?	**oma sülearvutit/iPhone'i/iPad'i/BlackBerry't laadida?** *oma suelearvutit/ai phouni/ai padi/blaekk berrit laadida*
access Skype?	**Skype'i kasutada** *skaipi kasutada*
What is the WiFi password?	**Mis on WiFi salasõna?** *mis on wifi salasoena*
Is the WiFi free?	**Kas WiFi on tasuta?** *kas wifi on tasuta*
Do you have bluetooth?	**Kas teil on bluetooth?** *kas teil on bluutuuth*
Do you have a scanner?	**Kas teil on skänner?** *Kas teil on skaenner*

Social Media

Are you on Facebook/ Twitter?	**Kas kasutate Facebooki/Twitterit?** *kas kasutate feissbuuki/tvitterit*
What's your username?	**Mis on teie kasutajanimi?** *mis on teie kasutajanimi*
I'll add you as a friend.	**Lisan teid oma sõbraks.** *lisan teid oma soebraks*
I'll follow you on Twitter.	**Hakkan teid Twitteris jälgima.** *hakkan teid tvitteris jaelgima*
Are you following…?	**Kas te jälgite…?** *kas te jaelgite…?*
I'll put the pictures on Facebook/Twitter.	**Panen pildid üles Facebooki/Twitterisse.** *panen pildid ewles feissbuuki/tvitterisse*
I'll tag you in the pictures.	**Märgin teid piltidel.** *maergin teid piltidel*

Conversation

Hello!/Hi!	**Tere.** *tere*
How are you?	**Kuidas teil läheb?** *kuidas teil laeheb*
Fine, thanks.	**Tänan küsimast, hästi!** *taenan kewsimast, haesti*
Excuse me!	**Vabandage!** *Vabandage*
Do you speak English?	**Kas te räägite inglise keelt?** *kas te reaegite inglise keeelt*
What's your name?	**Kuidas teie nimi on?** *kuidas teie nimi on*
My name is...	**Minu nimi on...** *minu nimi on*
Nice to meet you.	**Meeldiv kohtuda.** *meeldiv kohhtuda*
Where are you from?	**Kust te pärit olete?** *kust te paerit olete*
I'm from the U.K./U.S.	**Ma olen Ühendkuningriigist/USAst.** *Ma olen ewhendkuningriigist/uu-ess-aast*
What do you do for a living?	**Kellena te töötate?** *kellena te tuewtate*
I work for...	**Ma töötan...** *ma tuewtan...*
I'm a student.	**Ma olen õpilane/üliõpilane.** *ma olen oepilane/ewlioepilane*
I'm retired.	**Ma olen pensionär.** *ma olen pensionaer*

Romance

Would you like to go out for a drink/dinner?	**Kas sooviksite dringile/õhtusöögile minna?** *kas sooviksite dringile/oehtusuewgile minna?*
What are your plans for tonight/tomorrow?	**Mis plaanid teil tänaseks õhtuks/homseks on?** *mis plaanid teil taenaseks oehtuks/hommseks on?*
Can I have your (phone) number?	**Kas annaksite mulle oma (telefoni)numbri?** *kas annaksite mulle oma (telefoni) nummbri?*
Can I join you?	**Kas ma võin teiega ühineda?** *kas ma voein teiega ewhineda?*
Can I buy you a drink?	**Kas ma võin teile ühe joogi osta?** *kas ma voein teile ewhe joogi ossta?*
I love you.	**Ma armastan sind.** *ma armastan sind*

Accepting & Rejecting

I'd love to.	**See meeldiks mulle väga!** *see meeldiks mulle vaega*
Where should we meet?	**Kus me kokku saame?** *kus me kokku saame?*
I'll meet you at the bar/your hotel.	**Saame kokku baaris/teie hotellis.** *saame kokku baaris/teie hotellis*
I'll come by at...	**Ma tulen kell...** *ma tulen kell...*

I'm busy.	**Mul on kiire!** *mul on kiire*
I'm not interested.	**Ma ei ole huvitatud!** *ma ei ole huvitatud*
Leave me alone.	**Jätke mind rahule!** *jaetke mind rahule*
Stop bothering me!	**Ärge tülitage mind!** *aerge tewlitage mind*

Food & Drink

Eating Out

Can you recommend a good restaurant/bar?	**Kas oskate soovitada head restorani/baari?** *Kas oskate soovitada head restorani/baari?*
Is there a traditional/an inexpensive restaurant nearby?	**Kas läheduses asub mõni rahvustoitu pakkuv/odav restoran?** *kas laeheduses asub moeni rahvustoitu pakkuv/odav restoran?*
A table for…, please.	**Palun lauda…inimesele!** *palun lauda…inimesele*
Can we sit…?	**Kas saame istuda…?** *kas saame istuda…?*
here/there	**siia/sinna** *siia/sinna*
outside	**välja** *vaelja*
in a non-smoking area	**mittesuitsetajate alasse** *mitte suitsetajate alasse*
I'm waiting for someone.	**Ma ootan kaaslast.** *ma oootan kaaslast*
Where are the toilets?	**Kus asuvad tualettruumid?** *kus asuvad tualettruumid*
The menu, please.	**Palun menüüd!** *palun menewd*
What do you recommend?	**Mida te soovitate?** *mida te soovitate*
I'd like…	**Ma sooviksin…** *ma sooviksin …*
Some more…, please.	**Palun veel…** *palun veel …*
Enjoy your meal!	**Head isu!** *head isu*

YOU MAY SEE…

restorani lisatasu *restorani lisatasu*	cover charge
püsiv hind *pewsiv hind*	fixed price
(päeva)menüü *(peaeva) menew*	menu (of the day)
hind sisaldab (ei sisalda) tasu teeninduse eest *hinnd sisaldab (ei sisalda) tasu teeninduse eeest*	service (not) included
eripakkumised *eripakkumised*	specials

The check [bill], please.	**Palun arvet!** *palun arvet*
Is service included?	**Kas hind sisaldab tasu teeninduse eest?** *kas hinnd sisaldab tasu teeninduse eeest?*
Can I pay by credit card/have a receipt?	**Kas ma saan maksta krediitkaardiga?/Palun tšekki!** *Kas ma saan makssta krediit kaardiga?/Palun tšekki*

Breakfast

peekon *peekon*	bacon
leib/ röstsai *libe/ rostsai*	bread/toast
rukkileib *rookkeeleeb*	rye bread
või *vouy*	butter
kilud *keelud*	sprats
lihalõigud/ juust *leehaloygood/ yuuust*	cold cuts/ cheese
muna *moona*	...egg
hüübinud	scrambled
praetud *praaytood*	fried
kõvaks/pehmeks keedetud *kovaks/pehmeks keedetud*	hard boiled/soft boiiled
keedis *keedis*	jam [jelly]
omlett *omlett*	omelette
jogurt *yohgurt*	yogurt

Appetizers

heeringas *heeringas*	herring
juustu-munasalat küüslauguga *yuustumunasalat kewslauguga*	cheese and egg salad with garlic
kanalihasalat *kanalihasalat*	chicken salad
kartulisalat *kartulisalat*	potato salad
krevetisalat *krevetisalat*	prawn cocktail
rosolje *rosolye*	beet, potato, egg, pickle salad
segasalat *segasalat*	mixed salad
soojad võileivad *sooyad veileivad*	hot sandwiches

Meat

loomaliha/lambaliha *loomaliha/lambaliha*	beef/lamb
kana/biiifsteek *kana/beefsteak*	chicken/steak
sealiha/vasikaliha *sealiha/vasikaliha*	pork/veal
vorst *vorst*	sausage

YOU MAY HEAR...

kergelt läbiküpsetatud *kergelt laebikewpsetatud*	underdone (rare)
keskmiselt läbiküpsetatud	medium
keskmiselt laebikewpsetatud	
hästi läbiküpsetatud *haesti laebikewpsetatud*	well-done

Fish & Seafood

haug *haug*	pike
tursk *tursk*	cod
lest *lest*	plaice
heeringas *heeringas*	herring
vähk *vaehk*	lobster
lõhe *loehe*	salmon
krevetid *krevetid*	shrimp [prawns]

Vegetables

oad *oad*	beans
kapsas *kapsas*	cabbage
kurk *kurk*	cucumber
lauk *lauk*	leek
seen *seeen*	mushroom
sibul *sibul*	onion
herned *herned*	peas
kartulid *kartulid*	potatoes
tomat *tomat*	tomato

Sauces & Condiments

Sool *sool*	Salt
Pipar *pipar*	Pepper
Sinep *sinep*	Mustard
Ketšup *ketšupp*	Ketchup

Fruit & Dessert

õun *eun*	apple
banaan *banaaan*	banana
sidrun *sidrun*	lemon
apelsin *apelsin*	orange
ploom *plooom*	plum
maasikad *maasikad*	strawberries
jäätis *yaeaetis*	ice-cream
kohupiimakook *kohupiimakoook*	cheesecake
puuviljakook *puuvilyakoook*	fruit cake
rummikook *rummikoook*	rumcake
tarretis *tarretis*	jelly with
vahukoorega *vahukoorega*	whipped cream
tort *tort*	gateau

Drinks

The wine list/drink menu, please.	**Palun veinikaarti/joogimenüüd!** *palun veinikaarti/joogimenyyd*
What do you recommend?	**Mida te soovitate?** *mida te soovitate?*
I'd like a bottle/glass of red/white wine.	**Palun ühe pudeli/klaasi punast/valget veini.** *palun ewhe pudeli/klaasi punast/valget veini*
The house wine, please.	**Palun majaveini.** *palun mayaveini*
Another bottle/glass, please.	**Veel üks pudel/klaas, palun!** *veel ewks pudel/klaas, palun*
I'd like a local beer.	**Sooviksin kohalikku õlut.** *sooviksin kohalikku oelut*
Can I buy you a drink?	**Kas ma tohin teile ühe joogi osta?** *kas ma tohin teile ewhe joogi ossta?*
Cheers!	**Terviseks!** *terviseks!*
A coffee/tea, please.	**Üks kohv/tee, palun!** *ewks koff/tee palun!*
Black.	**Must.** *musst*
With...	-
milk	**Piimaga** *piimaga*
sugar	**Suhkruga** *suhhkruga*
artificial sweetener	**Suhkruasendajaga** *suhhkru asendayaga*
A..., please.	**Palun üks...** *palun ewks...*
juice	**puuviljamahl** *puuvilyamahhl*

soda [soft drink]   **limonaad** *limonaaad*
(sparkling/still) water **(gaseeritud/gaasita) vesi** *(gaseeritud/gaasita) vesi*

Leisure Time

Sightseeing

Where's the tourist information office?	**Kus asub turismibüroo?** *kus asub turismibewroo*
What are the main sights?	**Mis on peamised vaatamisväärsused?** *mis on peamised vaaatamisvaeersused*
Do you offer tours in English?	**Kas te pakute ingliskeelseid tuure?** *kas te pakute ingliskeelseid tuure*
Can I have a map/ guide?	**Kas ma saaksin kaardi/teejuhi?** *kas ma saaksin kaardi/teeyuhi?*

YOU MAY SEE...

avatud/suletud *avatud/suletud*	open/closed
sissepääs/väljapääs *sissepaeas/vealjapaeas*	entrance/exit

Shopping

Where's the market/ mall?	**Kus on turg/kaubanduskeskus?** *kus on turg/ kaunanduskeskus*
I'm just looking.	**Ma ainult vaatan.** *ma aynult vaatan*
Can you help me?	**Kas saate mind aidata?** *kas saate mind aidata?*
I'm being helped.	**Mind juba teenindatakse.** *mind yuba teenindatakse*
How much?	**Kui palju see maksab?** *kui palyu see maksab?*
That one, please.	**See, palun!** *see, palun!*
I'd like...	**Ma sooviksin...** *ma sooviksin...*
That's all.	**See on kõik.** *see on koeik*
Where can I pay?	**Kus ma maksta saan?** *kus ma makssta saan?*
I'll pay in cash/ by credit card.	**Ma soovin maksta sularahas/krediitkaardiga.** *Ma soovin makssta sularahas/krediit kaardiga*
A receipt, please.	**Palun tšekki!** *palun tšekki!*

Sport & Leisure

When's the game?	**Millal mäng algab?** *millal maeng algab?*
Where's…?	**Kus asub…?** *kus asub…?*
the beach	**rand** *rannd*
the park	**park** *park*
the pool	**bassein** *bassein*
Is it safe to swim here?	**Kas siin on ohutu ujuda?** *kas siin on ohutu uyuda?*
Can I hire clubs?	**Kas ma saan golfiklubi üürida?**
	kas ma saan golfklubi ewwrida?
How much per hour/day?	**Kui palju see tunnis/päevas maksab?**
	kui palyu see tunnis/peaevas maksab?
How far is it to…?	**Kui kaugel asub…?** *kui kaugel asub…?*
Show me on the map, please.	**Palun näidake mulle kaardil!** *palun neaidake mulle kaardil*

Going Out

What's there to do at night?	**Mida õhtul teha on?** *mida oehtul teha on?*
Do you have a program of events?	**Kas teil on ürituste kava?** *kas teil on ewrituste kava?*
What's playing tonight?	**Kes täna õhtul esineb?/Mida täna õhtul näidatakse?**
	kes taena oehtul esineb?/Mida taena oehtul naeidatakse?
Where's…?	**Kus asub…?** *kus asub…?*
the downtown area	**kesklinn** *kesklinn*
the bar	**baar** *baar*
the dance club	**tantsuklubi** *tantssu klubi*
Is this area safe at night?	**Kas selles piirkonnas on öösel ohutu?**
	kas selles piirkonnas on ewwsel ohutu?

Baby Essentials

Do you have…?	**Kas teil on…?** *kas teil on…?*
a baby bottle	**lutipudeleid** *lutipudeleid*
baby food	**imikutoitu** *imikutoittu*
baby wipes	**pühkimislappe** *pewhkimis lappe*
a car seat	**auto turvatool** *auto turvatoool*
a children's menu/ portion	**lastemenüü/portsjonid** *lastemenew/portsyonid*

a child's seat/highchair	**lastetool** *lastetool*
a crib/cot	**häll/võrevoodi** *haell/voerevoodi*
diapers [nappies]	**mähkmeid** *maehkmeid*
formula	**imikutoitu** *imikutoittu*
a pacifier [dummy]	**lutte** *lutte*
a playpen	**mänguaed** *maenguaed*
a stroller [pushchair]	**jalutuskäru** *jalutus kaeru*
Can I breastfeed the baby here?	**Kas ma võin siin last rinnaga toita?** *kas ma voein siin lasst rinnaga toitta?*
Where can I breastfeed/ change the baby?	**Kus ma saan last rinnaga toita/mähkmeid vahetada?** *kus ma saan lasst rinnaga toita/maehkmeid vahetada?*

For Dining with Children, see page 102.

Disabled Travelers

Is there...?	**Kas teil on...?** *kas teil on...?*
access for the disabled	**ligipääs erivajadustega inimestele** *ligipaes erivayadustega inimestele?*
a wheelchair ramp	**kaldtee ratastoolile** *kaldtee ratas toolile*
a disabled-accessible toilet	**tualettruum erivajadustega inimestele** *tualettruum erivayadustega inimestele*
I need...	**Ma vajan...** *ma vajan...*
assistance	**abi** *abi*
an elevator [a lift]	**lifti** *liffti*
a ground-floor room	**tuba esimesel korrusel** *tuba esimesel korrusel*
Please speak louder.	**Palun rääkige valjemini.** *palun raeaekige valyemini*

Health & Emergencies

Emergencies

Help!	**Appi!** *apppi*
Go away!	**Minge ära!** *minge aera!*
Stop, thief!	**Peatage varas!** *peatage varas*
Get a doctor!	**Kutsuge arst!** *kutsuge arst*
Fire!	**Tulekahju!** *tulekahju!*
I'm lost.	**Ma olen ära eksinud.** *ma olen aera eksinud*

Can you help me?	**Kas te saate mind aidata?** *kas te saate minnd aidata?*
Call the police!	**Kutsuge politsei!** *kutsuge politsei*
Where's the police station?	**Kus asub politseijaoskond?** *kus asub politsey yaoskonnd?*
My child is missing.	**Mu laps on kadunud.** *mu lapps on kadunud*

In the event of an emergency, dial: **112**

Health

I'm sick.	**Ma olen haige** *ma olen haige*
I need an English-speaking doctor.	**Ma vajan inglise keelt kõnelevat arsti.** *ma vayan inglise keelt koenelevat arssti*
It hurts here.	**Siit on valus.** *siit on valus*
Where's the pharmacy?	**Kus asub apteek?** *kus asub apteek?*
I'm (...months) pregnant.	**Ma olen (...kuud) rase.** *ma olen (...kuud) rase*
I'm on...	**Ma manustan...** *ma manustan...*
I'm allergic to antibiotics/penicillin.	**Mul on antibiootikumide/penitsilliini allergia.** *Mul on antibyootikumide/penitsiliini allergya*

YOU MAY HEAR...

Täitke see vorm. *taeitke see vorm*	Fill out this form.
Palun esitage oma isikut tõendav dokument. *palun esitage oma isikut toendav dokument*	Your ID, please.
Millal/kus see juhtus? *millal/kus see yuhtus?*	When/Where did it happen?
Missugune ta välja näeb? *missugune ta vaelja naeeb?*	What does he/she look like?

Dictionary

adaptor **adapter**
aid worker **esmaabitöötaja**
and **ja**
antiseptic cream **antiseptiline kreem**
baby **imik, väikelaps**
a backpack **seljakott**
bad **halb**
bag **kott**
Band-Aid [plasters] **plaaastrid**
bandages **sidemed**
battleground **lahinguväli**
bee **mesilane**
beige **beež**
bikini **bikiinid**
bird **lind**
black **must**
bland (food) **maitsetu (toit)**
blue **sinine**
bottle opener **pudeliavaja**
bowl **kauss**
boy **poiss**
boyfriend **poiss-sõber**
bra **rinnahoidja**
brown **pruun**
cat **kass**
castle **kinndlus**
charger **laadija**
cigarettes **sigaretid**
cold **külm**
comb *n* **kamm**
computer **arvuti**
condoms **kondoomid**
contact lens solution **kontaktläätsede vedelik**

corkscrew **korgitser**
cup **tass**
dangerous **ohtlik**
deodorant **deodorant**
diabetic **diabeetik**
dog **koer**
doll **nukk**
fly **kärbes**
fork **kahvel**
girl **tüdruk**
girlfriend **tüdruksõber**
glass **klaas**
good **hea**
gray **hall**
great **suurepärane/suur**
green **roheline**
a hairbrush **juuksehari**
hairspray **juukselakk**
horse **hobune**
hot **kuum**
husband **mees (abikaasa)**
ice **jää**
icy **jäine**
injection **süst**
I'd like... **Ma sooviksin...**
insect repellent **putukatõrjevahend**
jeans **teksapüksid**
(steak) knife **lauanuga (liha lõikamiseks)**
lactose intolerant **laktoositalumatu**
large **suur**
lighter **tulemasin**
lion **lõvi**

lotion [moisturizing cream] **niisutav kreem**

love **armastus**

matches **tikud**

medium **keskmine**

monkey **ahv**

museum **muuseum**

my **minu**

a nail file **küüneviil**

napkin **salvrätik**

nurse **meditsiiniõde**

or **või**

orange **oranž**

park **park**

partner **partner**

pen **pastakas**

pink **roosa**

plate **taldrik**

purple **lilla**

pyjamas **pidžaama**

rain **vihm**

a raincoat **vihmamantel**

a (disposable) razor **(ühekordselt kasutatav) žilett**

razor blades **žiletiterad**

red punane **punane**

safari **safari**

salty **soolane**

a sauna **saun**

sandals **sandaalid**

sanitary napkins [pads] **hügieenisidemed**

scissors **käärid**

shampoo/conditioner **šampoon/palsam**

shoes **kingad**

small **väike**

snake **madu**

sneakers **ketsid**

snow **lumi**

soap **seep**

socks **sokid**

spicy **vürtsikas**

spider **ämblik**

spoon **lusikas**

a sweater **sviiter**

stamp(s) **mark (mitm. margid)**

suitcase **kohver**

sun **päike**

sunglasses **päikseprillid**

sunscreen **päiksekreem**

a sweatshirt **dressipluus**

a swimsuit **ujumisriided**

a T-shirt **T-särk**

tampons **tampoonid**

terrible *adj* **kohutav**

tie **lips**

tissues **salvrätikud**

toilet paper **tualettpaber**

toothbrush **hambahari**

toothpaste **hambapasta**

tough (meat) **vintske (liha)**

toy **mänguasi**

underwear **aluspesu**

vegetarian **taimetoitlane**

vegan **veegan**

white **valge**

with k **oos**

wife **naine (abikaasa)**

without **ilma**

yellow **kollane**

your **teie**

zoo **loomaaed**

Hungarian

Essentials

Hello/Hi.	**Szia!/Sziasztok!** *seeo/seeostawk*
Goodbye.	**Viszontlátásra!** *veesawntlaataashro*
Yes.	**igen.** *eegæn*
No.	**Nem.** *næm*
Excuse me! (to get attention, to get past)	**Elnézést!** *ælnayzaysht*
I'm sorry.	**Sajnálom.** *shoynaalawm*
I'd like…	**Szeretnék…** *Særætnayk…*
How much?	**Mennyibe kerül?** *Mænyeebæ kærewl?*
Where is…?	**Hol van a…?** *hawl von o…*
Please.	**Kérem.** *kayraem*
Thank you.	**Köszönöm.** *kursurnurm*
You're welcome.	**Szívesen.** *séevaeshaen*
Can you speak more slowly?	**Elmondaná lassabban?** *ælmawndonnaa losh-shob-bon*
Can you repeat that, please?	**Megismételné?** *mægheeshmaytælnay*
I don't understand.	**Nem értem.** *næm ayrtæm*
Do you speak English?	**Beszél angolul?** *bæsayl ongawlool*
I don't speak (much) Hungarian.	**Nem tudok (jól) magyarul.** *næm toodawk (yawl) moð'orrool*
Where's the restroom [toilet]?	**Hol van a W.C.?** *hawl von o vaytsay*
Help!	**Segítség!** *shægheetshayg*

You'll find the pronunciation of the Hungarian letters and words written in gray after each sentence to guide you. Simply pronounce these as if they were English, noting that any overlines and bolds indicate an additional emphasis or stress or a lengthening of a vowel sound. As you hear the language being spoken, you will quickly become accustomed to the local pronunciation and dialect.

Numbers

0	**nulla**	*noollo*
1	**egy**	*æd^y*
2	**kettő**	*kættūr*
3	**három**	*haarawm*
4	**négy**	*nayd^y*
5	**öt**	*ūrt*
6	**hat**	*hot*
7	**hét**	*hayt*
8	**nyolc**	*n^yawlts*
9	**kilenc**	*keelænts*
10	**tíz**	*tēēz*
11	**tizenegy**	*teezænæd^y*
12	**tizenkettő**	*teezænkættūr*
13	**tizenhárom**	*teezænhaarawm*
14	**tizennégy**	*teezænnayd^y*
15	**tizenöt**	*teezænurt*
16	**tizenhat**	*teezænhot*
17	**tizenhét**	*teezænhayt*
18	**tizennyolc**	*teezænn^yawlts*
19	**tizenkilenc**	*teezænkeelænts*
20	**húsz**	*hōōs*
21	**huszonegy**	*hoosawnæd^y*
22	**huszonkettő**	*hoosawnkættūr*
30	**harminc**	*hormeents*
31	**harmincegy**	*hormeentsæd^y*
40	**negyven**	*næd^yvæn*
50	**ötven**	*urtvæn*
60	**hatvan**	*hotvon*
70	**hetven**	*hætvæn*
80	**nyolcvan**	*n^yawltsvon*
90	**kilencven**	*keelæntsvæn*
100	**száz**	*saaz*
101	**százegy**	*saazæd^y*
200	**kétszáz**	*kaytsaaz*
500	**ötszáz**	*urtsaaz*
1,000	**ezer**	*æzær*

| 10,000 | **tízezer** *tēezæzær* |
| 1,000,000 | **milliárd** *meelleeaard* |

Time

Excuse me. Can you tell me the time?	**Elnézést, megmondaná mennyi az idő?** *ælnayzaysht mægmawn- donnaa* **mæn**ʸ*-nyee oz eedūr*
It's...	**Most van...** *mawst von...*
five past one	**egy óra öt perc*** *æd*ʸ *aw̄ro ūrt pærts*
ten past two	**két óra tíz perc** *kayt aw̄ro teez pærts*
a quarter past three	**negyed négy** *næd*ʸ*æd nayd*ʸ
twenty past four	**négy óra húsz** *nayd*ʸ *aw̄ro hōos*
twenty-five past five	**öt óra huszonöt** *ūrt aw̄ro hoosawnurt*
half past six	**fél hét** *fayl hayt*
twenty-five to seven	**öt perccel múlt fél hét** *ūrt pærtsæl mōolt fayl hayt*
twenty to eight	**öt perc múlva háromnegyed nyolc** *ūrt pærts mōolvo haarawm- næd*ʸ*æd nvawlts*
a quarter to nine	**háromnegyed kilenc** *haarawmnæd*ʸ*æd keelænts*
ten to ten	**tíz perc múlva tíz** *tēez pærts mōolvo tēez*
five to eleven	**öt perc múlva tizenegy** *ūrt pærts mōolvo teezæn-æd*ʸ
twelve o'clock	**tizenkét óra** *teezænkayt aw̄ro*
noon/midnight	**dél/éjfél** *dayl/ay*ʸ*fayl*
in the morning	**délelőtt** *daylælūrt*
in the afternoon	**délután** *daylootaan*
in the evening	**este** *æshtæ*

Days

Monday	**hétfő** *haytfūr*
Tuesday	**kedd** *kæd*
Wednesday	**szerda** *særdo*
Thursday	**csütörtök** *tshewturrturk*
Friday	**péntek** *payntæk*
Saturday	**szombat** *sawmbot*
Sunday	**vasárnap** *voshaarnop*

Dates

| yesterday | **tegnap** *tægnop* |
| today | **ma** *mo* |

tomorrow	**holnap** *hawlnop*
day	**nap** *nop*
week	**hét** *hayt*
weekend	**hétvége** *haytvayghæ*
month	**hónap** *hawnop*
year	**év** *ayv*
Happy New Year!	**Boldog új évet!** *bawldawg ōoy ayvæt*
Happy Birthday!	**Boldog születés napot!** *bawldawg sewlætaysh-noppawt*

Months

January	**január** *yonnooaar*
February	**február** *fæbrooaar*
March	**március** *maartseeoosh*
April	**április** *aapreeleesh*
May	**május** *maayoosh*
June	**június** *yōoneeoosh*
July	**július** *yōoleeoosh*
August	**augusztus** *o-oogoostoosh*
September	**szeptember** *sæptæmbær*
October	**október** *awktawbær*
November	**november** *nawvæmbser*
December	**december** *dætsæmbær*

Arrival & Departure

I'm on vacation.	**A szabadságomat töltöm itt.** *o sobodshaagawmot turlturm eet*
I'm here on business.	**Üzleti úton vagyok itt.** *ewzlætee ōotawn vod'awk eet*
I'm going to...	**...megyek/utazom** *...mædyæk/ootozom*
I'm staying at the...Hotel.	**...szállodában szálltam meg.** *...saalawdaabon saaltom mæg*

Money

Where's...?	**Hol van...?** *hawl von*
the ATM	**ATM automata** *AA-TAY-ÆM o-oo-taw-moto*
the bank	**bank** *bonk*
the currency exchange office	**pénzváltó** *panyzvaaltaw*

When does the bank open/close?	**Hány órakor nyitnak/zárnak a bankok?** *Haany awrokawr nyeetnok/zaarnok o bonkok?*
I'd like to change dollars/euros/pounds sterling into forint	**Forintra szeretném váltani a dollárt/eurót/font sterlinget.** *Fawreentro særætnaym vaaltoni o dawllaart/æ-oo-rawt/fawnt shtærleengæt.*
I'd like to cash traveler's cheques.	**Be szeretném váltani az utazási csekkeket.** *Bæ særætnaym vaaltonee oz ootozaashee chækækæt.*

For Numbers, see page 114.

YOU MAY SEE...

The basic unit of currency in Hungary is the **Forint** *(fawreent)*, abbreviated **Ft**. It is divided into **100 fillér** *(feellayr)*.
Notes: 500, 1000, 2000, 5000, 10000, and 20000 **Forints**.
Coins: 5,10, 20, 50, 100 and 200 **Forints**.

Getting Around

How do I get to town?	**Hogyan jutok a városba?** *Hawdyon yootawk ovaaroshbo?*
Where's...?	**Hol van a...?** *hawl von o...*
the airport	**a repülőtérre** *o ræpewlūrtayr-ræ*
the train station	**a vasútállomásra** *o voshōōtaal-lawmaashro*
the bus station	**buszpályaudvarra** *boospaayo-oodvorro*
the subway [underground] station	**metró állomásra** *mætrāw aallawmaashro*
Is it far from here?	**Messze van innen?** *Massæ von eenæn?*
Where do I buy a ticket?	**Hol lehet jegyet venni?** *Hawl læhæt yædyæt vænnee?*
A one-way/return-trip ticket to...	**Egy útra szóló/retúr jegy...** *æd ootro sawl-aw/rætōor yædy*
How much?	**Mennyibe kerül?** *mænyeebæ kærewl*
Which gate/line?	**Melyik kijárat/vonal?** *Mæyeek keeyaarot/vawnol?*
Which platform?	**Melyik vágány?** *Mæyeek vaagaany?*
Where can I get a taxi?	**Hol lehet taxit fogni?** *Hawl læhæt toxeet fawgnee?*
Take me to this address.	**Kérem vigyen el erre a címre.** *kayræm veedyæn æl ær-ræ o tséemræ*
Do you have a map?	**Van térképe?** *von tayrkaypæ*

Tickets

When's...to Budapest?	**Mikor indul...Budapestre?**	*meekawr eendool...*
		boodoppæshtræ
the (first) bus	**(az első) busz** *(oz ælshūr) boos*	
the (next) flight	**(a következő) járat** *(o kurvætkæzūr) yaarot*	
the (last) train	**(az utolsó) vonat** *(oz ootawlshāw) vawnot*	
Where do I buy a ticket?	**Hol lehet jegyet venni?** *Hawl læhæt yædyæt vænnee?*	
One/Two ticket(s) please.	**Kérek egy/két jegyet.** *Kayræk æd¹/kayt yædyæt.*	
For today/tomorrow.	**Mára/holnapra.** *Maaro/hawlnopro.*	
A...ticket.	**Egy...jegy.** *æd¹...yædy*	
one-way	**útra szóló** *ootro sawl-aw*	
return trip	**retúr** *rætōōr*	
first class	**első osztályra** *ælshur awstaayro*	
business class	**business osztályra** *beeznees awstaayro*	
economy class	**economy-osztály** *economy-awstaay*	
How much?	**Mennyibe kerül?** *mænyeebæ kærewl*	
Is there a discount for...?	**...számára van kedvezmény?**	
	...saamaaro von kædvæzmayny?	
children	**gyerekek** *dyærækæk*	
students	**diákok** *deeaakawk*	
senior citizens	**nyugdíjasok** *nyoogdeeyashok*	
tourists	**turisták** *toorishtaak*	

The express bus/express train, please.	**Expressz buszra/Expressz vonatra kérek.** *Express boosro/express vawnotro keerek.*	
The local bus/train, please.	**Helyi buszra/vonatra kérek.** *Heeye boosro/vawnotro keerek.*	
I have an e-ticket.	**E-jegyem van.** *Æ-yædyæm von.*	
Can I buy...	**Vehetek...** *Væhætæk...*	
a ticket on the bus/train?	**jegyet a buszon/vonaton?** *yædyæt o boosawn/vawnotawn?*	
the ticket before boarding?	**felszállás előtt jegyet?** *Fælsaallaash elüt yædyæt?*	
How long is this ticket valid?	**Meddig érvényes a jegy?** *Mædeeg ayrvaynyesh o yædy?*	
Can I return on the same ticket?	**Visszaútra is érvényes ez a jegy?** *Veesso-ootro eesh ayrvaynyæsh æz o yædy?*	
I'd like to...	**Szeretném...a jegyfoglalásomat.**	
my reservation.	*særætnaym...o yædvfawglollaashawmot*	

cancel	**töröltetni** *turrurltætnee*
change	**megváltoztatni** *mægvaaltawstotnee*
confirm	**megerősíteni** *mægærūrsheetænee*

For Days, see page 115.

Car Hire

Where's the car hire?	**Hol van az autókölcsönző?** *Hawl von oz-oottaw-kurlchurnza*
I'd like...	**Szeretnék...** *Særætnayk...*
a cheap/small car	**egy olcsó/kicsi autót** *ædy awlchaw/keechee o-ootawt*
an automatic/	**egy automata/kézi váltós autót** *ædy o-oo-tawmoto/*
a manual	*kayzee vaaltowsh o-ootaswt*
air conditioning	**légkondicionáló** *laygkawndeetceeawnaalaw*
a car seat	**gyerekülés** *dyærækurlaysh*
How much...?	**Mennyibe kerül a...?** *Mænyeebæ kærewl o...*
per day/week	**egy napra/hétre** *ædy nopro/haytræ*
per kilometer	**per kilométer** *pær keelawmaytær*
for unlimited mileage	**korlátlan távolságra** *kawrlaatlon taavawlshaagro*
with insurance	**biztosítással** *beeztawsheetaashol*
Are there any discounts?	**Vannak-e kedvezmények?** *Vonnok-æ kædvæzmaynyæk?*

YOU MAY HEAR...

egyenesen *ædyænæshæn*	straight ahead
balra *bolro*	left
jobbra *yawbro*	right
a sarok mögött *o shorawk murgurt*	around the corner
szemben *sæmbæn*	opposite
mögött *murgurt*	behind
mellett *mælæt*	next to
után *ootaan*	after
észak/dél *aysok/dayl*	north/south
kelet/nyugat *kælæt/nyoogot*	east/west
a lámpáknál *o laampaaknaal*	at the traffic light
a kereszteződésnél *o kæræstæzurdayshnayl*	at the intersection

Places to Stay

Can you recommend a hotel?	**Ajánlana nekem szállodát?**	*Ajaanlono nækæm saalawdaat?*
I made a reservation.	**Előre foglaltam szobát.**	*æʃurræ fawgloltom sawbaat*
My name is…	**…vagyok.**	*… voɟawk*
Do you have a room…?	**Van szobájuk…?**	*Von sawbaayook…?*
for one/two	**egy/két fő számára**	*ædy/kayt fur saamaaro?*
with a bathroom	**fürdőszobával**	*fewrdursawbaavol?*
with air conditioning	**légkondicionált**	*laygkawndeetseeawnaalt*
For…	**a…**	*o…*
tonight	**ma éjszakára**	*mo aysokaaro*
two nights	**két éjszakára**	*kayt aysokaaro*
one week	**egy hétre**	*edy haytræ*
How much?	**Mennyibe kerül…?**	*mænveebæ kærewl*
Is there anything cheaper?	**Volna olcsóbb szobájuk?**	*vawlno awlchāwb sawbaayook*
When's checkout?	**Meddig kell kijelentkezni?**	*Mædeeg kæl keeyælæntkæznee?*
Can I leave this in the safe?	**Ezt hagyhatom a széfben?**	*Æzt hodhotawm o sayf-bæn?*
Can I leave my bags?	**Itt hagyhatom a csomagomat?**	*Eet hodyhotawm o chawmogawmot?*
Can I have my bill/ a receipt?	**Megkaphatom a számlámat/bizonylatomat?**	*Mægkophotawm o saamlaamot/beezawnylotawmot?*
I'll pay in cash/ by credit card.	**Készpénzzel/kártyával fizetek.**	*Kayspaynzæl/ kaartyaabol feezætæk.*

Communications

Where's an internet cafe?	**Hol van az internet cafe?**	*Hawl von oz eentærnæt kofay?*
Does it have wireless internet?	**Van WiFi internetes hozzáférése?**	*Von vee-fee eentærnætæs hawz-zaafayraysh?*
What is the WiFi password?	**Mi a WiFi jelszava?**	*Mee o vee-fee yælsovo?*
Is the WiFi free?	**A WiFi használata ingyenes?**	*O vee-fee hosnaaloto eendyænæsh?*
Do you have bluetooth?	**Van Bluetooth-a?**	*Von Bluetooth-o?*
Can you show me how to turn on/off the computer?	**Megmutatná, hogyan kapcsoljam be/ki a számítógépet?**	*mægmoototnaa, hawdyon kopchawl-yom bæ-kee o saameetawgaypæt?*
Can I access the internet?	**Kaphatok internetes hozzáférést?**	*Kophotawk eentærnætæsh hawz-zaafayraysht?*

Can I check my email?	**Megnézhetem az e-mail üzeneteimet?** *mægnayz-hætæm oz e-mail ewzætæ-eemæt?*
Can I print?	**Nyomtathatok?** *Nyawmtothotawk?*
Can I plug in/charge my laptop/iPhone/ iPad/BlackBerry?	**Bekapcsolhatom/feltölthetem a laptopomat/ iPhone-omat/iPadomat/BlackBerry-met?** *Bækopchawlhotawm/fælturlthætæm o loptop-awmot/iPhone-awmot/iPad-awmoat/BlackBerry-mæt?*
Can I access Skype?	**Használhatom a Skype-ot?** *Hosnaalhotom o skype-awt?*
How much per half hour/hour?	**Mennyibe kerül a félóras/egy órás használata?** *mænyeebæ kærewl o faylawrash/edyawrash hosnaaloto?*
How do I...?	**Hogyan...?** *Hawdyon*
connect/disconnect	**csatlakozhatok/kapcsolhatom szét-** *chotlokawz hotok/kopchawlhotom sayt?*
log on/off	**bejelentkezés/kijelentkezés** *bæyælæntkæzaysh/keeyælæntkæzaysh*
type this symbol	**írd be ezt a jelet** *eerd bæ æzt o yælæt*
What's your email?	**Mi az e-mail címe?** *Mee oz email tseemæ?*
My email is...	**Az én e-mail címem...** *Oz ayn email tseemæm...*
Do you have a scanner?	**Van szkennerük?** *Von skænærewk?*

Social Media

Are you on Facebook/ Twitter?	**Megtalálhatom Önt a Facebookon/Twitteren?** *Maegtolaalhotawm urnt o Facebook-awn/Tveettaeraen?*
What's your username?	**Mi a felhasználó neve?** *Mee o faelhosnaalaw naevae?*
I'll add you as a friend.	**Hozzáadom az ismerőseimhez.** *Hawzaa-odawm awz eeshmaerurshae-eemhaez*
I'll follow you on Twitter.	**A Twitteren követni fogom.** *A Tveettaeraen kurveatnee fawgawm*
Are you following...?	**Ön is követ...?** *Urn eesh kurvaet?*
I'll put the pictures on Facebook/Twitter.	**Felteszem a képeket a Facebookra/Twitterre.** *Fealtaesaem o kaypaekaet o Facebbok-ro/Tveettaerae*
I'll tag you in the pictures.	**Megjelöllek a képeken.** *Meagyaelurlaek o kaypaekaen*

Conversation

Hello!/Hi!	**Szia!/Sziasztok!** *seeo/seeostawk*
How are you?	**Hogy van?** *hawdⁿ von*
Fine, thanks.	**Köszönöm jól.** *kursurnurm yāwl*

Excuse me!	**Elnézést!** *ælnayzaysht*
Do you speak English?	**Beszél angolul?** *bæsayl ongawlool*
What's your name?	**Hogy hívják?** *hawd^y heevyaak*
My name is…	**…vagyok.** *…vod^{y}awk*
Nice to meet you.	**Örülök, hogy megismerhetem.** *urrewlurk hawd^y mægeeshmærhætæm*
Where are you from?	**Honnan jött?** *hawn-non jurt*
I'm from the U.K./U.S.	**Nagy Britanniából/Egyesült Államokból jöttem.** *Nod^y Breetonneeaabawl/Ædyæshewlt Aalomawkbawl yurttem*
What do you do for a living?	**Mivel foglalkozik?** *Meevel fawglolkawzeek?*
I work for…	**…dolgozom** *…dawlgawzawm*
I'm a student.	**Diák vagyok.** *deeaak vod^{y}awk*
I'm retired.	**Nyugdíjas vagyok.** *N^{y}oogdeeyosh vod^{y}awk*
Do you like…?	**Szereti a…?** *Særætee aw…?*
Goodbye.	**Viszontlátásra!** *veesawntlaataashro*
See you later.	**Viszlát!** *veeslaat*

Romance

Would you like go out for a drink/dinner?	**El szeretnél menni italozni vagy vacsorázni?** *æl særætnayl mænnee eetolawznee vod^y vochawraaznee?*
What are your plans for tonight/tomorrow?	**Milyen terveid vannak estére/holnapra?** *meeyæn tærvæ-eed vonnok æshtayræ/hawlnopro?*
Can I have your (phone) number?	**Megadod a telefonszámodat?** *mægheevhotlok o/tælæfawnsaamawdot?*
Can I join you?	**Csatlakozhatok?** *Chotlokawz-hotawk?*
Can I buy you a drink?	**Meghívhatlak egy italra?** *Mægheevhotlok æd^y eetolro?*
I love you.	**Szeretlek.** *Særætlæk.*

Accepting & Rejecting

I'd love to.	**Szívesen, köszönöm.** *Seevæshæn kursurnurm*
Where should we meet?	**Hol találkozzunk?** *hawl tollaalkawz-zoonk*
I'll meet you at bar/your hotel.	**Találkozzunk a bárban/szállodában.** *Tolaalkawzoonk o baarbon/saallawdaabon.*
I'll come by at…	**Ott leszek…-kor.** *awt læsæk…-kawr.*
I'm busy.	**Köszönöm nem, sok dolgom van.** *kursurnurm næm, shawk dawlgawm von*

I'm not interested.	**Köszönöm, nem érdekel.** *kursurnurm næm ayrdækæl*
Leave me alone.	**Kérem, hagyjon békén!** *kayræm hoďawn baykayn*
Stop bothering me!	**Ne zavarj többé!** *næ zovory turbay!*

Food & Drink

Eating Out

Can you recommend a good restaurant/bar?	**Tudna ajánlani egy jó éttermet/bárt?** *toodno oyaanlonnee æď yaw ayt-tærmæt/bar*
Is there a traditional/ an inexpensive restaurant nearby?	**A közelben van helyi ételeket kínáló étterem/ nem drága étterem?** *O kurlælbæn von hæyee aytælækæt keenaalaw/næm draago ayt-tæræm.*
A table for..., please.	**Kérek...fős asztalt.** *Kayræk...füsh ostolt.*
Can we sit...?	**Leülhetünk...?** *Læwlhætewnk...?*
here/there	**itt/ott** *eet/awt*
outside	**kint** *keent*
in a non-smoking area	**nem dohányzó részben** *næm dawhaanv –zaw raysbæn*
I'm waiting for someone.	**Várok valakit.** *Vaarawk volokeet.*
Where are the toilets?	**Hol van a W.C.?** *hawl von o vaytsay*
The menu, please.	**Egy étlapot kérnék.** *ædv aytloppawt kayrnayk*
What do you recommend?	**Mit ajánlana?** *meet oyaanlonno*
I'd like...	**Kérnék...** *kayrnayk...*
Some more..., please.	**Kaphatnék még...?** *kophotnayk mayg...*
Enjoy your meal!	**Jó étvágyat!** *Yaw aytvaadv ot.*
The check [bill], please.	**Kérem a számlát.** *Kayræm o saamlaat.*

YOU MAY SEE...

BELÉPŐ DÍJ	cover charge
ÁLLANDÓ ÁR	fixed price
NAPI MENÜ	menu (of the day)
FELSZOLGÁLÁST (NEM)TARTALMAZZA	service (not) included
SPECIALITÁS	specials

Is service included?	**Az ár tartalmazza a kiszolgálást?** *Az aar tortolmozo o keesawlgaalaasht?*	
Can I pay by credit card/have a receipt?	**Fizethetek kártyával/kérhetek számlát?** *Feezæthætæk kaartyaavol/kayrhætæk saamlaat?*	

Breakfast

kenyeret *kæn^yæræt*	bread
vajat *voyot*	butter
tojást *tawyaasht*	eggs
tükörtojást *tewkurrtawyaasht*	fried eggs
rántottát *raantawt-taat*	scrambled eggs
főtt tojást *fūrt tawyaasht*	boiled egg
lágy/kemény *laad^y/kæmayny*	soft/hard
sonkát tojással *shawnkaat taw^waash-shol*	ham and eggs
lekvárt *lækvaart*	jam
piritóst *peereetāwsht*	toast
joghurtot *yawghoortawt*	yogurt

Appetizers

bécsi heringsaláta *baychee haereeng- shollaato*	herring salad, Vienna-style
francia saláta *frontseeo shollaato*	Russian salad
kaszinó tojás *kosseenāw taw^yaash*	egg mayonnaise
kaviár *kovveeaar*	caviar
daragaluska *dorroggollooshko*	semolina dumplings
galuska *gollooshko*	dumplings
hasábburgonya *hoshaabboorgawn^yo*	chips (french fries)
hortobágyi húsos palacsinta *hawrtawbaad^yee hōōshawsh pollocheento*	stuffed pancakes Hortobágy-style: filled with veal or pork and sour cream
libamáj pástétom *leebommaay paashtaytawm*	goose-liver paté mixed with béchamel, spices and brandy, served in a flaky pastry shell
magyaros ízelítő *mod^yorawsh eezæleetūr*	a mix of salami, sausages, goose liver, eggs, green pepper
májgombóc *maaygawmbāwts*	liver dumplings
nokedli *nawkædlee*	noodles

tormás sonkatekercs	slices of ham filled with
*taw*rmaash **shawn**-kotækærch	horseradish, ewe's cheese
	butter, mustard, paprika.
rántott sajt *raan*tawt shoyt	fried cheese
tarhonya *tor*hawnyo	egg barley
tormás sonkatekercs	slices of ham filled with
*taw*rmaash **shawn**-kotækærch	horseradish
zsemlegombóc *zhæm*lægawmbawts	white-bread dumplings

Meat

Marhahúst *mor*hohо̄о̄sht	beef
Bárányhúst *baa*raanʸhо̄о̄sht	lamb
csirke*cheer*kas	chicken
fiié *feel*ay	fillet
Sertéshúst *shær*taysh-hо̄о̄sht	pork
Borjúhúst *bawr*yо̄о̄hо̄о̄sht	veal
kolbászfélék *kawl*baasfaylayk	sausages

Fish & Seafood

csuka *choo*ko	pike
tőkehal *tū*rkæhol	cod
harcsa *hor*cho	catfish
nyelvhal *nʸælv*hol	sole
pisztráng *pees*traang	trout
ponty *pawnt*ʸ	carp
tonhal *tawn*hol	tunny (tuna)
rákpörkölt *raak*purrkurlt	broiled crab

Vegetables

bab *bob*	beans
káposzta *kaa*pawsto	cabbage
gomba *gawm*bo	mushrooms
hagyma *hod*ʸmo	onions
zöldborsó *zurld*bawrshāw	peas
burgonya *boor*gawnʸo	potatoes
burgonyapüré *boor*gawnʸoppewray	mashed potatoes
paradicsom *por*roddeechawm	tomatoes

Sauces & Condiments

sót *shāwt*	salt
borsot *bawrshawt*	pepper
mustár *mooshtaar*	mustard
ketchup *kæchop*	ketchup

Fruit & Dessert

alma *olmo*	apple
banán *bonnaan*	banana
citrom *tseetrawm*	lemon
narancs *norronch*	orange
szilva *seelvo*	plum
eper *æpær*	strawberries
Fagylaltjuk *fod[y]lolt[y]ook*	ice-cream
dobostorta *dawbawshtawrto*	caramel-topped chocolate cake
gesztenyepüré tejszínhabbal *Gæstæn[y]æpewray tæ[y]ssēēnhob-bol*	chestnut puree with whipped cream
aranygaluska *orron[y]gollooshko*	sweet dumpling

Drinks

The wine list/drink menu, please.	**Kérem a bor/itallapot.** *Kayream o bawr/eetol lopot*
What do you recommend?	**Mit ajánl?** *Meet oyaanl?*
I'd like a bottle/glass of red/white wine.	**Kérek egy üveg vizet/vörös bort/fehér bort.** *Kayræk ed[y] ewvæg veezæt/vur-rursh bawrt/fæhayr bawrt*
The house wine, please.	**Házi bort kérek.** *Haazee bawrt kayræk*
Another bottle/glass, please.	**Kérek még egy üveg/pohár bort.** *Kayræk mayg ed[y] ewvæg/pawhaar bawrt*
I'd like a local beer.	**Helyi sört szeretnék megkóstolni.** *Hæyee shurt særætnayk mæg-kawshtawlnee*
Can I buy you a drink?	**Meghívhatom Önt egy italra?** *Mæheevhotom urnt ed[y] eetolro?*
Cheers!	**Egészségére!** *Egays-shaygayræ?*
A coffee/tea, please.	**Kávét/teát kérek.** *Kaavayt/tæ-aat kayræk*
Black.	**Feketét.** *Faykaytayt*
With...	**-al/-el** *-ol/-æl*
milk	**tejjel** *tæyyæl*

sugar	**cukorral** *tsookawrrol*
artificial sweetener	**édesítővel** *aydæsheeturvæl*
A…, please.	**Kérek….** *Kayræk…*
juice	**gyümölcslét** *d'ewmurlchlayt*
soda [soft drink]	**üdítőitalt** *ewdeetur-eetolt*
(sparkling/still)	**szénsavas/szénsavmentes vizet.**
water	*saynshovosh/saynshovmæntæsh veezæt*

Leisure Time

Sightseeing

Where's the tourist information office?	**Hol van az utazási iroda?** *hawl von oz ootozaashee eerawdo*
What are the main sights?	**Mik a legfontosabb látnivalók?** *meek o lægfawntawshob laatneevollawk*
Do you offer tours in English?	**Tudnak-e ajánlani kirándulásokat angol vezetéssel?** *Toodnok-æ ayaanlonee keeraandoolaashawkot ongawl væzætaysshæl?*
Can I have a map/ guide?	**Kérhetnék térképet/útikönyvet?** *Kayrhætnayk tayrkaypæt/ooteekurnyvæt?*

Shopping

Where's the market/ mall?	**Hol van a piac/bevásárló központ?** *hawl von o peeots/bævaashaarlaw kurzpawnt bevásárló kōzpont*
I'm just looking.	**Csak nézelődök.** *chok nayzælūrdurk*
Can you help me?	**Segítene?** *shægheetænæ*
I'm being helped.	**Már kiszolgálnak** *Maar keesawlgaalnok*
How much is this?	**Mennyibe kerül ez?** *mænveebæ kærewl æz*
That one, please.	**Azt kérem.** *Ozt kayræm.*
That's all.	**Ez minden.** *æz meendæn*
Where can I pay?	**Hol lehet fizetni?** *Hawl læhæt feezætnee?*
I'll pay in cash/ by credit card.	**Készpénzzel/kártyával fizetek.** *Kayspaynzæl/kaarty aavol feezætæk*
A receipt, please.	**Blokkot kaphatnék?** *blawk-kawt kophotnayk*

YOU MAY SEE...

NYITVA/ZÁRVA	open/closed
KIJÁRAT	exit

Sport & Leisure

When's the game?	**Mikor lesz a játszma?**	*Meekawr les o yaatsmo?*
Where's...?	**Hol van a...?**	*Hawl von o...?*
the beach	**strand**	*shtrawnd*
the park	**park**	*pork*
the pool	**uszoda**	*oosawdo*
Is it safe to swim here?	**Biztonságos itt fürdeni?**	*beestawnshaagawsh eet fewrdænee*
Can I hire clubs?	**Bérelhetek golfütőket?**	*Bayrælhætæk gawlfewtükæt?*
How much per hour/day?	**Mennyi a bérleti díj...?**	*mæn'ee o bayrlætæ déey*
How far is it to...?	**Milyen messze van a...?**	*Meeyæn mæssæ von o...?*
Show me on the map, please.	**Kérem, mutassa meg a térképen.**	*Kayræm, mootosho mæg o tayrkaypæn.*

Going Out

What's there to do	**Mit lehet ott éjszaka csinálni?**	
	Meet læhæt awt aysoko cheenaalnae?	
Do you have a program of events?	**Eseménynaptárt tud adni?**	*ÆshæmaynY-noptaart tood odnee?*
What's playing tonight?	**Mi megy ma este?**	*mee mædy mo æshtæ*
Where's...?	**Hol van a...?**	*Hawl von o...?*
the downtown area	**városközpont**	*vaarawshkurzpawnt*
the bar	**bár**	*baar*
the dance club	**táncklub**	*taantskloob*

Baby Essentials

Do you have...?	**Van-e...?**	*Von-ae...?*
a baby bottle	**cumisüvege**	*tsoomeesh-ewvaegae*
baby food	**bébiétele**	*baby-aytaelae*
baby wipes	**baba-törlőkendője**	*bobo-turrlükaendüyae*
a car seat	**gyerekülése**	*dyaeraek-ewlayshae*

a children's menu/ portion	**gyerekmenü/gyerekadag** *dyaeraek-maenew/ dyaeraek-odog*
a child's seat/highchair	**gyerekszék** *dyaeraek-sayk*
a crib/cot	**gyerekágy** *dyaeraek-aady*
diapers [nappies]	**pelenka** *paelaenko*
formula	**tápszer** *taapsaer*
a pacifier [dummy]	**cumi** *tsoomee*
a playpen	**járóka** *yaarawko*
a stroller [pushchair]	**gyerekkocsi (üléssel)** *dyaeraek-kawchee (ewlayshael)*
Can I breastfeed the baby here?	**Megszoptathatom itt a gyereket?** *Maegsawpthothotawm eet o dyaeraekaet?*
Where can I breastfeed/ change the baby?	**Hol szoptathatom meg/tehetem tisztába a gyerekemet?** *Hawl sawpthothotawm maeg/taehaetaem teestaabo a dyaeraekaemaet?*

Disabled Travelers

Is there…?	**Van itt…** *Von eet…*
access for the disabled	**mozgássérülteknek bejárat** *mawzgaash shayrewltaeknaek baeyaarot*
a wheelchair ramp	**kerekesszékes rámpa** *kaeraekaesh-saykaesh raampo*
a disabled-accessible toilet	**WC mozgáskorlátozottak számára** *vaytsay mawzgaash-kawrlaatawzawttok saamaaro*
I need…	**Szükségem van…** *Sewkshaygaem von…*
assistance	**segítségre** *haegeetsaygrae*
an elevator [a lift]	**liftre** *leeftrae*
a ground-floor room	**földszinti szobára** *furldseentee sawbaaro*

Health & Emergencies

Emergencies

Help!	**Segítség!** *shæghēētshayg*
Go away!	**Távozzék!** *taavawzzayk*
Stop, thief!	**Fogják meg, tolvaj!** *fawgyaak mæg tawlvoy*
Get a doctor!	**Hívjon orvost!** *hēēvyawn awrvawsht*

Fire!	**Tüz!** _tewz_
I'm lost.	**Eltévedtem.** _æltayvædtæm_
Can you help me?	**Tudna segíteni?** _Toodno shægeetænee?_
Call the police!	**Hívja a rendőrséget!** _heevyo o rændörrshaygæt_
Where's the police station?	**Hol van a rendőrség?** _hawl von o rændürrshayg_
My child is missing.	**Eltűnt a gyerekem.** _Æltewnt o dyærækæm_

In an emergency, dial **112**.

Health

I'm sick.	**Beteg vagyok.** _bætæg vod'awk_
I need an English-speaking doctor.	**Angolul beszélő orvosra van szükségem.** _Ongawlool bæsaylur awrvawrshro von sewkshaygæm_
It hurts here.	**Itt fáj.** _Eet faay_
Where's the pharmacy?	**Hol van a patika?** _Hawl von o poteeko?_
I'm (...months) pregnant.	**(...hónapos) Terhes vagyok.** _(...) tærhæsh vod'awk_
I'm on...	**...szedek** ..._sædæk_
I'm allergic to... antibiotics/ penicillin.	**Allergiás vagyok...** _Allærgeeash vod'awk..._ **antibiotikumra/penicillinre.** _Ænteebeeawteekoomawkræ/pæneetseeleenræ_

YOU MAY HEAR...

Töltse ki az űrlapot. _Turltshæ kee oz ewrlopawt._ — Fill out this form.

Kérem a személyi igazolványát. — Your ID, please.
Kayræm o sæmayyee eegozawlvaanyaat.

Mikor/Hol történt? _Meekawr/Hawl turtaynt?_ — When/Where did it happen?

Hogy néz ki a gyerek? _Hawd nayz kee a dyæræk?_ — What does he/she look like?

a **egy**
adaptor **adapter**
and **és**
baby **kisbaba**
bad **rossz**
bag **táska; szatyor**
Band-Aid **sebtapasz**
beige **drapp, beige**
black **fekete**
blue **kék**
bottle-opener **sörnyitó**
boy **fiú**
boyfriend **barát**
bra **melltartó**
brown **barna**
camera **fényképezőgép**
castle **vár**
cold **hideg**
corkscrew **dugóhúzó**
deodorant **dezodor**
diabetic **cukorbeteg**
doll **baba**
fork **villa**
girl **lány;**(child) **kislány**
girlfriend **barátnő**
glass **pohár**
great (excellent) **nagyszerű**
green **zöld**
hot **meleg; forró**
husband **férj**
ice **jég**
insect repellent **rovarirtó**
jeans **farmer**
knife **kés**

large **nagy**
lighter **öngyújtó**
love, to **szeretni**
match **gyufa;** (sport) **meccs**
napkin **szalvéta**
nurse **nővér**
or **vagy**
pen **toll**
plate **tányér**
rain **eső**
raincoat **esőkabát**
razor **borotva**
razor blade **borotvapenge**
red **vörös, piros**
salty **sós**
sanitary towel/napkin **papírtörülköző**
scissors **olló**
shampoo **sampon**
shoe **cipő**
small **kicsi, kis**
snow **hó**
sock **zokni**
spoon **kanál**
stamp (postage) **bélyeg**
suncream **napozókrém**
tampon **tampon**
tissue **papírzsebkendő**
toilet paper **W.C. papír**
toothbrush **fogkefe**
toothpaste **fogkrém**
toy **játék**
wife **feleség**
with **-val, -vel**
without **nélkül**

Latvian

Essentials

Hello/Hi.	**Sveiki** *sveyky*
Good morning.	**Labrīt.** *labreet*
Good afternoon.	**Labdien.** *labdeean*
Good night.	**Ar labu nakti.** *ar laboo nakti*
Goodbye.	**Uz redzēšanos.** *ooz redzehshanwas*
Yes/No/Okay.	**Jā/Nē/Labi.** *jah/neh/labee*
Excuse me!	**Es atvainojos!** *ess atvaynwaywass*
(to get attention)	
Excuse me. (to get past)	**Atvainojiet!** *atvaynwayeeat*
I'm sorry.	**Es atvainojos!** *ess atvaynwaywass*
I'd like…	**Es vēlos…** *ess ve'lwass…*
How much?	**Cik daudz?** *tsik dowdz*
And/or.	**Un/vai.** *oon/vay*
Please.	**Lūdzu.** *loohdzoo*
Thank you.	**Paldies.** *paldeeass*
You're welcome.	**Vienmēr laipni.** *veeanmehr laypni*
Where is…?	**Kur ir?** *koor ir*
I'm going to…	**Es eju uz…** *ess eyu ooz…*
My name is…	**Mani sauc…** *mani sowts…*
Please speak slowly.	**Lūdzu, runājiet lēnām.** *loohdzoo roonahyeeat lehnahm*
Can you repeat that?	**Vai variet atkārtot?** *vay vareeat atkahrtwat*
I don't understand.	**Es nesaprotu.** *ess nesaprwatoo*
Do you speak English?	**Vai jūs runājat angliski?** *vai yoohss roonahyat angliski*
I don't speak Latvian.	**Es nerunāju latviski.** *ess neroonayoo latviski.*
Where's the restroom [toilet]?	**Kur ir labierīcības?** *kur ir labeeareetseebass*
Help!	**Palīgā!** *paleegah*

Numbers

0	**nulle** *noolle*
1	**viens** *veeanss*
2	**divi** *divi*

You'll find the pronunciation of the Latvian letters and words written in gray after each sentence to guide you. Simply pronounce these as if they were English. As you hear the language being spoken, you will quickly become accustomed to the local pronunciation and dialect.

3	**trīs**	*treess*
4	**četri**	*chetri*
5	**pieci**	*peeatsi*
6	**seši**	*seshi*
7	**septiņi**	*septinyi*
8	**astoņi**	*astwanyi*
9	**deviņi**	*devinyi*
10	**desmit**	*desmit*
11	**vienpadsmit**	*veeanpatsmit*
12	**divpadsmit**	*divpatsmit*
13	**trīspadsmit**	*treespatsmit*
14	**četrpadsmit**	*chetrpatsmit*
15	**piecpadsmit**	*peeatspatsmit*
16	**sešpadsmit**	*seshpatsmit*
17	**septiņpadsmit**	*septin'patsmit*
18	**astoņpadsmit**	*astwan'patsmit*
19	**deviņpadsmit**	*devin'patsmit*
20	**divdesmit**	*divdesmit*
21	**divdesmit viens**	*divdesmit veeanss*
30	**trīsdesmit**	*treezdesmit*
40	**četrdesmit**	*chetrdesmit*
50	**piecdesmit**	*peeatsdesmit*
60	**sešdesmit**	*seshdesmit*
70	**septiņdesmit**	*septin'desmit*
80	**astoņdesmit**	*astwan'desmit*
90	**deviņdesmit**	*deviņ'desmit*
100	**simts**	*simts*
101	**simtu viens**	*simtoo veeanss*
200	**divsimt**	*divsimt*

500	**piecsimt** *peeatssimt*
1,000	**tūkstots** *toohkstwats*
10,000	**desmit tūkstoši** *desmit toohkstwashi*
1,000,000	**miljons** *milyohnss*

Time

What time is it?	**Cik pulkstenis?** *tsik poolksteniss*
It's midday.	**Tagad ir divpadsmit dienā.** *tagad ir divpatsmit deeanah*
Five past three.	**Piecas pāri trijiem** *peeatsass pahri triyeeam*
A quarter to ten.	**Bez piecpadsmit desmit** *bez peeatspatsmit desmit*
5:30 a.m./p.m.	**Pusseši no rīta/vakarā** *pooss seshi nwa reeta/vakarah*

Days

Monday	**pirmdiena** *pirmdeeana*
Tuesday	**otrdiena** *watrdeeana*
Wednesday	**trešdiena** *trezhdeeana*
Thursday	**ceturtdiena** *tsa'toordeeana*
Friday	**piektdiena** *peeagdeeana*
Saturday	**sestdiena** *sezdeeana*
Sunday	**svētdiena** *svehdeeana*

Dates

yesterday	**vakar** *vakar*
today	**šodien** *shwadeean*
tomorrow	**rīt** *reet*
day	**dienu** *deeanoo*
week	**nedēļu** *nedehlyoo*
month	**mēnesis** *mehnesiss*
year	**gads** *gadss*
Happy New Year!	**Laimīgu jauno gadu!** *laymeegoo yownwa gadoo*
Happy Birthday!	**Daudz laimes dzimšanas dienā!** *daoodz laymess dzimshanass deeanah*

Months

January	**janvāris** *yanvahris*
February	**februāris** *febroahris*
March	**marts** *marts s*

April	**aprīlis** *apreeliss*
May	**maijs** *maiyss*
June	**jūnijs** *yoohniyss*
July	**jūlijs** *yoohliyss*
August	**augusts** *owgoostss*
September	**septembris** *septembris*
October	**oktobris** *oktobris*
November	**novembris** *novembris*
December	**decembris** *detsembris*

Arrival & Departure

I'm on vacation [holiday]/business.	**Es esmu atvaļinā jumā/komandējumā.** *ess a'smoo atvalyinah yoomah/komandehyoomah*
I'm going to…	**Es eju uz…** *ess eyoo ooz…*
I'm staying at the…Hotel.	**Es palieku …viesnīcā.** *ess paleeakoo… veeasneetsah*

Money

Where's…?	**Kur ir…?** *Koor ir…*
the ATM	**bankomāts** *bankomahtss*
the bank	**banka** *banka*
the currency exchange office	**valūtas maiņas punkts** *valoohtass maynyass poonktss*
When does the bank open/close?	**No/līdz cikiem strādā banka?** *nwa/leedz tsikeeam strahdah banka*
I'd like to change dollars/pounds sterling/into euros.	**Es vēlos apmainīt dažus dolārus/mārciņas euros.** *ess ve'lwass apmaineet dazhooss dolahrooss/mahrtsinyas euros*
I'd like to cash traveler's cheques.	**Es vēlētos apmainīt ceļojuma čeku pret naudu.** *ess vehlehtwass apmayneet tselywayooma chekoo pret naoodoo*
Can I pay in cash?	**Vai es varu maksāt skaidrā naudā?** *vay ess varoo maksaht skaydrah naoodah*
Can I pay by (credit) card?	**Vai es varu maksāt ar (kredīt-) karti?** *vay ess varoo maksaht ar (kredeet-) karti?*

For Numbers, see page 133.

YOU MAY SEE...

The Latvian currency is the **euro**, **€**, which is divided into 100 **cents**.
Coins: 1, 2, 5, 10, 20 and 50 **cents**; €1, 2
Bills: €5, 10, 20, 50, 100, 200 and 500

Getting Around

How do I get to town?	**Kā es varu nokļūt līdz pilsētai?** *kah ees varoo nwaklyooht leedz pilsehtai*
Where's...?	**Kur ir...?** *Koor ir...?*
the airport	**lidosta** *lidwasta*
the train station	**dzelzceļa stacija** *dzelztselya statsiya*
the bus station	**autoosta** *aootowasta*
the subway station	**metro stacija** *metro statsiya*
Is it far from here?	**Vai tas ir tālu no šejienes?** *vay tas ir tahloo noh sheyeenes*
Where do I buy a ticket?	**Kur es varu nopirkt biļeti?** *koor ehs varoo nopreekt beelyetee*
A one-way/return-trip ticket to...	**Vienvirziena biļeti/biļeti turp-atpakaļ uz...** *vyen-veer-zee-eh-nah beelyetee/beelyetee toorp-atpakal ooz*
How much?	**Cik jāmaksā?** *seek jahmaksah?*
Which gate/line?	**Kura ieeja/kurš ceļš?** *koorah eeya/koorsh celyeesh?*
Which platform?	**Kura platforma?** *koorah platformah?*
Where can I get a taxi?	**Kur es varu dabūt taksometru?** *koor ehs varoo daboot taksohmetroo*
Take me to this address.	**Aizvediet mani uz šo adresi.** *ayzveedyet manee ooz sho adressee*
To...Airport, please.	**Uz...lidostu, lūdzu.** *ooz...lidwastoo, loohdzoo*
I'm in a rush.	**Es steidzos.** *ehs steydzoss*
Can I have a map?	**Vai es varu palūgt karti?** *vay ehs varoo paloogt kartee?*

Tickets

When's...to Riga?	**Kad atiet...uz Riga?** *kad ateeat...ooz Reega*
the (first) bus	**(pirmais) autobuss** *(peermaysch) autobus*
the (last) train	**(pēdējais) vilciens** *(pedayas) veelcheens*
When's the (next) flight to London?	**Kad ir (nākamais) lidojums uz London?** *kad ir (nahkamays) leedoyooms ooz London?*

One/Two ticket(s) please.	**Vienu biļeti/divas biļetes, lūdzu.** *veeanoo beelyetee/ divahs beelyetees, loohdzoo*
For today/tomorrow.	**Uz šodienu/rītdienu.** *ooz shwadeeanoo/reetdeeynoo*
A…ticket.	**…biļeti.** *… beelyetee*
one-way	**vienvirziena** *veenveerzeenah*
return trip	**turp-atpakaļ** *toorp-atpakay*
first class	**pirmās klases** *peermays klasehs*
I have an e-ticket.	**Man ir e-biļete.** *man ir e-beelyetee*
How long is the trip?	**Cik ilgs ir brauciens?** *seek eelgs ir browcheens*
Is it a direct train?	**Vai tas ir tiešais vilciens?** *vay tas ir teeshays veelcheenz*
Is this the bus to…?	**Šis ir autobuss uz…?** *shees ir autobus ooz…*
Can you tell me when to get off?	**Vai Jūs varat man pateikt, kad man jāizkāpj?** *vay yooz varat man pateykt, kad man yayzkahp*
I'd like to…	**Es vēlos…savu rezervāciju.**
my reservation.	*ehs vehlos…savoo reservahceeyoo*
cancel	**atcelt** *atcelt*
change	**mainīt** *mayneet*
confirm	**apstiprināt** *apsteepreenaht*

YOU MAY HEAR…

taisni uz priekšu *taysni ooz preeakshoo*	straight ahead
pa kreisi *pa kreysi*	left
pa labi *pa labi*	right
ap stūri *ap stoohri*	around the corner
pretī *pretee*	opposite
aiz *ayz*	behind
blakus *blakooss*	next to
pēc *pehts*	after
uz ziemeļiem/uz dienvidiem *ooz zeeamelyeeam/ooz deeanvideeam*	north/south
uz austrumiem/uz rietumiem *ooz owstroomeeam/ooz reeatoomeeam*	east/west
pie luksofora *peea looksofora*	at the traffic light
pie krustojuma *peea kroostwayooma*	at the intersection

Car Hire

Where's the car hire?	**Kur ir auto noma?**	*koor ir aooto nwama*
I'd like…	**Es vēlētos**…	*ess vehlehtwass*…
a cheap/small car	**lētu/nelielu auto**	*lehtoo/neleealoo aooto*
an automatic/	**automātisko/manuālo kārbu**	*aootomahtiskwa/*
a manual		*manooalwa kahrboo*
air conditioning	**gaisa kondicionieri**	*gaysa konditsiwaneeari*
a car seat	**…sēdvietu**	*…sehdveetoo*
How much…?	**Cik tas maksās…?**	*tsik tass maksahss?*
per day/week	**dienā/nedēļā**	*deeanah/nedelyah*
Are there any discounts?	**Vai iespējamas kādas atlaides?**	*vay eeaspehyamass kahdass atlaydess?*

Places to Stay

Can you recommend a hotel?	**Vai varat ieteikt kādu viesnīcu?**	*vay varat eeateykt kahdoo veeasneetsoo?*
I made a reservation.	**Esmu veicis/veikusi f rezervāciju.**	*esmoo veytsiss/veykoosi rezervahtsiyoo*
My name is…	**Mani sauc…**	*mani saoots*…
Do you have a room…?	**Vai ir pieejams numuriņš…?**	*vay ir peeaeyamss noomoorinysh*
for one/two	**vienam/diviem**	*veeanam/diveeam*
with a bathroom	**ar vannas istabu**	*ar vannass istaboo*
with air conditioning	**ar gaisa kondicionieri**	*ar gaysa konditsioneeari*
For…	**Uz…**	*ooz*…
tonight	**šodienu**	*shwadeeanoo*
two nights	**divām naktīm**	*divahm nakteem*
one week	**vienu nedēļu**	*vehnoo nedehlyoo*
How much?	**Cik tas maksā?**	*tsik tass maksah?*
Is there anything cheaper?	**Vai ir arī kaut kas lētāks?**	*vay ir aree kowt kass lehtahkss?*
When's checkout?	**Kad ir jāizrakstās?**	*kad ir yahizrakstahss?*
Can I leave this in the safe?	**Vai šo es varu atstāt seifā?**	*vay shwa ess varoo atstaht seyfah?*
Can I leave my bags?	**Vai es varu atstāt savas somas?**	*vay ess varoo atstaht savass swamass?*
Can I have my bill/ a receipt?	**Vai es varētu saņemt čeku/kvīti?**	*vay ess varehtoo sanyemt chekoo/kveeti?*
I'll pay in cash/by credit card.	**Es maksāšu -skaidrā naudā/-ar kredītkarti**	*ess maksahshoo -skaydrah nowdah/-ar kredeetkarti*

Communications

Where's an internet cafe?	**Kur atrodas interneta kafejnīca?** *koor atrwadass interneta kafeyneetsa?*
Can I access the internet/check my email?	**Vai es varu tikt pie interneta/pārbaudīt savu e-pastu?** *vay ess varoo tikt pea interneta/pahrbowdeet savoo epastoo?*
How much per half hour/hour?	**Cik tas maksā pusstundā/stundā?** *tsik tass maksah poostoondah/stoondah?*
How do I connect/log on?	**Kā es varu pieslēgties?** *kah ess varoo peeaslehgteeass?*
A phone card, please.	**Lūdzu, vienu telekarti.** *loohdzoo veeanoo telekarti*
Can I have your phone number?	**Vai es varētu palūgt jūsu telefona numuru?** *vay ess varehtoo palooght joohsoo telefona noomooroo?*
Here's my number/email.	**Šis ir mans telefons/e-pasts.** *shiss ir mans telefons/epasts*
Call me/text me.	**Pazvani/atraksti man.** *pazvani/atraksti man*
I'll text you.	**Es tev atrakstīšu.** *ess tev atraksteeshoo*
Email me.	**Atsūti man e-pastu.** *atsoohti man epastoo*
Hello. This is...	**Sveiki, te...** *sveyki te...*
Can I speak to...?	**Vai es varu runāt ar...?** *vay ess varoo roonaht ar...?*
Can you repeat that?	**Vai jūs varētu to atkārtot?** *vay joohss varehtoo twa atkahrtwat?*
I'll call back later.	**Es jums pārzvanīšu.** *ess joomss pahrzvaneeshoo*
Bye.	**Atā!** *atah!*
Where's the post office?	**Kur ir pasta nodaļa?** *koor ir pasta nwadalya?*
I'd like to send this to...	**Es šo vēlētos nosūtīt uz...** *ess shwa vehlehtwass nwasoohteet ooz*
Can I...?	**Vai es varētu ...** *vay ess varehtoo ...*
access the internet	**piekļūt internetam** *peeaklyooht internetam*
check my email	**pārbaudīt savu e-pastu** *pahrbowdeet savoo epastoo*
print	**izprintēt** *izprinteht*
plug in/charge my laptop/iPhone/iPad/BlackBerry?	**pieslēgt/uzlādēt savu datoru/iPhone/iPad/BlackBerry?** *peeaslehgt/oozlahdeht savoo datoroo/iPhone/iPad/BlackBerry?*
access Skype?	**izmantot Skype?** *izmantwat Skype?*
What is the WiFi password?	**Kāda ir WiFi parole?** *kahda ir WiFi parole?*
Is the WiFi free?	**Vai WiFI ir bez maksas?** *vay WiFi ir bez maksass?*
Do you have bluetooth?	**Vai jums ir bluetooth?** *vay yoomss ir bluetooth?*
Do you have a scanner?	**Vai jums ir skeneris?** *vay yoomss ir skeneriss?*

Social Media

Are you on Facebook/Twitter?	**Vai esi reģistrējies Facebook/Twitter?** *vay essi regystrehyeeass Facebook/Twitter?*
What's your username?	**Kāds ir tavs lietotājvārds?** *kahdss ir tavss leeatotahyvahrdss?*
I'll add you as a friend.	**Es tevi pievienošu saviem draugiem.** *ess tevi peeaveeanwashoo saveeam draoogeeam*
I'll follow you on Twitter.	**Es sekošu tev Twitter.** *ess sekwashoo tev Twitter*
Are you following...?	**Vai tu seko...?** *vay too seko...?*
I'll put the pictures on Facebook/Twitter.	**Es ielikšu bildes Faceboook/Twitter.** *ess eealikshoo bildess Faceboook/Twitter*
I'll tag you in the pictures.	**Es atzīmēšu tevi bildēs.** *ess atzeemehshoo tevi bildehss*

Conversation

Hello!/Hi!	**Labdien!/Sveiki!** *labdeean!/sveyki!*
How are you?	**Kā jums klājas?** *kah yoomss klahyass*
Fine thanks.	**Paldies, labi.** *paldeeass labi*
Excuse me!	**Es atvainojos!** *ess atvaynwaywas!*
Do you speak English?	**Vai jūs runājat angliski?** *vai yoohss roonahyat angliski*
What's your name?	**Kā jūs sauc?** *kah yoohss sowts?*
My name is...	**Mani sauc...** *mani sowts...*
Nice to meet you.	**Prieks jūs satikt.** *preeakss yoohss satikt*
Where are you from?	**No kurienes jūs esat?** *nwa kooreeanes yoohss a'sat*
I'm from the U.K./U.S.	**Es esmu no...** *ess esmoo nwa ...*
What do you do for a living?	**Ar ko jūs nodarbojaties?** *ar kwa yoohss nwadarbwayateeass*
I work for...	**Es strādāju...** *ess strahdahyoo...*
I'm a student.	**Esmu students *m*/studente *f*.** *esmoo stoodentss/stoodente*
I'm retired.	**Esmu pensijā.** *esmoo pensiyah*

Romance

Would you like to go out for a drink/dinner?	**Vai vēlies aiziet -uz kādu dzērienu/-pavakariņot?** *vay vehlateeass aizeeat -ooz kahdoo dzehreeanoo/-pavakarinywat?*
What are your plans for tonight/tomorrow?	**Kādi ir jūsu plāni -šim vakaram/-rītdienai?** *kahdi ir yoohsoo plahni -shim vakaram/-reetdeeanay*
Can I have your (phone) number?	**Vai varu palūgt tavu telefona numuru?** *vay varoo paluhgt tavoo telefona noomooroo?*

Can I join you?	**Vai varu tev pievienoties?** *vay varoo tev peeaveeanwateeass?*
Can I buy you a drink?	**Vai varu izmaksāt tev dzērienu?** *vay varoo izmaksaht tev dzehreeanoo?*
I love you.	**Es tevi mīlu.** *ess tevi meelu*

Accepting & Rejecting

I'd love to.	**Labprāt.** *labpraht*
Where should we meet?	**Kur mēs varētu satikties?** *koor mehss varehtoo satikteeass?*
I'll meet you at the bar/your hotel.	**Satiekamies bārā/viesnīcā.** *sateeakameeass bahrah/veeasneetsah*
I'll come by at…	**Es tur būšu…** *ess toor booshoo*
I'm busy.	**Esmu aizņemts *m*/aizņemta *f*.** *esmoo ayznyemtssm/ayznyemta*
I'm not interested.	**Neesmu ieinteresēts *m*/ieinteresēta *f*.** *ne-esmoo eeainteresehtssm/eeainteresehtaf*
Leave me alone.	**Liec mani mierā.** *leeats mani meearah*
Stop bothering me!	**Beidz mani traucēt.** *beydz mani trowtseht*

Food & Drink

Eating Out

Can you recommend a good restaurant/bar?	**Vai variet ieteikt kādu labu restorānu/bāru?** *vay vareeat eeateykt kahdoo laboo restorahnoo/bahroo?*
Is there a traditional/ an inexpensive restaurant nearby?	**Vai tuvumā ir kāds tradicionālais/ne pārāk dārgs restorāns?** *vay toovoomah ir kaahdss tradicionahlss/ne pahrahk dahrgss restorahnss?*
A table for…, please.	**Galdiņu…lūdzu.** *galdinyoo…loohdzoo*
Can we sit…?	**Vai mēs varam sēsties** *vay mehss varam sehsteeass*
here/there	**šeit/tur** *sheyt/toor*
outside	**ārpusē** *ahrpooseh*
in a non-smoking area	**nesmēķētāju zonā** *nesmehkyehtahyoo zonah*
I'm waiting for someone.	**Es kādu gaidu.** *ess kahdoo gaydoo*
Where are the toilets?	**Kur ir labierīcības?** *koor ir labeeareetseebass?*
The menu, please.	**Ēdienkarti, lūdzu.** *ehdeeankarti loohdzoo*
What do you recommend?	**Ko jūs ieteiktu?** *kwa yoohss eeateyktoo?*

I'd like…	**Es vēlos…** *ess ve'lwass…*
Some more…, please.	**Vēl…, lūdzu.** *vehl…loohdzoo*
Enjoy your meal!	**Labu apetīti!** *laboo apeteeti*
The check [bill], please.	**Rēķinu, lūdzu!** *rehkyinoo loohdzoo*
Is service included?	**Vai apkalpošana ir iekļauta?** *vay apkalpwashana ir eeaklyowta?*
Can I pay by credit card/have a receipt?	**Vai es varu maksāt ar karti/palūgt kvīti?** *vay ess varoo maksaht ar karti/paloohgt kveeti?*

YOU MAY SEE…

ieejas maksa *eeaeyass maksa*	cover charge
viena cena *veeana tsena*	fixed price
dienas piedāvājums *deeanass peeadahvahyoomss*	menu (of the day)
apkalpošana (nav) iekļauta *apkalpwashana (now) eeaklyowta*	service (not) included
īpašie piedāvājumi *eepasheea peeadahvahyoomi*	specials

Breakfast

maizi/sviestu *maizi/sveeastoo*	bread/butter
sieru *seearoo*	cheese
olu/šķiņķi *waloo/shtyin'tyi*	egg/ham
ievārījumu *eeavahreeyoomoo*	jam
maizīti *maizeeti*	rolls
grauzdiņš *growzdinysh*	toast
bekons *bekonss*	bacon
desiņa *desinya*	sausage

Appetizers

marinētas sēnes *marina'tas sehness*	pickled mushrooms
nēģi *nehdyi*	lamprey
šprotes *shprwatess*	smoked sprats
žāvēts lasis *zhahve'ts lasiss*	smoked salmon
žāvēts zutis *zhahve'ts zootiss*	smoked eel

Meat

Es vēlos... *ess ve'lwass*	I'd like some...
vēršgaļu *vehrshgalyoo*	beef
vistu/pīli *vistoo/peeli*	chicken/duck
jērgaļu *ye'rgalyoo*	lamb
cūkgaļu *tsoohkgalyoo*	pork
teļgaļu *tel'galyoo*	veal
karbonāde *karbonahde*	pork chop
kotletes *kotletess*	meat balls
mežcūkas cepetis *mezhtsoohkas tsepetis*	wild boar steak
sautēta vista *sowte'ta vista*	braised chicken
sīpolu sitenis *seepwaloo sitenis*	steak (beef) with onions
teļgaļas cepetis *tel'galyas tsepetis*	roast veal

YOU MAY HEAR...

labi izcepts *labi iztsa'pts*	(rare)
vidējs *videhyss*	medium
labi izcepts *labi iztsa'pts*	well-done

Fish & Seafood

cepts lasis *tsa'ptss lasiss*	fried/grilled salmon
cepta forele *tsa'pta forele*	fried/grilled trout
cepta bute *tsa'pta boote*	fried plaice
sālīta siļķe *sahleeta sil'tye*	salt herring
cepta karpa *tsa'pta karpa*	fried carp
līdaka želējā *leehdaka zhelehyah*	pike in jelly

Vegetables

pupiņas *poopinyass*	beans
kāposti *kahpwasti*	cabbage
burkāni *boorkahni*	carrots
sēnes *sehness*	mushroom
sīpoli *seepwali*	onion

zirņi *zirnyi*	peas
kartupeļi *kartoopelyi*	potatoes
tomāti *tomahti*	tomato
burkānu *boorkahnoo*	carrot
omlete ar sēnēm *omlete ar sehnehm*	mushroom omelet
omlete ar sieru *omlete ar seearoo*	cheese omelet
sautētas saknes ar mērci *sowte'tas sakness ar mehrtsi*	stewed vegetables with cream sauce

Sauces & Condiments

sāls *sahlss*	Salt
pipari *pipari*	Pepper
sinepes *sinepess*	Mustard
kečups *kechoopss*	Ketchup

Fruit & Dessert

āboli/banāni *ahbwali/banahni*	apple/banana
plūmes/citroni *ploohmess/tsitrwani*	plum/lemon
apelsīni/zemenes *apelseeni/zemenes*	orange/strawberries
ābolkūka *ahbwalkoohka*	apple tart
buberts *boobertss*	egg mousse with fruit sauce
maizes zupa *maizess zoopa*	rye bread soup with fruit, spices
saldējums *saldehyooms*	ice-cream
torte *torte*	gateau
pankūkas *pankookass*	pancakes

Drinks

The wine list/drink menu, please.	**Vīnu/dzērienu karti, lūdzu.** *veenoo/dzehreeanoo karti loohdzoo*
What do you recommend?	**Ko jūs iesakāt?** *kwa yoohss eeasakaht?*
I'd like a bottle/glass of red/white wine.	**Es vēlētos pudeli/glāzi sarkanvīna/baltvīna.** *ess vehlehtwass poodeli/glahzi sarkanveena/baltveena.*
The house wine, please.	**Mājas vīnu, lūdzu.** *mahyass veenoo loohdzoo*
Another bottle/glass, please.	**Vēl vienu glāzi/pudeli, lūdzu.** *vehl veeanoo glahzi/poodeli loohdzoo*
I'd like a local beer.	**Es vēlētos vietējo alu.** *ess vehlehtwass veeatehywa aloo.*

Can I buy you a drink?	**Vai es varu izmaksāt tev dzērienu?** *vay ess varoo tev izmaksaht dzehreeanoo?*
Cheers!	**Priekā!** *preeakah*
A coffee/tea, please.	**Kafiju/tēju, lūdzu.** *kafiyoo/tehyoo loohdzoo.*
Black.	**Melnu.** *melnoo*
With…	**Ar…** *ar…*
milk	**pienu** *peeanoo*
sugar	**cukuru** *tsookooroo*
artificial sweetener	**saldinātāju** *saldinahtahyoo*
A…, please.	**…, lūdzu** *…loohdzoo*
juice	**sulu** *sooloo*
soda [soft drink]	**limonādi** *limonahdi*
(sparkling/still) water	**(gāzētu/negāzētu) ūdeni** *(gahzehtoo/negahzehtoo) oohdeni*

Leisure Time

Sightseeing

Where's the tourist information office?	**Kur atrodas tūristu informācijas centrs?** *koor atrwadass toohristoo informahtsiyass tsentrss?*
What are the main sights?	**Kas ir galvenie apskates objekti?** *kas ir galveneea apskatess obyekti?*
Do you offer tours in English?	**Vai jūs piedāvājat tūres angļu valodā?** *vay yoohss peeadahvahyat toohress anglyoo valwadah?*
Can I have a map/guide?	**Vai es varu iegādāties karti/ceļvedi?** *vay ess varoo eeagahdahteeass karti/tselyvedi?*

> #### YOU MAY SEE…
>
> | **atvērts/slēgts** *atvehrtss/slehgtss* | open/closed |
> | **ieeja/izeja** *eeaeya/izeya* | entrance/exit |

Shopping

| Where's the market/mall? | **Kur atrodas tirgus/lielveikals?** *koor atrwadas tirgooss/leealveykalss?* |
| I'm just looking. | **Es tikai skatos.** *ess tikay skatwass* |

Can you help me?	**Vai varat man palīdzēt?** *vay varat man paleedzeht?*
I'm being helped.	**Man jau kāds palīdz.** *man yaoo kahdss paleedz*
How much?	**Cik tas maksā?** *tsik tass maksah?*
That one, please.	**Tas, lūdzu.** *tass loohdzoo*
I'd like…	**Es vēlētos…** *ess vehlehtwass…*
That's all.	**Tas ir viss.** *tass ir viss*
Where can I pay?	**Kur es varu samaksāt?** *koor es varoo samaksaht?*
I'll pay in cash/by credit card.	**Es maksāšu skaidrā naudā/ar kredītkarti.** *ess maksahshoo skaydrah naoodah/ar kredeetkarti*
A receipt, please.	**Kvīti, lūdzu.** *kveeti loohdzoo*

Sport & Leisure

When's the game?	**Kad ir spēle?** *kad ir spehle?*
Where's…?	**Kur atrodas…?** *koor atrwadass…?*
the beach	**pludmale** *ploodmale*
the park	**parks** *parkss*
the pool	**baseins** *baseynss*
Is it safe to swim here?	**Vai šeit ir droši peldēt?** *vay sheyt ir drwashi peldeht?*
Can I hire clubs?	**Vai es varu noīrēt nūjas?** *vay es varoo nwaeereht noohyass?*
How much per hour/day?	**Cik tas maksā stundā/dienā?** *tsik tass maksah stoondah/deeanah?*
How far is it to…?	**Cik tālu ir līdz…?** *tsik tahloo ir leedz…?*
Show me on the map, please.	**Parādiet, lūdzu, to kartē.** *parahdeeat loohdzoo twa karteh*

Going Out

What's there to do at night?	**Ko tur iespējams darīt naktīs?** *kwa toor eeaspehyamss dareet nakteess?*
Do you have a program of events?	**Vai jums ir pasākumu programma?** *vay yoomss ir pasahkoomoo programma?*
What's playing tonight?	**Kas šonakt uzstāsies?** *kas shwanakt oozstahseeass?*
Where's…?	**Kur atrodas…?** *koor atrwadass…?*
the downtown area	**pilsētas centrs** *pilsehtass tsentrss*
the bar	**bārs** *bahrss*
the dance club	**naktsklubs** *naktskloobss*
Is this area safe at night?	**Vai šis rajons naktīs ir drošs?** *vay shiss raywans naktees ir drwashss?*

Baby Essentials

Do you have...?	**Vai jums ir...?** *vay yoomss ir...?*	
a baby bottle	**bērnu pudelīte** *behrnoo poodeleete*	
baby food	**pārtika mazuļiem** *pahrtika mazoolyeeam*	
baby wipes	**mitrās salvetes mazuļiem** *mitrahss salvetess mazoolyeeam*	
a car seat	**automašīnas sēdeklītis** *aootomasheenass sehdekleetiss*	
a children's menu/ portion	**bērnu ēdienkarte/porcijas** *behrnoo ehdeeankarte/ portsiyas*	
a child's seat/ highchair	**bērnu sēdvieta/krēsliņš** *behrnoo sehdveeata/ krehslinysh*	
a crib/cot	**bērnu gultiņa** *behrnoo gooltinya*	
diapers [nappies]	**autiņi** *aootinyi*	
formula	**zīdaiņu pārtika** *zeedainyoo pahrtika*	
a pacifier [dummy]	**knupītis** *knoopeetiss*	
a playpen	**bērnu manēža** *behrnoo manehzha*	
a stroller [pushchair]	**ratiņi** *ratinyi*	
Can I breastfeed the baby here?	**Vai es varu šeit bērnu barot ar krūti?** *vay ess varoo sheyt behrnoo barwat ar kroohti?*	
Where can I breastfeed/change the baby?	**Kur es varu pabarot bērnu ar krūti/nomainīt autiņus?** *koor ess varoo pabarwat behrnoo ar kroohti/ nwamaineet aootinyooss?*	

For Eating Out, see page 142.

Disabled Travelers

Is there...?	**Vai tur ir...?** *vay toor ir...?*	
access for the disabled	**piekļuve invalīdiem** *peeaklyoove invaleedeeam*	
a wheelchair ramp	**uzbrauktuve ratiņkrēsliem** *oozbrowktoove ratinykrehsleeam*	
a disabled-accessible toilet	**tualete invalīdiem** *twalete invaleedeeam*	
I need...	**Man nepieciešama/nepieciešams...** *man nepeeatseeashama/nepeeatseeashamss...*	
assistance	**palīdzība** *paleedzeeba*	
an elevator [a lift]	**lifts** *liftss*	
a ground-floor room	**numuriņš pirmajā stāvā** *noomoorinysh pirmayah stahvah*	
Please speak louder.	**Lūdzu, runājiet skaļāk.** *loohdzoo roonahyeeat skalyahk*	

Health & Emergencies

Emergencies

Help!	**Palīgā!** *paleegah*
Go away!	**Ejiet projām.** *yeeat prwa-yahm*
Stop, thief!	**Ķeriet zagli!** *tyereeat zagli*
Get a doctor!	**Izsauciet ārstu.** *issowtseeat ahrsstoo*
Fire!	**Ugunsgrēks!** *oogoonsgrehkss*
I'm lost.	**Es nezinu kur atrodos.** *ess nezinoo koor atrwadwas*
Can you help me?	**Vai jūs varat man palīdzēt?** *vai yoohss varat man paleedzeht*
Call the police!	**Izsauciet policiju.** *issowtseeat politseeyoo*
Where's the police station?	**Kur ir policijas iecirknis?** *koor ir politsiyass eeatsirkniss?*
My child is missing.	**Mans bērns ir pazudis.** *manss behrnss ir pazoodiss*

YOU MAY HEAR...

Aizpildiet šo veidlapu. *aizpildeeat shwa veydlapoo.*	Fill out this form.
Jūsu dokumentus, lūdzu. *yoohsoo dokoomentoos loohdzoo*	Your ID, please.
Kad/kur tas notika? *kad/koor tass nwatika?*	When/Where did it happen?
Kā viņa/viņš izskatās? *kah vinya/viynsh izskatahss?*	What does he/she look like?

Health

I'm sick.	**Es esmu slims.** *ess a'smoo slimss* **(slima)** *(slima)*
I need an English-speaking doctor.	**Man nepieciešams ārsts, kas runā angļu valodā.** *man nepeeatseeashamss ahrsts kass roonah anglyoo valwadah*
It hurts here.	**Šajā vietā man sāp.** *shayah veeatah man sahp*
Where's the pharmacy?	**Kur ir aptieka.** *koor ir apteeaka*
I'm (...months) pregnant.	**Esmu...mēnesī.** *esmoo...mehnesee*
I'm on...	**Es lietoju...** *ess leeatwayoo...*
I'm allergic to antibiotics/penicillin.	**Man ir alerģija pret antibiotikām/penicilīnu** *man ir alergyiya pret antibiotikahm/penitsileenoo*

YOU MAY HEAR...

Aizpildiet šo veidlapu.
ayzpeekdeet cho vaydlapoo

Jūsu ID. *Yoosoo eed*

Kad/Kur tas notika? *kad/koor tas noteeka*

Kā viņš/viņa izskatījās?
kah veensch/veenah eezkateeyass

Fill out this form.

Your ID, please.

When/Where did it happen?

What does he/she look like?

Dictionary

adaptor **adapters**
and **un**
baby **mazulis**
bad **slikts** *m*/**slikta** *f*
bag **soma**
Band-Aid [plasters] **plāksteris**
bee **bite**
beige **smilškrāsas**
bikini **peldkostīms**
bird **putns**
black **melns**
bland (food) **viegls (ēdiens)**
blue **zils**
bottle opener **pudeļu attaisāmais**
bowl **bļoda**
boy **zēns**
boyfriend **puisis**
bra **krūšturis**
brown **brūns**
camera **fotoaparāts**
castle **pils**
charger **lādētājs**

computer **dators**
cold **auksti**
comb (n) **ķemm**
condoms **prezervatīvi**
contact lens solution
   kontaktlēcu šķidums
corkscrew **korķvilķis**
cup **glāze/tase**
dangerous **bīstami**
deodorant **dezodorants**
diabetic **diabētisks** *m*/**diabētiska** *f*
dog **suns**
doll **lelle**
fly n **muša**
fork **dakša**
girl **meitene**
girlfriend **meitene/draudzene**
glass **stikls/glāze**
good **labs** *m*/**laba** *f*
gray **pelēks** *m*/**pelēka** *f*
great **lielisks** *m*/**lieliska** *f*
green **zaļš**

a hairbrush **matu suka**

hot **karsts** m/**karsta** f

husband **vīrs**

ice **ledus**

icy **ledains** m/**ledaina** f

I'd like… **Es vēlētos…**

insect repellent **insektu atbaidītājs**

jeans **džinsi**

(steak) knife **(steika) nazis**

lactose intolerant **nepanes laktozi**

large **liels** m/**liela** f

lighter **šķiltavas**

love **mīlestība/mīla**

medium **vidējs** m/**vidēja** f

museum **muzejs**

my **mans** m/**mana** f

a nail file **nagu vīlīte**

napkin **salvete**

nurse **māsiņa**

or **vai**

orange **oranžs**

park **parks**

partner **partneris**

pen **pildspalva**

pink **rozā**

plate **šķīvis**

rain **lietus**

a raincoat **lietusmētelis**

a (disposable) razor **(vienreizlietojamais) skuveklis**

razor blades **skuvekļa asmeņi**

red **sarkanss**

salty **sāļš** m/**sāļa** f

sanitary napkins [pads] **biksīšu ieliktnīši**

scissors **šķēres**

shampoo/conditioner **šampūns/ kondicionieris**

shoes **apavi**

small **mazs** m/**maza** f

sneakers **teniskurpes**

snow **sniegs**

soap **ziepes**

socks **zeķes**

spicy **ass** m/**asa** f

spider **zirneklis**

spoon **karote**

a sweater **džemperis**

stamp(s) **zīmogs**

suitcase **ceļasoma**

sun **saule**

sunglasses **saulesbrilles**

sunscreen **sauļošanās krēms**

a sweatshirt **sporta krekls**

a swimsuit **peldkostims**

a T-shirt **t-krekls**

tampons **tamponi**

terrible adj **drausmīgs** m/**drausmīga** f

tissues **salvetes**

toilet paper **tualetes papīrs**

toothbrush **zobu birste**

toothpaste **zobu pasta**

tough (meat) **sīksts** m/**sīksta** f

toy **rotaļlieta**

underwear **apakšveļa**

vegetarian **veģetārietis** m/ **veģetāriete** f

white **balts**

with **ar**

wife **sieva**

without **bez**

yellow **dzeltens**

your **tavs** m/**tava** f

zoo **zoodārzs**

Lithuanian

Essentials

Hello/Hi.	**Sveiki/slabas.**	*Sweyihkyi/lahbahs*
Good morning.	**Labas rytas.**	*laabahs reetahs*
Good afternoon.	**Laba diena.**	*lahbah dienah*
Good night.	**Labanakt.**	*lahbaanahkt*
Goodbye.	**Viso gero.**	*vyiso gyero*
Yes/No/Okay.	**Taip/ene/Gerai.**	*Taip/ne/ghyerayi*
Excuse me!	**Atsiprašau!/Atleiskite!**	
(to get attention)	*Atsyiprahsha00!/Athleyiskhyithe*	
Excuse me. (to get past)	**Atsiprašau.**	*Atsyiprahshaoo*
I'm sorry.	**Aš atsiprašau.**	*Ahsh atsyiprahshaoo*
I'd like…	**Aš norėčiau…**	*ahsh noryehchiaoo…*
How much?	**Kiek?**	*kyiek*
And/or.	**Ir (arba).**	*Irh/arhbha*
Please.	**Prašau.**	*prashaoo*
Thank you.	**Ačiū.**	*aachyioo*
You're welcome.	**Nėra už ką.**	*Nhehrha uzh khaah*
Where's…?	**Kur yra…?**	*Kur eerah…*
I'm going to…	**Aš vykstu į…**	*Ahsh eyihnu ee…*
My name is…	**Mano vardas yra…**	*mahno vahrdahs eerah*
Please speak slowly.	**Kalbėkite lėtai.**	*Phrashome kalbehtH lhyethayi*
Can you repeat that?	**Ar galite pakartoti?**	*Ahr galyithe pakarthothyi*
I don't understand.	**Nesuprantu.**	*nesuprahntu*
Do you speak English?	**Ar Jūs kalbate angliškai?**	*ahr yoos kahlbahte ahnglHshkai*
I don't speak	**Gerai negaliu**	*gyerai negahlHu*
Lithuanian.	**Kalbėti lietuviškai.**	*kalbehtH lyietuvyishkai*
Where's the restroom [toilet]?	**Kur yra tualeto kambarys (tualetas)?**	*Kurh eerha thualetoh kambarees (thualethas)?*
Help!	**Gelbėkite!**	*gyelbehkyite*

Numbers

0	**nulis** *nuleis*
1	**vienas** *vienahs*
2	**du/dvi** *du/dvyi*

3	**trys**	*treess*
4	**keturi**	*keturi*
5	**penki**	*pengkyi*
6	**šeši**	*sheshvi*
7	**septyni**	*septeenyi*
8	**aštuoni**	*ashtuonyi*
9	**devyni**	*deveenyi*
0	**dešimt**	*dashimt*
11	**vienuolika**	*vienuolyikah*
12	**dvylika**	*dveelyikah*
13	**trylika**	*treelyikah*
14	**keturiolika**	*keturyolyikah*
15	**penkiolika**	*pengkyolyikah*
16	**šešiolika**	*shyeshyolyikah*
17	**septyniolika**	*septeenyolyikah*
18	**aštuoniolika**	*ashtunyolyikah*
19	**devyniolika**	*deveenyolyikah*
20	**dvidešimt**	*dvyideshimt*
21	**dvidešimt vienas**	*dvyideshimt vienahs*
30	**trisdešimt**	*tryisdeshimt*
40	**keturiasdešimt**	*katuriasdeshimt*
50	**penkiasdešimt**	*pengkiasdeshimt*
60	**šešiasdešimt**	*shyashiasdeshimt*
70	**septyniasdešimt**	*septeeniasdeshimt*
80	**aštuoniasdešimt**	*ashtuoniasdeshimt*
90	**devyniasdešimt**	*deveeniasdeshimt*
100	**šimtas**	*shyimtahs*
101	**šimtas vienas**	*shyimtahs vienahs*
200	**du šimtai**	*du shyimtayi*

You'll find the pronunciation of the Lithuanian letters and words written in gray after each sentence to guide you. Simply pronounce these as if they were English. As you hear the language being spoken, you will quickly become accustomed to the local pronunciation and dialect.

500	**penki šimtai** *pengkyi shyimtayi*
1,000	**tūkstantis** *tookstahntis*
10,000	**dešimt tūkstančių** *dashimt tookstahnchyioo*
1,000,000	**milijonas** *mhilijhonhahs*

Time

What time is it?	**Kiek dabar valandų?** *Kyiekh dahbaar vahlandoo*
It's midday.	**Dabar vidurdienis.** *Dahbaar vyidurdienis*
Five past three	**Po trijų penkios.** *Po thryiyoo phankhyios.*
A quarter to ten.	**Be penkiolikos dešimt.** *Be penkyiolikhos dashimt*
5:30 a.m./p.m.	**pusė šešių ryto/vakaro** *pusyeh shashyioo*

Days

Monday	**pirmadienis** *pyirmaadienis*
Tuesday	**antradienis** *ahntraadienis*
Wednesday	**trečiadienis** *trechiahdienis*
Thursday	**ketvirtadienis** *kyetvyirtaadienis*
Friday	**penktadienis** *penktaadienis*
Saturday	**šeštadienis** *shyeshtaadienis*
Sunday	**sekmadienis** *syekmaadienis*

Dates

yesterday	**vakar** *wahkar*
today	**šiandien** *shyiahndyiehn*
tomorrow	**rytoj** *reetoy*
day	**diena** *dienah*
week	**savaitė** *savayihtye*
month	**mėnuo** *myehnuo*
year	**metai** *matahayi*
Happy New Year!	**Laimingų Naujųjų metų!** *Lahyimingoo Naooyooyoo matoo!*
Happy Birthday!	**Su gimimo diena!** *Soo gimimo dienah!*

Months

January	**sausio** *saoosyo*
February	**vasario** *vahsahryo*
March	**kovo** *kohvoh*
April	**balandžio** *bahlahndzhyo*

May	**gegužės** *gyeguzhyehs*
June	**birželio** *byirzhalyo*
July	**liepos** *liepos*
August	**rugpiučio** *rugpyiuchyo*
September	**rugsėjo** *rugsyehyo*
October	**spalio** *spahlio*
November	**lapkričio** *laapkryichyo*
December	**gruodžio** *gruodzhyo*

Arrival & Departure

I'm on holiday (vacation)/on business.	**Aš atostogauju/komandiruotėje.** *ahsh ahtostogaooyu/komahndiruotehyeh*
I'm going to...	**Aš vykstu į...** *Ahsh weekstoo ee...*
I'm staying at the...Hotel.	**Aš apsistosiu ...viešbutyje.** *Ahsh ahpsyistosyioo ...wyieshbooteeye*

Money

Essential

Where's...?	**Kur yra...?** *kur eerah...*
the ATM	**bankomatas** *bahnkomahtahs*
the bank	**bankas** *bahnkahs*
the currency exchange office	**valiutos keitykla punktas?** *wahlyiuhtohs kayiteehklah poonktahs*
When does the bank open/close?	**Kada atsidaro/užsidaro bankas?** *Kahda uzhsyidaahro baahnkahs?*
I'd like to change dollars/pounds sterling/euros into litas.	**Norėčiau pasikeisti dolerius/svarus sterlingų/eurus į litus.** *Nohryechyiaoo pahsyikaystyi dolahryioos/swahroos starlingoo/aooroohs ee lyithuhs*
I'd like to cash traveler's cheques.	**Norėčiau išgryninti kelionės čekius.** *Nohryechyiaoo yishgreenyinthyi kyelionhyehs chyekhyioos*
Can I pay in cash?	**Ar galiu sumokėti grynaisiais?** *Ahr gahlyioo mokyethyi greenhayisyiayihs phyinyighayihs?*
Can I pay by (credit) card?	**Ar galiu sumokėti (kreditine) kortele?** *Ahr gahlyioo mokyethyi (kryedyitho) kortyelye?*

For Numbers, see page 153.

YOU MAY SEE...

The Lithuanian currency is the **litas, Lt**, which is divided into 100 **cents**.
Coins: 1, 2, 5, 10, 20 and 50 **cents**; **Lt**1, 2, 5
Bills: **Lt** 10, 20, 50, 100, 200 and 500

Getting Around

How do I get to town?	**Kaip man nuvykti į miestą?** *Khayiph mahn nuveekhtyi ee mhyiesthaa?*
Where's...?	**Kur yra...?** *kur eerah ...?*
the airport	**oro uostas** *ohro uosthahs*
the train station	**traukinių stotis** *thraookhyinyioo stothyihs*
the bus station	**autobusų stotis** *aoothobuhsoo stothyihs*
the subway [underground] station	**metro (metropolitenas)** *myethro (myethropolyithyehnahs)* **stotis** *stothyihs*
Is it far from here?	**Ar toli nuo čia?** *Ahr tholyi nhuo chyiah?*
Where do I buy a ticket?	**Kur galiu nusipirkti bilietą?** *Khurh gahlyiu nusyiphyirkhthyi byilyiethaa?*
A one-way/return-trip ticket to...	**Bilietas į vieną pusę/į abi puses** *Byilyiethahs ee wyienaa phusa/ee abhyi phusahs*
How much?	**Kiek kainuoja?** *Khyiekh khayinuoya?*
Which gate/line?	**Kurie vartai/linija?** *Khurhyie warhthayi/lyinyiyah?*
Which platform?	**Kuri platforma?** *Khurhyi plathforhmah?*
Where can I get a taxi?	**Kur galėčiau išsikviesti taksi?** *Khurh gahlyechyiau yishsyikwyiesthyi takhsyi?*
Take me to this address.	**Nuvežkite mane I šį adresą.** *nuvyezhkyite mahne ee shee aadresaa*
To...Airport, please.	**Prašyčiau į...oro uostą.** *Phrasheechyiau ee...ohro uosthaa*
I'm in a rush.	**Aš labai skubu.** *Ahsh labhayi skubhu*
Can I have a map?	**Ar galėčiau gauti žemėlapį?** *Arh gahlyechyiau ghauthyi zhamyehlaphee?*

Tickets

When's...to Vilnius?	**Kada...į Vilnių?** *Khadah...ee Wyilnhyioo?*
the (first) bus	**(pirmas) autobusas** *(phyirhmahsyis) aoothobuhsahs*

the (next) flight	**(kitas) skrydis** *(khyithahs) skhreedyis*
the (last) train	**(paskutinis) traukinys** *(pahskuthyinyihs) thraukhyinees*
One/Two ticket(s) please.	**Prašau vieną/du bilietus.** *Phrashau wyiehnaa/du byilyiethuhs*
For today/tomorrow.	**Šiandienai/rytojui.** *Shyiandyiehnay/reethoyuy*
A…ticket.	**…bilietas.** *…byilyiethahs*
one-way	**į vieną pusę** *ee wyehnaa phusee*
return trip	**į abi puses** *ee abhyi phusahs*
first class	**pirmos klasės** *phyirmohs klaahsyes*
I have an e-ticket.	**Aš turiu elektroninį bilietą.** *Ahsh thuryiu elektrohnyinee bhyilyiethaa*
How long is the trip?	**Kiek laiko trunka kelionė?** *Khyiek layikho thrunka kalyiohnye?*
Is it a direct train?	**Ar tai tiesioginis traukinys?** *Arh thayi thyiesyioghyinyihs thraookhyineehs?*
Is this the bus to…?	**Ar tai traukinys į…?** *Arh thayi thraookhyineehs ee…?*
Can you tell me when to get off?	**Prašau man pasakyti kur išlipti?** *prashaoo mahn pahsahkeeti kur ishlipti?*
I'd like to…	**Aš norėčiau rezervuoti vietą…** *ahsh norehchiaoo rezervuoti vietaa…*
my reservation.	
cancel	**anuliuoti** *ahnuliuoti*
change	**mainyti** *maineeti*
confirm	**patvirtinti** *pahtvirtinti*

Car Hire

Where's the car hire?	**Kur yra automobilių nuomos punktas?** *Khur eerah aootomobyilyioo nhuomah?*
I'd like…	**Aš norėčiau…** *Ahsh nhoryechyiaoo…*
a cheap/small car	**pigaus/mažo automobilio** *pyighaoohs/maazho aootomobhyilyioh*
an automatic/a manual	**automatinės/rankinės** *aoothomaathyinyehs/rankyinyehs*
air conditioning	**oro kondicionieriaus** *ohro kondyicyionyierhyiaoohs*
a car seat	**automobilio kėdutės** *aootomobhyilyioh kyeduthyehs*
How much…?	**Kiek kainuoja…?** *Kyiekh kayinuoya…?*
per day/week	**dienai/savaitei** *dienay/savayihtey*
Are there any discounts?	**Ar suteiksite nuolaidų?** *Arh suteyikhsyith nuohlayidhoo?*

YOU MAY HEAR...

tiesiai *thyiesyiayi*	straight ahead
į kairę *ee kaeerye*	left
į dešinę *ee dashyinee*	right
už kampo *oozh kampoh*	around the corner
priešais *phryieshaeehs*	opposite
už *oozh*	behind
šalia *shahlyiah*	next to
paskui... *pahskuyi*	after
į šiaurę/į pietus *ee shyiaooree/ee phyiethuhs*	north/south
į rytus/į vakarus *ee rheethuhs/ee waakahruhs*	east/west
prie šviesoforo *phryie shwyiesaphoroh*	at the traffic light
sankryžoje *saankreezhoye*	at the intersection

Places to Stay

Can you recommend a hotel?	**Gal galite rekomenduoti viešbutį?** *Gahl galyithe rekomendhuotyi vyieshbutee?*
I made a reservation.	**Aš rezervavau.** *Ahsh rezerwawaoo*
My name is...	**Mano vardas yra...** *Mahno warhdahs eerah...*
Do you have a room...?	**Ar turite kambarį...?** *Arh turyitheh kambharee...?*
for one/two	**vienam/dviem** *wyienaam/dwyiem*
with a bathroom	**su vonios kambariu** *su wonyiohs kambahryiu*
with air conditioning	**su kondicionieriumi** *su kondyicyionyierhyiumh*
For...	-
tonight	**šiai naktiai** *shyiayih nakchyiayaih*
two nights	**dviem naktims** *dwyiem naktyimhs*
one week	**vienai savaitei** *wyienayi savayihteyi*
How much?	**Kiek kainuoja?** *Kyiekh kayinuoya...?*
Is there anything cheaper?	**Ar turite ką nors pigiau?** *Arh turyithee kaa norhs pyigyiaoo?*
When's checkout?	**Kada reikia išsiregistruoti?** *Kada reyikyia yishsyiryegyistruotyi?*
Can I leave this in the safe?	**Ar galiu tai palikti seife?** *Arh gahlyioo tayi palikhtyi seyifye?*
Can I leave my bags?	**Ar galiu palikti savo krepšius?** *Arh gahlyioo palikhtyi sahwo kryepshyiuhs?*

| Can I have my bill/ a receipt? | **Ar galėčiau gauti sąskaitą/kvitą?** *Nohryechyiaoo ghaootyi saaskayitaa/kwyitaa?* |
| I'll pay in cash/by credit card. | **Aš mokėsiu grynaisiais/kreditine kortele.** *Ahsh mokyehsyioo greenhayisyiayihs phyinyighayihs/kryedyitho kortyelye* |

Communications

Where's an internet cafe?	**Kur yra interneto kavinė?** *Kurh eerah internetho kawyinye?*
Can I access the internet/check my email?	**Ar galiu prisijungti prie interneto/pasitikrinti savo el. paštą?** *Ahr gahlyioo pryisyiyunghtyi phryie inthyernyetho/pasyityikryinthyi elektrohnyinee pashtaa?*
How much per half hour/hour?	**Kiek kainuoja pusvalandis/valanda?** *Khyiekh khayinuoya puswalandyis/walanda?*
How do I connect/log on?	**Kaip man prisijungti?** *Kayiph mahn pryisyiyunghtyi?*
A phone card, please.	**Prašyčiau telefono kortelės.** *Phrasheechyiau telephono korthyelyehs*
Can I have your phone number?	**Ar galite pasakyti savo telefono numerį?** *Arh ghalyitye pasakheetyi telephono numyeree?*
Here's my number/ email.	**Štai mano numeris/el. paštas.** *Shtayi mano numehryis/ elektrohnyinyihs pashtahs*
Call me/text me.	**Paskambink (paskambinkite) man/parašyk (parašykite) žinutę.** *Paskambyinkh (paskambyinkhyith) manh/parasheekh (parasheekyith) zhyinuthee*
I'll text you.	**Aš parašysiu Tau/Jums žinutę.** *Ash parasheesyiu Thaoo/ Yumhs zhyinuthee*
Email me.	**Parašyk (parašykite) el. laišką.** *Parasheekh (parasheekyith) elektrohnyinee layishkhaa*
Hello. This is. . .	**Sveiki. Tai. . .** *Sweyihkyi. Thayi. . .*
Can I speak to. . .?	**Ar galiu kalbėti su. . .?** *Ahr gahlyioo kalbyetyi soo. . .?*
Can you repeat that?	**Ar galite pakartoti?** *Arh galyitye pakarthothyi?*
I'll call back later.	**Paskambinsiu vėliau.** *Paskambyinsyiu vyelyiaoo*
Bye.	**Viso!** *Wyiso!*
Where's the post office?	**Kur yra paštas?** *Kurh eerha pashths?*
I'd like to send this to. . .	**Norėčiau išsiųsti tai į. . .** *Nohryechyiaoo pasyioostyi tayi ee. . .*
Can I. . .?	**Ar galiu. . .?** *Ahr gahlyioo. . .?*
access the internet	**prisijungti prie interneto** *pryisyiyunghtyi phryie inthyernyetho*

check my email	**pasitikrinti el.** *paštą pasyityikryinthyi elektrohnyinee pashtaa*
print	**atspausdinti** *atspaoosdyintyi*
plug in/charge my laptop/iPhone/iPad/BlackBerry?	**įsijungti/įkrauti savo nešiojamąjį kompiuterį/iPhone/iPad/BlackBerry?** *eesiyiounghtyi/ pakraootyi neshyioyamaayee kompyiyutyeree/iPhone/iPad/ BlackBerry?*
access Skype?	**pasinaudoti Skype?** *pasyinaoodotyi Skype*
What is the WiFi password?	**Koks yra Wi Fi slaptažodis?** *Koks eerah Wi Fi slaptaazhodyihs?*
Is the WiFi free?	**Ar Wi Fi yra nemokamas?** *Arh Wi Fi eerah nemokhamahs?*
Do you have bluetooth?	**Ar turite Bluetooth?** *Arh tooryithe Bluetooth?*
Do you have a scanner?	**Ar turite skaitytuvą?** *Arh tooryithe skanehree?*

Social Media

Are you on Facebook/Twitter?	**Ar turite Facebook/Twitter paskyrą?** *Arh yoos esathe Facebook/Twitter?*
What's your username?	**Koks yra Jūsų vartotojo vardas?** *Koks yoosoo wartotoyo wardahs?*
I'll add you as a friend.	**Aš priimsiu Jus į draugus.** *Ahsh pryiyimsyiu yoos ee draooghoos*
I'll follow you on Twitter.	**Aš seksiu Jus Twitter.** *Ahsh syeksyioo yoos Twitter*
Are you following...?	**Ar Jūs sekate...?** *Arh yoos syekathe...?*
I'll put the pictures on Facebook/Twitter.	**Aš įkelsiu nuotraukas į Facebook/Twitter.** *Ahsh eedyesyiu nuotraookahs ee Facebook/Twitter*
I'll tag you in the pictures.	**Aš pažymėsiu Jus nuotraukose.** *Ahsh pazheemyesyioo yoos nuotraookosye*

Conversation

Hello!/Hi!	**Sveiki!/Labas!** *Sweyihkyi/lahbahs*
How are you?	**Kaip gyvenate?** *kaip geeWanahte*
Fine, thanks.	**Ačiū, gerai.** *aachyioo gyerai*
Excuse me!	**Atsiprašau!** *atsyiprahshaoo*
Do you speak English?	**Ar Jūs kalbate angliškai?** *ahr yoos kahlbahte ahnglHshkai*
What's your name?	**Koks Jūsų vardas?** *koks yoosoo vahrdahs*
My name is...	**Mano vardas yra...** *mahno vahrdahs eerah...*
Nice to meet you.	**Malonu susipažinti.** *Malohnoo su yoomyihs susyipazhyinthyi*
Where are you from?	**Iš kur Jūs?** *ish kur yoos*

I'm from the U.K./U.S.	**Aš esu iš Jungtinės Karalystės/Jungtinių Valstijų** *ahsh esu ish Yoongtyinyehs Karaleestyehs/Yoonghtyinyioo Walstyiyou*
What do you do for a living?	**Kuo Jūs užsiimate?** *Kuo yoos oozhsyimatye?*
I work for...	**Aš dirbu...** *Ahsh dyirboo...*
I'm a student.	**Aš studentas** *m*/**studentė** *f*. *Ahsh studentahs /studentye*
I'm retired.	**Aš pensininkas** *m*/**pensininkė** *f*. *Ahsh pansyinyinkahs/ pansyinyinkyeh*

Romance

Would you like to go out for a drink/dinner?	**Ar norėtumėte su manimi išgerti/pavakarieniauti?** *Arh noryehtoomyehtye soo manyim eyityi ishgyerthyi/ pawakaryienyiaootyi?*
What are your plans for tonight/tomorrow?	**Kokie Jūsų planai šiam vakarui/rytojui?** *Kokyie yoosoo planayi shyiam wakarooy/reethoyuy?*
Can I have your (phone) number?	**Gal galite pasakyti savo telefono numerį?** *Galh ghalyitye pasakheetyi sawo telephono numyeree?*
Can I join you?	**Ar galiusprisidėti prie Jūsų?** *Arh ghalyiu su yoomyihs?*
Can I buy you a drink?	**Gal galėčiau nupirkti Jumsąišgerti?** *Ghal ghalyechyiaoo nupyirktyi yoomhs gyeryimaa?*
I love you.	**Aš Tave myliu.** *Ahsh tawye meelyiu*

Accepting & Rejecting

I'd love to.	**Norėčiau.** *Noryechyiay*
Where should we meet?	**Kur susitiksime?** *Kur susityiksyimye?*
I'll meet you at the bar/your hotel.	**Susitiksime bare/tavo (Jūsų) viešbutyje.** *Susyitixyimye bahrye/tawo (yoosoo) yieshbooteeye.*
I'll come by at...	**Aš ateisiu...valandą.** *Ahsh ateyisyioo...wahlahndaa*
I'm busy.	**Aš užsiėmęs** *m*/**užsiėmusi** *f*. *Ahsh uzhsyiyemahs/uzhsyiyemoosyi*
I'm not interested.	**Mauęs tai nedomina.** *mahn naeedomoo*
Leave me alone.	**Atstokite nuo manęs.** *Atstokhyitye nuo mahnyehs*
Stop bothering me!	**iNetrukdykite man!** *Nustokyitye mahn trookdeetyi!*

Food & Drink

Eating Out

Can you recommend a good restaurant/bar?	**Ar galite man rekomenduoti gerą restoraną/barą?** *Ahr gahlyitye mahn rakomahnduotyi gyeraa rastorahnaa/baahraa?*
Is there a traditional/an inexpensive restaurant nearby?	**ar yra tradicinis/nebrangus restoranas netoliese?** *arh yis trahdyihcyinyihs/brangoos arh rastorahnahs nahtolyi?*
A table for..., please.	**prašau staliuką...** *prahshaoo stahlyiookaa...*
Can we sit...?	**Ar galime prisėsti...?** *Arh gahlyimh peryisyesth...?*
here/there	**čia/ten** *chyia/tahn*
outside	**lauke** *laookhye*
in a non-smoking area	**nerūkančiųjų zonoje** *nahrookanchyiooyou zohnoye*
I'm waiting for someone.	**Aš laukiu...** *Ahsh laookyiu...* **kai ko.** *kay ko*
Where are the toilets?	**Kur yra tualetai?** *Kur eerah thualethay*
The menu, please.	**Prašyčiau meniu.** *Prahsheechyiau mahnyiu*
What do you recommend?	**Ką Jūs rekomenduotumėte?** *Kaa yoos rekomyenduotoomyeteh?*
I'd like...	**Aš nor...** *ahsh nor...*
Some more..., please.	**Prašau...šiek tiek daugiau.** *Perashau...shyiek tyiek daoogyiaoo*
Enjoy your meal!	**Skanaus!** *Skanaoohs!*
The check [bill], please.	**Prašyčiau sąskaitos.** *Prasheechyiaoo saaskaytohs*
Is service included?	**Ar aptarnavi assjskaičiuotas?** *Arh aptahrnawyimo paslaoogohs eeskayichyiuotohs?*
Can I pay by credit card/ have a receipt?	**Ar galiu sumokėti kreditine kortele/gauti kvitą?** *Arh gahlyioo mokyetyi kryedyitho kortyelye/gaootyi kwyitaa?*

Breakfast

bekonas *bakhonahs*	bacon
duonos/sviesto *duonohs/sviestoh*	bread/butter
sūrio *sooryoh*	cheese
kiaušinio *kya00shinyoh*	egg
kumpio *kumpyoh*	ham
uogienės *wuogienehs*	jam

YOU MAY SEE...

įėjimo mokestis *eeyeyimo mokyestyihs*	cover charge
fiksuota kaina *fyixuota kayina*	fixed price
(dienos) meniu *(dyienohs) menu*	menu (of the day)
aptarnavimas (ne) skai iuotas *aptahrnahwyimo pahslaoogos (ne)eeskayichyiotos*	service (not) included
ypatingi pasiūlymai *pasyiooleemay*	specials

bandeliu *bahndehlyoo*	rolls
skrebutis *skhrabutyihs*	toast
dešrelė *dashralye*	sausage
jogurtas *yogoortahs*	yogurt

Appetizers

ikrai *ikrai*	caviar
kumpis *kumpyis*	ham
marinuoti grybai *mahryinuoti greebai*	pickled mushrooms
mišrainė *mishrainyeh*	salad
rūkyta dešra *rookyeetah dyeshrah*	smoked sausage
silkė *silkyeh*	herring

Meat

jautienos/avienos *ya00tienos/ah vienos*	beef/lamb
vištienos *vyishtiėnos*	chicken
antienos *ahntienos*	duck
kaulienos *kya00lyienos*	pork
veršienos *vershienos*	veal
balandėliai *bahlahndehlyei*	stuffed cabbage rolls
galkos *gahlkos*	meat balls
karbonadas su kopūstais *kahrbonahdahs su kopoostais*	pork chop with cabbage
pyragas *peerahgahs*	meat pie
troškinta mėsa *troshkyintah myesah*	meat stew

YOU MAY HEAR...

ne visai iškeptas *ne visai ishkeptahs*	(rare)
viduriniai iškeptas *viduryinyei ishkeptahs*	medium
labai sukepintas *lahbai sukyahpintahs*	well-done

Fish & Seafood

keptas karpis *kyaptahs kahrpyis*	fried carp
marinuotos žuvys su bulvėmis *mahryinuotos zhuvees su bulvyehmis*	marinated fish with potatoes
silkių ir daržovių sriuba *syilkyoo ir dahrzhovyoo sriubah*	herring and vegetable soup
troškinta žuvis *troshkyintah zhuvyes*	fish stew
žuvų blyneliai *zhuvoo bleenehlyei*	fish pancakes
žuvų galkos *zhuvoo gahlkos*	fried fish dumplings

Vegetables

pupos *pupos*	beans
kopūstas *kopoostahs*	cabbage
svogūnai *svogoonai*	onions
žirniai *zhirnyei*	peas
bulvės *bulvehs*	potatoes
pomidoras *pomidorahs*	tomato
bulviniai blynai *bulvyinyei bleenai*	potato pancakes
kopūstu sriuba *kopustoo sryubah*	cabbage soup
šaltibarščiai *shahltibahrshchyei*	cold beetroot soup
varškės/grybu virtinukai *vahrshkyehs/greeboo virtinukai*	curd cheese/mushroom dumplings

Sauces & Condiments

Druska *Drhuska*	Salt
Pipirai *Phyiphyiray*	Pepper
Garstyčios *Garsteechyiohs*	Mustard
Ketčupas *Kachuphahs*	Ketchup

Fruit & Dessert

obuolys *ohbuolees*	apple
bananas *bahnahnahs*	banana
citrina *tsyitreenah*	lemon
apelsinas *ahpyelseenahs*	orange
slyva *slyeevah*	plum
žemuogės *zhyemuogyehs*	strawberries
blyneliai *blinehlyei*	small pancakes
grietininiai ledai *gryietininyei lyadai*	ice-cream
obuolinis pyragas *ohbuoPinis peerahgahs*	apple pie
tortas *tortahs*	gateau
uogu virtinukai *wuogoo virtinukai*	fruit dumplings

Drinks

The wine list/drink menu, please.	**Prašyčiau vynų sąrašo/gėrimų meniu.** *Prahshaoo veenoo saarashaa/gyeryimoo menu*
What do you recommend?	**Ką Jūs rekomenduotumėte?** *Kaa yoos rekomendootumety?*
I'd like a bottle/glass of red/white wine.	**Norėčiau butelį/taurę raudono/balto vyno.** *Noryechyaoo butahlee/taoora raoodono/baalto veeno*
The house wine, please.	**Prašyčiau naminio vyno.** *Prahshaoo nahmynyo veeno*
Another bottle/glass, please.	**Prašyčias dar vieno butelio/taurės.** *Perahshaoo kyto butyelyo/taooryes*
I'd like a local beer.	**Norėčiau vietinio alaus.** *Noryechyaoo wyetynyo ahlaoos*
Can I buy you a drink?	**Ar galiu nupirkti Jums išgerti?** *Arh gahlyoo nupyrkty yooms gyerymaa?*
Cheers!	**Į sveikatą!** *Ee sweykataa!*
A coffee/tea, please.	**Prašyčiau kavos/arbatos.** *Prahshaoo kahwos/ahrbahtos.*
Black.	**Juoda.** *yuodah*
With…	**Su…** *su…*
milk	**pienu** *pyienu*
sugar	**cukrumi** *cukrumy*
artificial sweetener	**dirbtiniu saldikliu** *dirbtinyu saldyklyu*
A…, please.	**Prašyčiau…** *Perahshaoo…*
juice	**vaisiu sultys** *vaisyoo sultyees*
soda [soft drink]	**gazuoto gėrimo** *gahzuoto gyerymo*
(sparkling/still) water	**(gazuoto/negazuoto) vandens** *(gahzuoto/nyegahzuoto) vahndyens*

Leisure Time

Sightseeing

Where's the tourist information office?	**Kur yra turizmo informacijos centras?** *Kur eehra turyzmo inphormacyos byoorahs?*
What are the main sights?	**Kokios yra pagrindinės įžymybės?** *Kokyos eehra pagryndynyes eezheemeebyes?*
Do you offer tours in English?	**Ar Jūs siūlote ekskursijas anglų kalba?** *Ahr yoos syoolote exkursyias ahngloo kahlba?*
Can I have a map/ guide?	**Ar galėčiau gauti žemėlapį/gidą?** *Arh gahlyechyiau ghauthyi zhamyehlaphee/gydaa?*

Shopping

Where's the market/ mall?	**Kur yra turgus/prekybos centras?** *Koor eerha toorgoos/prekeebos centrahs?*
I'm just looking.	**Aš tik žiūrinėju.** *Ahsh tik yeshkaoo*
Can you help me?	**Ar galite man padėti?** *Arh galyithe maan padyetyi?*
I'm being helped.	**Man jau padeda.** *Mahn padyeyo*
How much?	**Kiek?** *Kyiek?*
That one, please.	**Prašyčiau šitą.** *Prahshaoo, shyitaa.*
I'd like…	**Norėčiau…** *Nhoryechyiaoo…*
That's all.	**Tai viskas.** *Tayi vyiskahs*
Where can I pay?	**Kur galiu sumokėti?** *Kur gahlyioo sumokyetyi?*
I'll pay in cash/ by credit card.	**Aš mokėsiu grynaisiais/kreditine kortele.** *Ahsh mokyehsyioo greenhayisyiayihs phyinyighayihs/kryedyitho kortyelye*
A receipt, please.	**Prašyčiau kvito.** *Perasheechyau kwyito*

YOU MAY SEE…

atidaryta/uždaryta *atydaeeta/uzhdareeta*	open/closed
įėjimas/išėjimas *eeyeyimas/yishyieyimas*	entrance/exit

Sport & Leisure

When's the game?	**Kada varžybos?** *Kada varzhheebohs?*
Where's…?	**Kur yra…?** *Kur eera…?*
the beach	**paplūdimys** *pahploodeyimees*
the park	**parkas** *pahrkas*
the pool	**baseinas** *baseyinahs*
Is it safe to swim here?	**Ar čia saugu maudytis?** *Arh chya saoogu maoodeetis?*
Can I hire clubs?	**Ar galiu išsinuomoti klubą?** *Arh galyu yishsyinuomotyi kloobaa?*
How much per hour/day?	**Kiek kainuoja valanda/diena?** *Kyiek kayinuoya vahlahnda/dyiena?*
How far is it to…?	**Ar toli iki…?** *Kayip toli eerha yikyi?*
Show me on the map, please.	**Parodykite man žemėlapyje.** *Pahrodeekyite mahn, prahshaoo, zhemyelapeeye*

Going Out

What's there to do at night?	**Ką čia galima veikti vakare?** *Kaa chya gahlyima veyiktyi vahkahre?*
Do you have a program of events?	**Ar turite renginių programą?** *Ahr tuhryite rengyinyioo programmaa?*
What's playing tonight?	**Kas žaidžia šį vakarą?** *Kahs zhaidzhya shee vakahraa?*
Where's…?	**Kur yra…?** *Koor…?*
the downtown area	**miesto centras** *myiesto cehntras*
the bar	**baras** *baahrahs*
the dance club	**šokių klubas** *shokyioo kloobahs*
Is this area safe at night?	**Ar šiame rajone saugu naktį?** *Ahr shyiamye rahyonye saoogu naaktee?*

Baby Essentials

Do you have…?	**Ar turite…?** *Ahr turyite…?*
a baby bottle	**buteliuką kūdikiams** *bootelyiookaa koodyikyiams*
baby food	**kūdikių maisto** *koodyikyioo mayisto*
baby wipes	**kūdikių servetėlių** *koodyikyioo servethyelyioo*
a car seat	**automobilio kėdutę** *aootomobyilyio kyedoota*
a children's menu/portion	**vaikų meniu/vaikišką porciją** *wayikoo menu/porcyiya*

a child's seat/ highchair	**vaikišką kėdutę/aukštą kėdę** *wayikyishkaa kyeda/ aookshtaa kyeda*
a crib/cot	**lopšį/vaikišką lovelę** *lopshee/wayikyishkaa lowala*
diapers [nappies]	**vystyklų (sauskelnių)** *weesteekloo (saooskelnyioo)*
formula	**pieno mišinį** *pyieno mishinee*
a pacifier [dummy]	**žinduką (čiulptuką)** *zhindookaa (chyiulptookaa)*
a playpen	**aptvarą vaikams (maniežą)** *aptwahraa (manyiezhaa)*
a stroller [pushchair]	**kėdutę su rateliais (vežimėlį)** *kyedoota su rahtalyiayis (wazhyimyelee)*

| Can I breastfeed the
baby here? | **Ar galiu čia žindyti kūdikį?** *Ahr galyioo cha zhyindeetyi
koodyikee?* |
| Where can I
breastfeed/change
the baby? | **Kur galėčiau pažindyti kūdikį/pakeisti kūdikio
sauskelnes?** *Koor galyioo zhyindeetyi koodyikee/
pahkayistyi koodyikyio saooskalnas?* |

Disabled Travelers

Is there…?	**Ar čia yra…?** *Ahr cha eerah…?*
access for the disabled	**privažiavimas neįgaliesiems** *pryiwahzhahwyimahs naeegahlyiesyiems*
a wheelchair ramp	**pandusas invalidų vežimėliams** *pahndoosahs inwalyidoo wazhimyelams*
a disabled-accessible toilet	**tualetas neįgaliesiems** *tooaleathahs naeegahlyiesyiems*
I need…	**Man reikia…** *Mahn raikyia…*
assistance	**pagalbos** *pahgalbos*
an elevator [a lift]	**keltuvo (lifto)** *liphto*
a ground-floor room	**kambario pirmame aukšte** *kahmbahryio pirmahmye aookshte*
Please speak louder.	**Kalbėkite garsiau.** *Prahshomye kalbyethi gahrsyiaoo*

Health & Emergencies

Emergencies

| Help! | **Gelbėkite!** *gyelbehkyite* |
| Go away! | **Eikit šalin.** *eikit chahlin* |

Stop, thief!	**Laikykite vagį!** *laikeekyite vaagee*
Get a doctor!	**Pakvieskite gydytoją.** *Pahkvieskyite geedeetoyaa*
Fire!	**Gaisras!** *Gayisrahs!*
I'm lost.	**Aš esu paklydęs** *ash esu pahkleedas*
	(paklydusi). *(pahkleedusyi)*
Can you help me?	**Ar galite man padėti?** *Ahr galithe mahn pahdyeti?*
Call the police!	**Pakvieskite policiją.** *Pahkvieskyite poPitsiyaa*
Where's the police station?	**Kur yra policijos nuovada?** *Koor eehra politsiyos nuowahda?*
My child is missing.	**Dingo mano vaikas.** *Dingho mahno vaeekahs*

Health

I'm sick.	**Aš nes veikuoju/sergu.** *ash nesveikuoyu/syergu*
I need an English-speaking doctor.	**Man reikia angliškai kalbančio gydytojo.** *Mahn reykyia ahnglyishkay kahlbanchyio geedeetoyo*
It hurts here.	**Man skauda čia.** *Mahn skaooda cha*
Where's the pharmacy?	**Kur yra vaistinė?** *Koor eera vayistyinye?*
I'm (…months) pregnant.	**Aš esu (…mėnesius)** *Ash ehsoo (…myenesyioos)* **nėščia.** *nyeshcha*
I'm on…	**Aš vartoju…** *Ash wahrtoyoo…*
I'm allergic to antibiotics/penicillin.	**Aš esu alergiškas *m*/alergiška *f* antibiotikams/penicilinui.** *Ash ehsoo ahlergyishkahs/ahlergyishkah ahntyibyiotyikahms/pehnyicyilyinooyi*

YOU MAY HEAR…

Užpildykite šią formą. *Oouzhpildeekyithe sha formaa.*	Fill out this form.
Pasakykite savo asmens kodą. *Prahshaoo pahsakeetyi sahwo ahsmens kodaa.*	Your ID, please.
Kada/kur tai atsitiko? *Kahda/koor tayi atsyityiko?*	When/Where did it happen?
Kaip jis/ji atrodo? *Kaeep yis/yi atrodo?*	What does he/she look like?

Dictionary

adaptor **adapteris**
and **ir**
baby **kūdikis**
bad **blogas/bloga**
bag **krepšys**
Band-Aid [plasters] **tvarstis su marle**
bee **bitė**
black **juodas**
blue **mėlynas**
bottle opener **butelių atidariklis**
boy **berniukas**
boyfriend **mylimasis**
brown **rudas**
charger **kroviklis**
cold **šalta**
comb *(n)* **šukos**
condoms **prezervatyvai**
contact lens solution **kontaktinių lęšių tirpalas**
diabetic **diabetikas/diabetikė**
doll **lėlė**
fork **šakutė**
girl **mergaitė**
girlfriend **mylimoji**
good **gerai**
great **puiku**
green **žalias**
a hairbrush **plaukų šepetys**
hot **karšta**
husband **vyras**
ice **ledas**
insect repellent **vabzdžių repelento**
jeans **džinsai**
(steak) knife **peilis (kepsniui)**

lactose intolerant **netoleruoju laktozės**
large **didelis**
lighter **žiebtuvėlis**
love **meilė**
or **arba**
orange **oranžinis**
pen **rašiklis**
pink **rožinis/rožinė**
plate **lėkštė**
purple **purpurinis/purpurinė**
rain **lietus**
a raincoat **lietpaltis**
razor **skustuwahs**
red **raudonas**
salty **sūrus/sūri**
sanitary napkins **higieninės servetėlės**
scissors **žirklės**
small **mažas/maža**
stamp(s) **antspaudas (-ai)**
sun **saulė**
sunglasses **akiniai nuo saulės**
sunscreen **kremas nuo saulės**
tampons **tamponai**
tissues **popierinės servetėlės**
toilet paper **tualetinis popierius**
toothbrush **dantų šepetukas**
toothpaste **dantų pasta**
toy **žaislas**
vegetarian **vegetaras/vegetarė**
white **baltas**
with s**u**
wife **žmona**
without **be**
yellow **geltona**

Polish

Essentials

Hello./Hi.	**Dzień dobry./Cześć.**
	dj'yehn' dohb•ryh/chehsh'ch'
Goodbye.	**Do widzenia.** *doh vee•dzeh•n'yah*
Yes.	**Tak.** *tahk*
No.	**Nie.** *n'yeh*
Okay.	**Okay.** *oh•kay*
Excuse me.	**Przepraszam.** *psheh•prah•shahm*
I'm sorry.	**Przepraszam.** *psheh•prah•shahm*
I'd like…	**Poproszę…** *poh•proh•sheh…*
How much?	**Ile to kosztuje?** *ee•leh toh kohsh•tuh•yeh*
Where is/are…?	**Gdzie jest/są…?** *gdj'yeh yehst/sohm…*
Please.	**Proszę.** *proh•sheh*
Thank you.	**Dziękuję.** *dj'yehn'•kuh•yeh*
You're welcome.	**Nie ma za co.** *n'yeh mah zah tsoh*
Please speak slowly.	**Proszę mówić wolniej.** *proh•sheh muh•veech'vohl•n'yehy*
Please repeat that.	**Proszę powtórzyć.** *proh•sheh pohf•tuh•zhyhch'*
I don't understand.	**Nie rozumiem.** *n'yeh roh•zuh•myehm*
Do you speak English?	**Mówi pan po angielsku?** *muh•vee pahn poh ahn•gyehls•kuh*
I don't speak much Polish.	**Słabo znam polski.** *swah•boh znahm pohl•skee*
Where are the restrooms [toilets]?	**Gdzie są toalety?** *gdj'yeh sohm toh•ah•leh•tyh*
Help!	**Pomocy!** *poh•moh•tsyh*

You'll find the pronunciation of the Polish letters and words written in gray after each sentence to guide you. Simply pronounce these as if they were English, noting that any underlines indicate an additional emphasis or stress or a lengthening of a vowel sound. As you hear the language being spoken, you will quickly become accustomed to the local pronunciation and dialect.

Numbers

0	**zero**	*zeh·roh*
1	**jeden**	*yeh·dehn*
2	**dwa**	*dvah*
3	**trzy**	*tshyh*
4	**cztery**	*chteh·ryh*
5	**pięć**	*pyehn'ch'*
6	**sześć**	*shehsh'ch'*
7	**siedem**	*sh'yeh·dehm*
8	**osiem**	*oh·sh'yehm*
9	**dziewięć**	*dj'yeh·vyehn'ch'*
10	**dziesięć**	*dj'yeh·sh'yehn'ch'*
11	**jedenaście**	*yeh·deh·nahsh'·ch'yeh*
12	**dwanaście**	*dvah·nahsh'·ch'yeh*
13	**trzynaście**	*tshyh·nahsh'·ch'yeh*
14	**czternaście**	*chtehr·nahsh'·ch'yeh*
15	**piętnaście**	*pyeht·nahsh'·ch'yeh*
16	**szesnaście**	*shehs·nahsh'·ch'yeh*
17	**siedemnaście**	*sh'yehdehm·nahsh'·ch'yeh*
18	**osiemnaście**	*oh·sh'yehm·nahsh'·ch'yeh*
19	**dziewiętnaście**	*dj'yeh·vyeht·nahsh'·ch'yeh*
20	**dwadzieścia**	*dvah·dj'yehsh'·ch'yah*
21	**dwadzieścia jeden**	*dvah·dj'yehsh'·ch'yah yeh·dehn*
22	**dwadzieścia dwa**	*dvah·dj'yehsh'·ch'yah dvah*
30	**trzydzieści**	*tshyh·dj'yehsh'·ch'ee*
40	**czterdzieści**	*chtehr·dj'yehsh'·ch'ee*
50	**pięćdziesiąt**	*pyehn'·dj'yeh·sh'yohnt*
60	**sześćdziesiąt**	*shehsh'·dj'yeh·sh'yont*
70	**siedemdziesiąt**	*sh'yeh·dehm·dj'yeh·sh'yohnt*
80	**osiemdziesiąt**	*oh·sh'yehm·dj'yeh·sh'yohnt*
90	**dziewięćdziesiąt**	*dj'eh·vyen'·dj'yeh·sh'ohnt*
100	**sto**	*stoh*
101	**sto jeden**	*stoh·yeh·dehn*
200	**dwieście**	*dvyehsh'·ch'yeh*
500	**pięćset**	*pyehnch'·seht*
1,000	**tysiąc**	*tyh·sh'yohnts*

| 10,000 | **dziesięć tysięcy** *dj'yeh•sh'yehn'ch' tyh•sh'yen•tsyh* |
| 1,000,000 | **milion** *meel•yohn* |

Time

What time is it?	**Czy może mi pan powiedzieć, która godzina?** *chyh moh•zheh mee pahn poh•vyeh•dj'yehch' ktoo•rah goh•dj'ee•nah*
five after [past] five	**pięć po piątej** *pyehn'ch' poh pyohn•tehy*
quarter to nine	**za piętnaście dziewiąta** *zah pyeht•nahsh'•ch'yeh dj'yeh•vyohn•tah*
ten to seven	**za dziesięć siódma** *zah dj'yeh•sh'yehn'ch' sh'yood•mah*
5:30 a.m./p.m.	**piąta trzydzieści rano/siedemnasta trzydzieści** *pyohn•tah tshyh•dj'yehsh'•ch'ee rah•noh/ sh'yeh•dehm•nahs•tah tshyh•dj'yehsh'•ch'ee*
It's noon [midday].	**Jest południe.** *yehst poh•wood•n'yeh*
It's midnight.	**Jest północ.** *yehst poow•nohts*

Days

Monday	**poniedziałek** *poh•n'yeh•dj'yah'•wehk*
Tuesday	**wtorek** *ftoh•rehk*
Wednesday	**środa** *sh'roh•dah*
Thursday	**czwartek** *chfahr•tehk*
Friday	**piątek** *pyohn•tehk*
Saturday	**sobota** *soh•boh•tah*
Sunday	**niedziela** *n'yeh•dj'yeh•lah*

Dates

yesterday	**wczoraj** *fchoh•rahy*
today	**dzisiaj** *dj'ee•sh'yahy*
tomorrow	**jutro** *yoot•roh*
day	**dzień** *dj'yehn'*
week	**tydzień** *tyh•dj'yehn'*
month	**miesiąc** *myeh•sh'ohnts*
year	**rok** *rohk*

Months

| January | **styczeń** *styh•chehn'* |
| February | **luty** *loo•tyh* |

March	**marzec** _mah_•zhehts
April	**kwiecień** _kfyeh_•ch'yehn'
May	**maj** mahy
June	**czerwiec** _chehr_•vyehts
July	**lipiec** _lee_•pyehts
August	**sierpień** _sh'yehr_•pyehn'
September	**wrzesień** _vzheh_•sh'yehn'
October	**październik** pahzh'•_dj'yehr_•n'eek
November	**listopad** lees•_toh_•paht
December	**grudzień** _groo_•dj'yehn'

Arrival & Departure

I'm here on vacation/business.	**Przyjechałem** m/**Przyjechałam** f **tutaj na wakacje/łużbowo.** pshyh•yeh•_hah_•wehm/pshyh•yeh•_hah_•wahm _too_•tahy nah vah•_kahts_•yeh/swoozh•_boh_•voh
I'm going to...	**Jadę do...** _yah_•deh doh...
I'm staying at the... Hotel.	**Zatrzymałem** m/**Zatrzymałam** f **się w Hotelu...** zah•tshyh•_mah_•wehm/zah•tshyh•_mah_•wahm sh'yeh fhoh•_teh_•loo...

Money

Where's...?	**Gdzie jest...?** gdj'yeh yehst...
the ATM	**bankomat** bahn•_koh_•maht
the bank	**bank** bahnk
the currency exchange office	**kantor** _kahn_•tohr
When does the bank open/close?	**O której otwierają/zamykają bank?** oh _ktoo_•rehy oht•fyeh•_rah_•yohm/zah•myh•_kah_•yohm bahnk

YOU MAY SEE...

Polish currency is currently the **złoty**; one **złoty** is made up of 100 **groszy**. Soon Poland may adopt the euro as its national currency; until then **złoty** is the accepted form of payment.
Coins: 1, 2, 5, 10, 20, 50 **groszy**; 1, 2, 5 **złoty**.
Bills: 10, 20, 50, 100, 200 **złoty**.

I'd like to change dollars/ pounds into zlotys.	**Chciałbym** *m* **/Chciałabym** *f* **wymienić dolary/funty na złotówki.** *hch'yahw·byhm/hch'yah·wah·byhm vyh·myeh·n'eech' do·lah·ryh/foon·tyh nah zwoh·toof·kee*
I want to cash some travelers checks.	**Chcę zrealizować czeki podróżne.** *htseh zreh·ah·lee·zoh·vahch' cheh·kee pohd·roozh·neh*

For Numbers, see page 174.

Getting Around

How do I get to town?	**Jak stąd dojechać do miasta?** *yahk stohnt doh·yeh·hahch' doh myahs·tah*
Where's…?	**Gdzie jest…?** *gdj'yeh yehst…*
the airport	*lotnisko loht·n'ees·koh*
the train [railway] station	**dworzec kolejowy** *dvoh·zhehts koh·leh·yoh·vyh*
the bus station	**dworzec autobusowy** *dvoh·zhehts ahw·toh·boo·soh·vyh*
the metro [underground] station	**stacja metra** *stahts·yah meht·rah*
Is it far from here?	**Czy to daleko stąd?** *chyh toh dah·leh·koh stohnt*
Where can I buy tickets?	**Gdzie mogę kupić bilety?** *gdj'yeh moh·geh koo·peech' bee·leh·tyh*
A one-way [single]/ round-trip [return] ticket to…	**Bilet w jedną stonę/powrotny do…** *bee·leht vyehd·nohm stroh·neh/pohv·roht·nyh doh…*
Are there any discounts?	**Czy są jakieś zniżki?** *chyh sohm yah·kyehsh' zn'eesh·kee*
Where can I get a taxi?	**Gdzie mogę złapać taksówkę?** *gdj'yeh moh·geh zwah·pahch' tahk·soof·keh*
Please take me to this address.	**Proszę mnie zawieźć pod ten adres.** *proh·sheh mn'yeh zah·vyehsh'ch' poht tehn ahd·rehs*
Where can I rent a car?	**Gdzie mogę wynająć samochód?** *gdj'yeh moh·geh vyh·nah·yohnch' sah·moh·hoot*
Can I have a map, please?	**Poproszę mapę.** *poh·proh·sheh mah·peh*

Tickets

When's…to Cracow?	**O której jest…do Krakowa?** *oh ktoo·rehy yehst… doh krah·koh·vah*
the (first) bus	**(pierwszy) autobus** *(pyehr·shyh) ahw·toh·boos*

the (next) flight	**(następny) samolot** (nahs-_tehm_-pnyh) sah-_moh_-loht
the (last) train	**(ostatni) pociąg** (ohs-_taht_-n'ee) poh-ch'yonk
Where can I buy a ticket?	**Gdzie mogę kupić bilet?** gdj'yeh moh-geh koo-peech' _bee_-leht
One/two ticket(s), please.	**Jeden bilet/Dwa bilety proszę.** _yeh_-dehn bee-leht/ dvah bee-_leh_-tyh proh-sheh
A...ticket.	**Bilet...** _bee_-leht...
one-way [single]	**w jedną stronę** _vyehd_-nohm stroh-neh
round-trip [return]	**powrotny** pohv-_roht_-nyh
first class	**w pierwszej klasie** _fpyehr_-shehy klah-sh'yeh
economy class	**w klasie turystycznej** fklah-sh'yeh too-ryhs-_tyhch_-nehy
How much?	**Ile to kosztuje?** ee-leh toh kohsh-_too_-yeh
Is there a discount for...?	**Czy jest zniżka dla...?** chyh yehst _zn'eesh_-kah dlah...
children	**dzieci** dj'ye-ch'ee
students	**studentów** stoo-_dehn_-toof
senior citizens	**emerytów** eh-meh-_ryh_-toof
I have an e-ticket.	**Mam bilet elektroniczny.** mahm bee-leht eh-lehk-troh-_n'eech_-nyh
Can I buy a ticket on the bus/train?	**Czy można kupić bilet w autobusie/pociągu?** chyh _mohzh_-nah koo-peech' bee-leht v ahw-toh-_boo_-sh'yeh/poh-ch'_yohn_-goo
I'd like to...my reservation.	**Chciałbym** m **/Chciałabym** f **...moją rezerwację.** hch'yahw-byhm/hch'yah-wah-byhm...moh-yohm reh-zehr-_vahts_-yeh
cancel	**odwołać** ohd-_voh_-wahch'
change	**zmienić** _zmyeh_-n'eech'
confirm	**potwierdzić** poh-_tfyehr_-dj'eech'

For Time, see page 175.

Car Hire

Where can I rent a car?	**Gdzie mogę wynająć samochód?** gdj'yeh moh-geh vyh-_nah_-yohnch' sah-_moh_-hoot
I'd like to rent...	**Chcę wynająć...** htseh vyh-_nah_-yohnch'...
an automatic/ a manual	**samochód z automatyczną/ręczną skrzynią biegów** sah-_moh_-hoot z ahw-toh-mah-_tyhch_-nohm/ _rehnch_-nohm skshyh-n'yohm byeh-goof
a car with air conditioning	**samochód z klimatyzacją** sah-_moh_-hoot sklee-mah-tyh-_zahts_-yohm

a car seat	**fotelik dziecięcy** foh·_teh_·leek dj'yeh·_ch'yehn_·tsyh
How much…?	**Ile to kosztuje…?** _ee_·leh toh kohsh·_too_·yeh…
per day/week	**za dzień/tydzień** zah dj'yehn'/_tyh_·dj'yehn'
per kilometer	**za kilometr** zah kee·_loh_·mehtr
for unlimited mileage	**bez limitu kilometrów** behs lee·_mee_·too kee·loh·_meht_·roof
with insurance	**z ubezpieczeniem** zoo·behs·pyeh·_cheh_·n'yehm
Are there any discounts?	**Czy są jakieś zniżki?** chyh sohm _yah_·kyehs' _zn'eezh_·kee

YOU MAY HEAR…

Proszę jechać… _proh_·sheh yeh_·hahch'…   You should go…
  prosto _prohs_·toh   straight
  w lewo _vleh_·voh   left
  w prawo _fprah_·voh   right
  na północ/południe nah _poow_·nohts/   north/south
  poh·_wood_·n'yeh
  na wschód/zachód na fs·hoot/_zah_·hoot   east/west
To jest… toh yehst…   It's…
  na rogu/za rogiem nah _roh_·goo/zah _roh_·gyehm   on/around the corner
  naprzeciwko… nah psheh·_ch'eef_·koh…   opposite…
  za… zah…   behind…
  przy… pshyh…   next to…

Places to Stay

Can you recommend a hotel?	**Czy może mi pan polecić jakiś hotel?** chyh _moh_·zheh mee pahn poh·_leh_·ch'eech' _yah_·keesh' _hoh_·tehl
I have a reservation.	**Mam rezerwację.** mahm reh·zehr·_vahts_·yeh
My name is…	**Nazywam się…** nah·_zyh_·vahm sh'yeh…
I would like a room…	**Chciałbym** m/**Chciałabym** f **wynająć pokój…** hch'_yahw_·byhm/hch'_yah_·wah·byhm vyh·_nah_·yohnch' _poh_·kooy…
for one/two	**jednoosobowy/dwuosobowy** yehd·noh·oh·soh·_boh_·vyh/dvoo·oh·soh·_boh_·vyh

with a bathroom	**z łazienką** zvah-_zh'yehn_-kohm
with air conditioning	**z klimatyzacją** sklee-mah-tyh-_zahts_-yohm
For...	**Na...** nah...
tonight	**tę noc** teh nohts
two nights	**dwie noce** dvyeh _noh_-tseh
one week	**tydzień** tyh-dj'yehn'
How much?	**Ile to kosztuje?** _ee_-leh toh kohsh-_too_-yeh
Do you have anything cheaper?	**Czy są jakieś tańsze pokoje?** chyh sohm yah-kyehsh' _tahn'_-sheh poh-_koh_-yeh
When's check-out?	**O której mamy zwolnić pokój?** oh _ktoo_-rehy _mah_-myh _zvohl_-n'eech' _poh_-kooy
Can I leave this in the safe?	**Mogę zostawić to w sejfie?** _moh_-geh zohs-_tah_-veech' toh _fsehy_-fyeh
Can I leave my luggage?	**Mogę zostawić mój bagaż?** _moh_-geh zohs-_tah_-veech' mooy _bah_-gahsh
Can I have the bill/ a receipt?	**Czy mogę prosić o rachunek/pokwitowanie?** chyh _moh_-geh _pro_-sh'eech' oh rah-_hoo_-nehk/poh-kfee-toh-_vah_-n'yeh
I'll pay in cash/ by credit card.	**Zapłacę gotówką/kartą kredytową.** zah-_pwah_-tseh goh-_toof_-kohm/_kahr_-tohm kreh-dyh-_toh_-vohm

Communications

Is there an internet cafe nearby?	**Czy jest tu gdzieś w pobliżu kafejka internetowa?** chyh yehst too gdj'yehsh' fpoh-_blee_-zhoo kah-_fehy_-kah een-tehr-neh-_toh_-vah
Does it have wireless internet?	**Jest tam bezprzewodowy internet?** yehst tahm behs-psheh-voh-_doh_-vyh een-_tehr_-neht
What is the WiFi password?	**Jakie jest hasło do sieci WiFi?** _yah_-kyeh yehst _hahs_-woh doh _sh'yeh_-ch'ee vee phee
Is the WiFi free?	**Czy korzystanie z WiFi jest bezpłatne?** chyh koh-zhyhs-_stah_-nyeh z vee phee yehst behs-_pwaht_-neh
Do you have bluetooth?	**masz funkcję Bluetooth?** mahsh foon-ktsyeh bloo-tooth
How do I turn the computer on/off?	**Jak włączyć/wyłączyć komputer?** yak _vwohn_-chyhch'/wyh-_wohn_-chyhch' kohm-_poo_-tehr
How much per hour/ half hour?	**Ile kosztuje godzina/pół godziny?** _ee_-leh kohsh-_too_-yeh goh-_dj'ee_-nah/poow goh-_dj'ee_-nyh
Can I...?	**Mogę...?** _moh_-geh...
access the internet	**skorzystać z internetu** skoh-_zhyhs_-tahch' zeen-tehr-_neh_-too

check e-mail	**sprawdzić pocztę** _sprahv_·dj'eech' pohch·teh	
print something	**coś wydrukować** tsohsh' vyh·droo·_koh_·vahch'	
access Skype?	**używać Skype'a?** ooh·_zhyh_·vahch' skahy·pah	
plug in/charge my laptop/iPhone/ iPad/BlackBerry?	**podłączyć/naładować laptopa/iPhone'a/ iPada/Blackberry?** pohd·_wohn_·chyhch'/nah·wah·_doh_·vach' lahp·_toh_·pah/ahy·_foh_·nah/ahy·_pah_·dah/blahk·_beh_·ryh	
How do I...?	**Jak mam się...?** yahk mahm sh'yeh...	
connect/disconnect	**połączyć z siecią/rozłączyć** poh·_wohn_·chyhch' ssh'yeh·ch'yohm/rohz·_wohn_·chyhch'	
log on/off	**zalogować/wylogować** zah·loh·_goh_·vahch'/ wyh·loh·_goh_·vahch'	
How do I type this symbol?	**Jak wpisać ten symbol?** yahk _fpee_·sahch' tehn _syhm_·bohl	
What's your e-mail?	**Jaki jest pana adres e-mail?** _yah_·kee yehst _pah_·nah _ahd_·rehs ee·mehyl	
My e-mail is...	**Mój e-mail to...** mooy ee·meyhl toh...	
Do you have a scanner?	**Czy jest tu skaner?** Chyh yehst too _skah_·nehr	

Social Media

Are you on Facebook/ Twitter?	**Masz konto na Facebooku/Twitterze?** mahsh _kohn_·toh nah fehys·_boo_·koo/twee·_teh_·zheh
What's your user name?	**Pod jaką nazwą masz konto?** pohd _yah_·kohm _nahz_·vohm mahsh _kohn_·toh
I'll add you as a friend.	**Dodam Cię do znajomych.** _doh_·dahm ch'yeh doh znah·_yoh_·myhh
I'll follow you on Twitter.	**Będę śledził/śledziła twoje wpisy na Twitterze.** _behn_·deh _sh'leh_·dj'eewh/sh'leh·_dj'ee_·wah _tfoh_·yeh _fpee_·syh nah twee·_teh_·zheh
Are you following....?	**Czy śledzisz wpisy....?** chyh _sh'leh_·dj'eesh _fpee_·syh...
I'll put the pictures on Facebook/Twitter.	**Wrzucę zdjęcia na Facebooka/Twittera.** _vzhoo_·tseh _zdyehn_·chy'ahh nah fehys·_boo_·kah/twee·_teh_·rah
I'll tag you in the pictures.	**Zaznaczę cię na zdjęciach.** zah·_znah_·cheh ch'yeh nah _zdyehn_·chy'ahh

Conversation

Hello	**Dzień dobry.** dj'yehn' _dohb_·ryh
How are you?	**Jak się pan ma?** yahk sh'yeh pahn mah
Fine, thanks.	**W porządku, dziękuję.** fpoh·_zhohnt_·koo dz'yehn·koo·yeh

Excuse me!	**Przepraszam!** psheh-_prah_-shahm
Do you speak English?	**Mówi pan po angielsku?** _moo_-vee pahn poh ahn-_gyehl_-skoo
What's your name?	**Jak się pan nazywa?** yahk sh'yeh pahn nah-_zyh_-vah
My name is…	**Nazywam się…** nah-_zyh_-vahm sh'yeh…
Pleased to meet you.	**Miło mi pana poznać.** _mee_-woh mee _pah_-nah pohz-nahch'
Where are you from?	**Skąd pan jest?** skohnt pahn yehst
I'm from the U.S./U.K.	**Jestem z USA/Wielkiej Brytanii.** _yehs_-tehm z oo-ehs-_ah_/ _vyehl_-kyehy bryh-_tah_-n'ee
What do you do for a living?	**Czym się pan zajmuje?** chyhm sh'yeh pahn zahy-_moo_-yeh
I work for…	**Pracuję w…** prah-_tsoo_-yeh v…
I'm a student.	**Studiuję.** stoo-_dyoo_-yeh
I'm retired.	**Jestem na emeryturze.** _yehs_-tehm nah eh-meh-ryh-_too_-zheh
Do you like…?	**Lubi pan…?** _loo_-bee pahn…
Goodbye.	**Do widzenia.** doh vee-_dzeh_-n'yah
See you later.	**Do zobaczenia.** doh zoh-bah-_cheh_-n'yah

Romance

Would you like to go out for a drink/meal?	**Może pójdziemy na drinka/coś zjeść?** _moh_-zheh _pooy_-dj'eh-myh nah _dreen_-kah/tsohsh' zyehsh'ch'
What are your plans for tonight/tomorrow?	**Masz jakieś plany na wieczór/jutro?** mahsh _yah_-kyehsh' _plah_-nyh nah _vyeh_-choor/_yoot_-roh
Can I have your number?	**Podasz mi swój numer telefonu?** _poh_-dahsh mee sfuy _noo_-mehr teh-leh-_foh_-noo
Can I join you?	**Mogę się dosiąść?** _moh_-geh sh'yeh _doh_-sh'yohn'sh'ch'
Can I buy you a drink?	**Mogę postawić ci drinka?** _moh_-geh pohs-_tah_-veech' ch'ee _dree_-nkah
I like/love you.	**Lubię/Kocham cię.** _loo_-bieh/_koh_-hahm ch'yeh

Accepting & Rejecting

I'd love to.	**Bardzo chętnie.** _bahr_-dzoh _chehnt_-n'yeh.
Where should we meet?	**Gdzie możemy się spotkać?** gdj'eh moh-_zheh_-myh sh'yeh _spoht_-kach'
I'll meet you at the bar/ your hotel.	**Spotkamy się w barze/twoim hotelu.** spoht-_kah_-myh sh'yeh v_bah_-zheh/_tfoh_-eem hoh-_teh_-loo
I'll come by at…	**Przyjdę o…** _pshyhy_-deh oh…
What's your address?	**Gdzie mieszkasz?** gdj'yeh _myehsh_-kahsh

I'm busy.	**Jestem zajęty** *m* /**zajęta** *f.* *yehs*·tehm zah·*yehn*·tyh/ *zah*·*yehn*·tah
I'm not interested.	**Nie jestem zainteresowany** *m* /**zainteresowana** *f.* *n'yeh yehs*·tehm zah·een·teh·reh·soh·*vah*·nyh/ *zah*·een·teh·reh·soh·*vah*·nah
Leave me alone, please!	**Zostaw mnie w spokoju!** *zohs*·tahf mn'yeh fspoh·*koh*·yoo
Stop bothering me!	**Odczep się!** *oht*·chehp sh'yeh

Food & Drink

Eating Out

Can you recommend a good restaurant/cafe?	**Czy może mi pan polecić dobrą restaurację/ kawiarnię?** *chyh moh*·zheh mee pahn poh·*leh*·ch'eech' *dohb*·rohm rehs·tahw·*rahts*·yeh/kah·*vyahr*·n'yeh
Is there a traditional Polish/an inexpensive restaurant nearby?	**Czy jest tu gdzieś w pobliżu tradycyjna polska/niedroga restauracja?** *chyh yehst too gdj'yehsh' fpoh·blee*·zhoo trah·dyh·*tsyhy*·nah *pohls*·kah/n'yeh·*droh*·gah rehs·tahw·*rahts*·yah
A table for one/two, please.	**Stolik dla jednej osoby/dwóch osób, proszę.** *stoh*·leek dlah *yehd*·nehy oh·*soh*·byh/dvooh *oh*·soop *proh*·sheh
Can we sit...?	**Możemy usiąść...?** moh·*zheh*·myh oo·sh'yohn'sh'ch'...
here/there	**tu/tam** too/tahm
outside	**na zewnątrz** nah *zehv*·nohntsh
in a non-smoking area	**w części dla niepalących** *fchehn'sh'*·ch'ee dlah n'yeh·pah·*lohn*·tsyhh
Where are the toilets?	**Gdzie są toalety?** *gdj'yeh* sohm toh·ah·*leh*·tyh
Can I have a menu?	**Mogę prosić menu?** *moh*·geh *proh*·sh'eech' meh·*n'ee*
What do you recommend?	**Co może pan polecić?** tsoh *moh*·zheh pahn poh·*leh*·ch'eech'
I'd like...	**Poproszę...** poh·*proh*·sheh...
Some more..., please.	**Poproszę trochę więcej...** poh·*proh*·sheh *troh*·heh *vyehn*·tsehy...
Enjoy your meal.	**Smacznego.** smahch·*neh*·goh
The check [bill], please.	**Poproszę rachunek.** poh·*proh*·sheh rah·*hoo*·nehk
Is service included?	**Czy obsługa jest wliczona w cenę?** chyh ohp·*swoo*·gah yehst vlee·*choh*·nah *ftseh*·neh

Can I pay by credit card?	**Czy mogę zapłacić kartą kredytową?** *chyh moh·geh zah·pwah·ch'eech' kahr·tohm kreh·dyh·toh·vohm*
Can I have a receipt?	**Czy mogę prosić paragon?** *chyh moh·geh pro·sh'eech' pah·rah·gohn*
Thank you.	**Dziękuję.** *dj'yehn·koo·yeh*

YOU MAY SEE...

DANIA DNIA	menu of the day
OBSŁUGA (NIE)WLICZONA W CENĘ	service (not) included
SZEF KUCHNI POLECA	specials

Breakfast

boczek *boh·chehk*	bacon
chleb *hlehp*	bread
masło *mahs·woh*	butter
ser *sehr*	cheese
jajecznica *yah·yehch·n'ee·tsah*	scrambled eggs
jajka sadzone *yahy·kah sah·dzoh·neh*	fried eggs
jajko na twardo/miękko *yahy·koh nah tfahr·doh/ myehnk·koh*	hard-boiled/soft-boiled egg
dżem *djehm*	jam
bułki *boow·kee*	rolls
tost *tohst*	toast
parówki *pah·roof·kee*	sausage
jogurt *yoh·goort*	yogurt

Appetizers

grillowany oscypek *gree·loh·vah·nyh ohs·tsyh·pehk*	grilled and smoked ewe's milk cheese
grzybki marynowane *gzhyhp·kee mah·ryh·noh·vah·neh*	marinated wild mushrooms
naleśniki z kapustą i grzybami *nah·lehsh'·n'ee·kee skah·poos·tohm ee gzhyh·bah·mee*	thin pancakes with sauerkraut and mushrooms

pieczarki w śmietanie pyeh·<u>chahr</u>·kee fsh'myeh·<u>tah</u>·n'yeh	mushrooms in a cream sauce
sałatka sah·<u>waht</u>·kah	mixed salad
sałatka jarzynowa sah·<u>waht</u>·kah yah·zhyh·<u>noh</u>·vah	mixed vegetable salad in mayonnaise
sałatka pomidorowa z cebulą sah·<u>waht</u>·kah poh·mee·doh·<u>roh</u>·vah stseh·<u>boo</u>·lohm	tomato and onion salad
sałatka ziemniaczana sah·<u>waht</u>·kah zh'yehm·n'yah·<u>chah</u>·nah	potato salad
śledź w oleju sh'lehdj' voh·<u>leh</u>·yoo	herring in oil
śledź w śmietanie sh'lehch' fsh'myeh·<u>tah</u>·n'yeh	herring in sour cream
węgorz wędzony <u>vehn</u>·gohsh vehn·<u>dzoh</u>·nyh	smoked eel

Meat

wołowina voh·woh·<u>vee</u>·nah	beef
jagnię <u>yahg</u>·n'yeh	lamb
kurczak <u>koor</u>·chahk	chicken
kaczka <u>kahch</u>·kah	duck
wieprzowina vyehp·shoh·<u>vee</u>·nah	pork
cielęcina ch'yeh·lehn'·<u>ch'ee</u>·nah	veal
baranina bah·rah·<u>n'eeh</u>·nah	mutton
gołąbki goh·<u>wohmp</u>·kee	cabbage leaves stuffed with ground meat and rice

YOU MAY HEAR...

krwisty kreh·<u>vee</u>·stuh	(rare)
średnio wysmażony sh'red·noh vys·mah·<u>vzho</u>·neh	medium
wysmażony vys·mah·<u>vzho</u>·neh	well-done

Fish & Seafood

dorsz dohrsh	cod
flądra <u>flohn</u>·drah	flounder [plaice]
homar <u>hoh</u>·mahr	lobster

karp *kahrp*	carp
krewetki *kreh-veht-kee*	shrimp [prawns]
łosoś <u>woh</u>-sohsh'	salmon
łupacz *woo-pahch'*	haddock
makrela *mahk-<u>reh</u>-lah*	mackerel
pstrąg *pstrohnk*	trout
sandacz <u>sahn</u>-dahch	perch
tuńczyk <u>toon'</u>-chyhk	tuna

Vegetables

kapusta *kah-<u>poos</u>-tah*	cabbage
pieczarka/grzyb *pyeh-<u>chahr</u>-kah/gzhyhb*	mushroom/wild mushroom
cebula *tseh-<u>boo</u>-lah*	onion
groszek <u>groh</u>-shehk	pea
ziemniak <u>z'yehm</u>-n'yahk	potato
pomidor *poh-<u>mee</u>-dohr*	tomato
placki ziemniaczane <u>plahts</u>-kee zyehm-n'yah-<u>chah</u>-neh	potato pancakes
pierogi z… *pyeh-<u>roh</u>-gee z…*	dumplings stuffed with…
grzybami *gzhyh-<u>bah</u>-mee*	mushrooms
kapustą *kah-<u>poos</u>-tohm*	sauerkraut
serem <u>seh</u>-rehm	curd cheese
owocami *oh-voh-<u>tsah</u>-mee*	fruit

Sauces & Condiments

sól *sool*	salt
pieprz <u>pyehpsh</u>	pepper
musztarda *moosh-<u>tahr</u>-dah*	mustard
keczup <u>keh</u>-choop	ketchup

Fruit & Dessert

jabłko <u>yahp</u>-koh	apple
banan <u>bah</u>-nahn	banana
cytryna *tsyh-<u>tryh</u>-nah*	lemon
pomarańcza *poh-mah-<u>rahn'</u>-chah*	orange
śliwka <u>sh'leef</u>-kah	plum
truskawka *troos-<u>kahf</u>-kah*	strawberry

racuchy z jabłkami rah·_tsoo_·hyh z yahp·_kah_·mee	small fried pancakes made with sliced apples
lody... _loh_·dyh...	...ice cream
szarlotka shahr·_loht_·kah	apple tart
sernik _sehr_·n'eek	cheesecake

Drinks

Can I see the wine list/ drink menu?	**Czy mogę prosić kartę win/listę drinków?** chyh _moh_·geh proh·sheech' _kahr_·teh veen/_lees_·teh _dreen_·koof
What do you recommend?	**Co może pan polecić?** tsoh _moh_·zheh pahn poh·_leh_·ch'eech'
I'd like a bottle/glass of red/white wine.	**Poproszę butelkę/kieliszek czerwonego/białego wina.** poh·_proh_·sheh boo·_tehl_·keh/kyeh·_lee_·shehk chehr·voh·_neh_·goh/byah·_weh_·goh _vee_·nah
The house wine, please.	**Poproszę wino stołowe.** poh·_proh_·sheh _vee_·noh stoh·_woh_·veh
Another bottle/glass, please.	**Poproszę jeszcze jedną butelkę/jeden kieliszek.** poh·_proh_·sheh yehsh·cheh _jehd_·nohm boo·_tehl_·keh/_yeh_·dehn kyeh·_lee_·shehk
I'd like a local beer.	**Poproszę lokalne piwo.** poh·_proh_·sheh loh·_kahl_·neh _pee_·voh
Can I buy you a drink?	**Mogę postawić panu drinka?** _moh_·geh pohs·_tah_·veech' _pah_·noo _dreen_·kah
Cheers!	**Na zdrowie!** nah _zdroh_·vyeh
A coffee/tea, please.	**Poproszę kawę/herbatę.** poh·_proh_·sheh _kah_·veh/ hehr·_bah_·teh
Black	**Czarną** _chahr_·nohm
A coffee with..., please.	**Poproszę kawę z...** poh·_proh_·sheh _kah_·veh z...
milk	**mlekiem** _mleh_·kyehm
sugar	**cukrem** _tsook_·rehm
artificial sweetener	**słodzikiem** swoh·_dj'ee_·kyehm
I'd like...	**Poproszę...** poh·_proh_·sheh...
a juice	**sok** sohk
a cola	**colę** _koh_·leh
a (sparkling/still) water	**wodę (gazowaną/niegazowaną)** _voh_·deh (gah·zoh·_vah_·nohm/n'yeh·gah·zoh·_vah_·nohm)
Is the tap water safe to drink?	**Można pić wodę z kranu?** _mohzh_·nah peech' _voh_·deh skrah·_noo_

Leisure Time

Sightseeing

Where's the tourist information office?	**Gdzie jest biuro informacji turystycznej?** *gdj'yeh yehst <u>byoo</u>·roh een·fohr·<u>mah</u>·tsyee too·ryhs·<u>tyhch</u>·nehy*
What are the main points of interest?	**Co tu warto zobaczyć?** *tsoh too <u>vahr</u>·toh zoh·<u>bah</u>·chyhch'*
Are there tours in English?	**Czy są wycieczki po angielsku?** *chyh sohm vyh·<u>ch'yech</u>·kee poh ahn·<u>gyehl</u>·skoo*
Can I have a map/guide please?	**Czy mogę prosić mapę/przewodnik?** *chyh <u>moh</u>·geh <u>proh</u>·sh'eech' <u>mah</u>·peh/psheh·<u>vohd</u>·n'eek*

> **YOU MAY SEE...**
>
> | | |
> |---|---|
> | **Zamknięte/otwarte** | open/closed |
> | **Wyjście** | exit |

Shopping

Where is the market/mall [shopping centre]?	**Gdzie jest targ/centrum handlowe?** *gdj'yeh yehst tahrk/<u>tsehn</u>·troom hahn·<u>dloh</u>·veh*
I'm just browsing.	**Tylko się rozglądam.** *tyhl·koh sh'yeh rohz·<u>glohn</u>·dahm*
Can you help me?	**Czy może mi pan pomóc?** *chyh <u>moh</u>·zheh mee pahn <u>poh</u>·moots*
I'm being helped.	**Jestem już obsługiwany m/obsługiwana f.** *yehs·tehm yoosh ohp·swoo·gee·<u>vah</u>·nyh/ohp·swoo·gee·<u>vah</u>·nah*
How much is this/that?	**Ile to/tamto kosztuje?** *ee·leh toh/<u>tahm</u>·toh kosh·<u>too</u>·yeh*
Can you show me...?	**Może mi pan pokazać...?** *<u>moh</u>·zheh mee pahn poh·<u>kah</u>·zahch'...*
This/That one, please.	**Proszę to/tamto.** *proh·sheh toh/<u>tahm</u>·toh*
That's all, thanks.	**To wszystko, dziękuję.** *toh <u>fshyhs</u>·tkoh dj'yehn·<u>koo</u>·yeh*
Where can I pay?	**Gdzie mogę zapłacić?** *gdj'yeh <u>moh</u>·geh zah·<u>pwah</u>·ch'eech'*
I'll pay in cash/by credit card.	**Zapłacę gotówką/kartą kredytową.** *zah·<u>pwah</u>·tseh goh·<u>toof</u>·kohm/<u>kahr</u>·tohm kreh·dyh·<u>toh</u>·vohm*
A receipt, please.	**Proszę paragon.** *<u>proh</u>·sheh pah·<u>rah</u>·gohn*

Sport & Leisure

Where's the game?	**Gdzie grają?** gdj'yeh <u>grah</u>·yohm
Where's…?	**Gdzie jest…?** gdj'yeh yehst…
the beach	**plaża** <u>plah</u>·zhah
the park	**park** pahrk
the pool	**basen** <u>bah</u>·sehn
Is it safe to swim/ dive here?	**Można tu bezpiecznie pływać/skakać?** <u>mozh</u>·nah too behs·<u>pyehch</u>·n'yeh <u>pwyh</u>·vahch'/<u>skah</u>·kahch'
I'd like to rent [hire] golf clubs.	**Chciałbym** m/**Chciałabym** f **wypożyczyć kije golfowe.** <u>hch'yahw</u>·byhm/<u>hch'yah</u>·wah·byhm fvyh·poh·<u>zhyh</u>·chyhch' <u>kee</u>·yeh gohl·<u>foh</u>·veh
What's the charge per hour?	**Jaka jest opłata za godzinę?** <u>yah</u>·kah yehst oh·<u>pwah</u>·tah zah goh·<u>dj'ee</u>·neh
How far is it to…from here?	**Jak daleko jest stąd do…?** yahk dah·<u>leh</u>·koh yehst stohnt doh…
Can you show me on the map?	**Czy może mi pan pokazać na mapie?** chyh <u>moh</u>·zheh mee pahn poh·<u>kah</u>·zahch' nah <u>mah</u>·pyeh

Going Out

What is there to do at night?	**Co można robić wieczorami?** tsoh <u>mozh</u>·nah <u>roh</u>·beech' vyeh·choh·<u>rah</u>·mee
Do you have a program of events?	**Czy jest program imprez?** chyh yehst <u>proh</u>·grahm <u>eem</u>·prehs
What's playing at the movies [cinema] today?	**Co dzisiaj grają w kinie?** tsoh <u>dj'ee</u>·sh'yay <u>grah</u>·yohm <u>fkee</u>·n'yeh
Where's…?	**Gdzie jest…?** gdj'yeh yehst…
the downtown area	**centrum** <u>tsehn</u>·troom
the bar	**bar** bahr
the dance club	**dyskoteka** dyhs·koh·<u>teh</u>·kah

Baby Essentials

Do you have…?	**Czy mają państwo…?** chyh <u>mah</u>·yohm pahn'·stfoh…
a baby bottle	**butelkę ze smoczkiem** boo·<u>tehl</u>·keh zeh <u>smohch</u>·kyehm
baby wipes	**wilgotne chusteczki pielęgnacyjne** veel·<u>goht</u>·neh hoos·<u>tehch</u>·kee pyeh·lehn·gnah·<u>tsyhy</u>·neh
a car seat	**fotelik samochodowy** foh·<u>teh</u>·leek sah·moh·hoh·<u>doh</u>·vyh

a child's seat/ highchair	**krzesełko dla dziecka/wysokie krzesełko** ksheh•<u>seh</u>•wkoh dlah <u>dj'yeh</u>•tskah/vyh•<u>soh</u>•kyeh ksheh•<u>seh</u>•wkoh
a crib/cot	**łóżko składane/łóżeczko dziecięce** <u>woo</u>•shkoh skwah•<u>dah</u>•neh/woo•<u>zhehch</u>•koh dj'yeh•<u>ch'ehn</u>•tseh
diapers [nappies]	**pieluszki** pyeh•<u>loosh</u>•kee
a pacifier [dummy]	**smoczek** smoh•chehk
a playpen	**kojec** <u>koh</u>•yehts
a stroller [pushchair]	**wózek spacerowy** <u>voo</u>•zehk spah•tseh•<u>roh</u>•vyh
Can I breastfeed the baby here?	**Czy mogę tutaj karmić dziecko piersią?** chyh moh•geh <u>too</u>•tay <u>kahr</u>•meech' <u>dj'yehts</u>•koh pyehr•sh'yohm
Where can I change the baby?	**Gdzie mogę przewinąć dziecko?** gdj'yeh <u>moh</u>•geh psheh•<u>vee</u>•nohn'ch' <u>dj'yehts</u>•koh

For Eating Out, see page 183.

Disabled Travelers

Is there…?	**Czy jest…?** chyh yehst…
access for the disabled	**dostęp dla niepełnosprawnych** <u>dohs</u>•tehmp dlah n'yeh•pehw•noh•<u>sprahv</u>•nyhh
a wheelchair ramp	**podjazd dla wózków inwalidzkich** <u>pohd</u>•yahst dlah <u>voos</u>•koof een•vah•<u>leets</u>•keeh
a disabled-accessible toilet	**toaleta dla niepełnosprawnych** toh•ah•<u>leh</u>•tah dlah n'yeh•pew•noh•<u>sprahv</u>•nyhh
I need…	**Potrzebuję…** poh•tsheh•<u>boo</u>•yeh…
assistance	**pomocy** poh•<u>moh</u>•tsyh
an elevator [lift]	**windy** <u>veen</u>•dyh
a ground-floor room	**pokoju na parterze** poh•<u>koh</u>•yoo nah pahr•<u>teh</u>•zheh

Health & Emergencies

Emergencies

Help!	**Pomocy!** poh•<u>moh</u>•tsyh
Go away!	**Proszę odejść!** <u>proh</u>•sheh oh•deysh'ch'
Leave me alone!	**Zostaw mnie w spokoju!** <u>zoh</u>•stahf mn'yeh fspoh•<u>koh</u>•yoo
Stop thief!	**Łapać złodzieja!** <u>wah</u>•pach' zwoh•<u>dj'yeh</u>•yah
Get a doctor!	**Wezwijcie lekarza!** vez•<u>veey</u>•ch'yeh leh•<u>kah</u>•zhah

Fire!	**Pali się!** _pah_-lee sh'yeh
I'm lost.	**Zgubiłem się** m **/Zgubiłam się** f. zgoo-_bee_-wehm sh'yeh/ zgoo-_bee_-wahm sh'yeh
Can you help me?	**Czy może mi pan pomóc?** chyh _moh_-zheh mee pahn _poh_-moots
Call the police!	**Wezwijcie policję!** vez-_veey_-ch'yeh poh-_leets_-yeh
Where's the police station?	**Gdzie jest komisariat?** gdj'yeh yehst koh-mee-_sahr_-yaht
My child is missing.	**Moje dziecko się zgubiło.** _moh_-yeh _dj'yeh_-tskoh sh'yeh zgoo-_bee_-woh

YOU MAY HEAR...

Proszę wypełnić ten formularz. _proh_-sheh vyh-_pehw_-n'eech' tehn fohr-_moo_-lash'

Please fill out this form.

Poproszę dowód tożsamości. poh-_proh_-sheh _doh_-voot tohsh'-sah-_mohsh'_-ch'ee

Your identification, please.

Gdzie/Kiedy to się stało? gdj'eh/_kyeh_-dyh toh sh'yeh _stah_-woh

When/Where did it happen?

Jak on/ona wygląda? yahk ohn/_oh_-nah vyh-_glohn_-dah

What does he/she look like?

In an emergency, dial: **112** for the police
998 for the fire brigade
999 for the ambulance.

Health

I'm sick [ill].	**Jestem chory** m **/chora** f. _yeh_-stehm _hoh_-ryh/_hoh_-rah
I don't feel well.	**Źle się czuję.** zh'leh sh'yeh _choo_-yeh
Is there an English-speaking doctor?	**Czy jest tu lekarz mówiący po angielsku?** chyh yehst too _leh_-kahsh moo-_vyohn_-tsyh poh ahn-_gyehls_-koo
It hurts here.	**Boli mnie tutaj.** _boh_-lee mn'yeh _too_-tay
I have a stomachache.	**Boli mnie brzuch.** _boh_-lee mn'yeh bzhooh

I'm (…months) pregnant. **Jestem w (…miesiącu) ciąży.** _yehs_·tehm fho _(…myeh·sh'ohntsoo)_ ch'yon·_zhyh_

I'm on… **Zażywam…** zah·_zhyh_·vahm…

I'm allergic to antibiotics/ penicillin. **Mam uczulenie na antybiotyki/penicylinę.** Mahm oo·choo·_leh_·n'yeh nah ahn·tyh·_byoh_·tyh·kee/ peh·nee·tsyh·_lee_·neh

Dictionary

adapter **przejściówka**
and **i**
antiseptic cream **krem aseptyczny**
aspirin **aspiryna**
baby **dziecko**
backpack _n_ **plecak**; _v_ **wędrować z plecakiem**
bad **zły**
bag **torba**
bandage **bandaż**
battle site **pole bitwy**
bikini **bikini**
bird **ptak**
black **czarny**
bland **mdły**
blue **niebieski**
bottle opener **otwieracz do butelek**
bowl **miska**
boy **chłopiec**
boyfriend **chłopak**
bra **biustonosz**
camera **aparat fotograficzny**
can opener **otwieracz do puszek**
castle **zamek**
cigarette **papieros**
cold _adj_ **zimny**; _adv_ **zimno**; _n_ (illness) **przeziębienie**

comb **grzebień**
computer **komputer**
condom **prezerwatywa**
corkscrew **korkociąg**
cup **filiżanka**
dangerous **niebezpieczny**
deodorant **dezodorant**
diabetic _n_ **cukrzyk**
doll **lalka**
fly _n_ **mucha**; _v_ **latać**
fork **widelec**
girl **dziewczyna**
girlfriend **dziewczyna**
glass (non-alcoholic) **szklanka**; (alcoholic) **kieliszek**
good **dobry**
gray **szary**
great _adj_ **świetny**; _adv_ **świetnie**
green **zielony**
hairspray **lakier do włosów**
horse **koń**
hot **gorący**
husband **mąż**
icy **oblodzony**
injection **zastrzyk**
insect repellent **środek na owady**
jeans **dżinsy**

knife **nóż**
large (size) **duży**
lighter *adj* **jaśniejszy**; *n* **zapalniczka**
love *n* **miłość**; *v* **kochać**
match (game) **mecz**; (light) **zapałka**
medium **średni**
museum **muzeum**
my **mój**
napkin **serwetka**
nurse **pielęgniarka**
or **albo**
orange (color) **pomarańczowy**
paracetamol *[BE]* **paracetamol**
park *n* **park**; *v* **parkować**
partner **partner**
pen **długopis**
pink **różowy**
plate **talerz**
purple **fioletowy**
rain *n* **deszcz**
raincoat **płaszcz przeciwdeszczowy**
razor **maszynka do golenia**
razor blade **żyletka**
red **czerwony**
sandal **sandał**
sanitary napkin **podpaska**
sauna **sauna**
scissors **nożyczki**
shampoo **szampon**
shoe **but**
small **mały**
sneaker **tenisówka**
snow **śnieg**
soap **mydło**
sock **skarpetka**
spicy **ostry**

spoon **łyżka**
stamp (postal) **znaczek**
suitcase **walizka**
sunglasses **okulary słoneczne**
suntan lotion **krem do opalania**
sweater **sweter**
sweatshirt **bluza**
swimsuit **kostium kąpielowy**
tampon **tampon**
terrible **okropny**
tie **krawat**
tissue **chusteczka**
toilet paper **papier toaletowy**
toothbrush **szczoteczka do zębów**
toothpaste **pasta do zębów**
toy **zabawka**
T-shirt **t-shirt**
underwear **bielizna**
vegetarian *adj* **wegetariański**; *n*
   wegetarianin
white **biały**

Romanian

Essentials

Hello.	**Bună.** *booner*
Goodbye.	**La revedere.** *la revedereh*
Yes.	**Da.** *da*
No.	**Nu.** *noo*
Fine.	**Bine.** *beeneh*
Excuse me! (to get attention, to get past)	**Pardon, vă rog!** *pardon ver rog*
I'm sorry.	**Scuzaţi-mă, vă rog.** *scoozatsee-mer, ver rog*
I'd like…	**Aş vrea…** *ash vreh-a…*
How much?	**Cât costă?** *cuht coster*
Where is…?	**Unde este…?** *oondeh yesteh…*
Please.	**Vă rog.** *ver rog*
Thank you.	**Mulţumesc.** *mooltsoomesc*
You're welcome.	**Nu aveţi pentru ce.** *noo avetsy pentroo cheh*
Please speak slowly.	**Puteţi să vorbiţi mai rar, vă rog?** *pootetsy ser vorbeetsy migh rar ver rog*
Can you repeat that, please?	**Puteţi să repetaţi asta?** *pootetsy ser repetatsy asta*
I don't understand.	**Nu înteleg.** *noo uhntseleg*
Do you speak English?	**Vorbiţi englezeşte?** *vorbeetsy englezeshteh*
I don't speak Romanian.	**Nu vorbesc româneşte.** *noo vorbesc romuhnehshteh*
Where's the restroom [toilet]?	**Unde este toaleta?** *oondeh yesteh twaleta*
Help!	**Ajutor!** *ajootor*

You'll find the pronunciation of the Romanian letters and words written in gray after each sentence to guide you. Simply pronounce these as if they were English, noting that any underlines and bolds indicate an additional emphasis or stress or a lengthening of a vowel sound. As you hear the language being spoken, you will quickly become accustomed to the local pronunciation and dialect.

Numbers

0	**zero**	*zero*
1	**unu**	*oonoo*
2	**doi**	*doy*
3	**trei**	*tray*
4	**patru**	*patroo*
5	**cinci**	*cheenchy*
6	**şase**	*shaseh*
7	**şapte**	*shapteh*
8	**opt**	*opt*
9	**nouă**	*no-wer*
10	**zece**	*zecheh*
11	**unsprezece**	*oonsprezecheh*
12	**doisprezece**	*doysprezecheh*
13	**treisprezece**	*traysprezecheh*
14	**paisprezece**	*pighsprezecheh*
15	**cincisprezece**	*cheenchysprezecheh*
16	**şaisprezece**	*shighsprezecheh*
17	**şaptesprezece**	*shaptesprezecheh*
18	**optsprecece**	*optsprezecheh*
19	**nouăsprezece**	*no-wersprezecheh*
20	**douăzeci**	*do-werzechy*
21	**douăzeci şi unu**	*do-werzechy shee oonoo*
22	**douăzeci şi doi**	*do-werzechy shee doy*
30	**treizeci**	*trayzechy*
31	**treizeci şi unu**	*trayzechy shee oonoo*
40	**patruzeci**	*patroo*
50	**cincizeci**	*cheenchyzechy*
60	**şaizeci**	*shighzechy*
70	**şaptezeci**	*shaptehzechy*
80	**optzeci**	*optzechy*
90	**nouăzeci**	*no-werzechy*
100	**o sută**	*o sooter*
101	**o sută unu**	*o sooter oonoo*
200	**două sute**	*do-wer sooteh*
500	**cinci sute**	*cheenchy sooteh*
1,000	**o mie**	*o mee-eh*

| 10,000 | **zece mii** *zecheh mee* |
| 1,000,000 | **un milion** *oon meelee-on* |

Time

What time is it?	**Cât e ora?** *cuht ye ohrah*
It's midday.	**Este amiază.** *yesteh ameeaser*
At midnight.	**la miezul nopţii.** *la myezool noptsee*
From one o'clock to two o'clock.	**De la ora unu la ora două.** *deh la ohrah oonoo la ora do-wer*
Five past three.	**Trei şi cinci.** *trey shee cheenchy*
A quarter to ten.	**Zece fără un sfert.** *zecheh fer-rer oon sfehrt*
5:30 a.m./p.m.	

Days

Monday	**luni** *loony*
Tuesday	**marţi** *martsy*
Wednesday	**miercuri** *myercoory*
Thursday	**joi** *zhoy*
Friday	**vineri** *veenery*
Saturday	**sâmbătă** *suhmberter*
Sunday	**duminică** *doomeeneecer*

Dates

yesterday	**ieri** *yery*
today	**azi** *azy*
tomorrow	**mâine** *muhyneh*
day	**zi** *zee*
week	**săptămână** *serptermuhner*
month	**lună** *looner*
year	**an** *an*

Months

January	**ianuarie** *yanoo-aree-eh*
February	**februarie** *febroo-aree-eh*
March	**martie** *martee-eh*
April	**aprilie** *apreelee-eh*
May	**mai** *migh*

June	**iunie** *yoonee-eh*
July	**iulie** *yoolee-eh*
August	**august** *aoogoost*
September	**septembrie** *septembree-eh*
October	**octombire** *octombree-eh*
November	**noiembrie** *noyembree-eh*
December	**decembrie** *dechembree-eh*

Arrival & Departure

I'm on vacation/ business.	**Sunt în vacanţă/Am venit în interes de serviciu.** *soont uhn vacantser/am veneet uhn eenteres deh serveechee-oo*
I'm going to...	**Merg la/Cu destinaţia spre...** *merg la/coo desteenats'a spreh*
I'm staying at the...Hotel.	**O să stau la hotelul...** *o ser sta°° la hotelool...*

Money

Where's...?	**Unde se află...?** *oondeh seh afler...*
the ATM	**bancomatul** *bancomatool*
the bank	**o bancă** *o bancer*
the currency exchange office	**birou de schimb** *beero-ool deh skeemb*
When does the bank open/close?	**Când se deschide/închide banca?** *Cuhnd seh deskeedeh/uhnkeedeh banca*
I'd like to change pounds dollars/sterling into Lei.	**Aş dori să schimb dolari/lire sterline în lei.** *Ash doree ser skeemb dolar'/leereh sterleeneh uhn ley*
I'd like to cash. traveler's cheques	**Acceptaţi cecuri de voiaj?** *accheptats' checoor' deh vo-yazh*

For Numbers, see page 196.

YOU MAY SEE...

Romania's currency is **Leu** (plural **Lei** *lay*), abbreviated to **RON**.
Notes: 1, 5, 10, 50, 100 and 500 **lei** *lay*
Coins: 1, 5, 10 and 50 **bani** *bahnee*
1 leu = 100 bani

Getting Around

How do I get to town?	**Cum să ajung în oraş?**	_coom_ ser _azhoong_ uhn or_ash_
Where's...?	**Unde este...?**	_oondeh yesteh_ ...
the airport	**aeroportul**	aero_portool_
the train station	**gara**	_gara_
the bus station	**staţia de autobuz**	_statsya_ deh _aootobooz_
the subway [underground] station	**staţia de metrou**	_statsyeh_ deh _metrooo_
Is it far from here?	**Este departe de aici?**	_yesteh_ departeh deh _aeechy_
Where do I buy a ticket?	**Unde pot să-mi cumpăr un bilet?**	_oondeh_ pot sermy _coomper_ oon bee_let_
A one-way/return-trip ticket to...	**(bilet) dus/dus-întors pentru...**	(beelet) doos/doos-uhn_tors_ _pentroo_
How much?	**Cât costă?**	cuht _coster_
Which gate/line?	**De la care poartă/linie?**	Deh la _careh_ _pwarter_/_leeneeeh_
Which platform?	**De la ce peron?**	deh la cheh pe_ron_
Where can I get a taxi?	**De unde pot lua taxi?**	deh _oondeh_ pot loo-_a_ taxee
Take me to this address.	**Vreau să merg la adresa aceasta.**	vra_oo_ ser merg la a_dresa_ a_chasta_
Can I have a map?	**Îmi puteţi da o hartă?**	uhm_y_ poo_tetsy_ da o _harter_

Tickets

When's...to Paris?	**La ce oră pleacă...spre Paris?**	la cheh _orer_ pleh-_acer_...spreh _Paris_
the (first) bus	**(primul) autobuz**	(_preemool_) aootobooz
the (next) flight	**(următorul) zbor**	(oormer_torool_) zbor
the (last) train	**(ultimul) tren regio**	(_oolteemool_) tren rejee-o
Where do I buy a ticket?	**De unde pot cumpăra un bilet?**	deh _oondeh_ pot coomperah oon beelet
One/Two ticket(s) please.	**Un/Două bilet(e), vă rog.**	_oon_/_dohooer_ bee_let_/beel_eteh_, ver _rog_
For today/tomorrow.	**azi/mâine**	az_y_/muh_y_neh
A...ticket.	**Un bilet...**	_oon_ beelet ...
one-way	**numai dus**	_noomigh_ doos
return trip	**dus-întors**	doos-uhn_tors_
first class	**clasa întâi**	clasa uhntuh_y_
business class	**business class**	business class
economy class	**clasa a doua**	_clasa_ _a_ dowa

How much?	**Cât costă?** *cuht coster*
Is there a discount for...?	**Există o reducere pentru...?**
	egzeester oh rehdoochehreh pentroo...
children	**copii** *copeeʸ*
students	**studenți** *stoodentsʸ*
senior citizens	**persoane în vârstă** *pehrswaneh uhn vuhrster*
tourists	**turişti** *tooreeshtʸ*
The express bus/ train, please.	**Autobuzul expres/Trenul inter-city, vă rog.**
	aootoboozool ekspres/trenool inter-city, ver rog
The local bus/train, please.	**Autobuzul local/Trenul regio, vă rog.**
	aootoboozool local/trenool rejee-o, ver rog
I have an e-ticket.	**Am un bilet electronic.** *am oon beelet electroneec*
Can I buy a ticket on the bus/train?	**Pot cumpăra un bilet în autobuz/tren?**
	pot coomperra oon beelet uhn aootobooz/tren
Do I have to stamp the ticket before boarding?	**Trebuie să compostez biletul înainte de îmbarcare?**
	trebooye ser compostez beeletool uhnaheenteh deh uhmbarcareh
How long is this ticket valid?	**Cât timp este valabil acest bilet?** *cuht teemp yesteh*
	valabeel achest beelet
Can I return on the same ticket?	**Pot să mă întorc utilizând acelaşi bilet?**
	poht ser mer uhntorc ooteeleezuhnd achelash beelet
I'd like to...	**Aş vrea să...rezervarea.** *ash vreh-a ser...rezervareh-a*
my reservation.	
cancel	**anulez** *anoolez*
change	**schimb** *skeemb*
confirm	**confirm** *confeerm*

For Time, see page 197.

Car Hire

Where's the car hire?	**Unde este biroul de închirieri auto?** *oondeh yesteh*
	beero-ool deh uhnkeeree-eree aᵒᵒto
I'd like...	**Aş dori...** *ash doree...*
a cheap/small car	**o maşină ieftină/mică** *o masheener yefteener/meecer*
an automatic/ a manual	**cu cutie automată/manuală**
	coo cootee-eh aootomater/manwaler
air conditioning	**aer condiţionat** *aer conditsyonat*
a car seat	**scaun pentru copil** *scaoon pentroo copeel*

How much…?	**Cât costă?** _cuht coster_
per day/week	**pe zi/săptămână** _pe/zee serptermerner_
per kilometer	**pe kilometru** _pe kilometroo_
for unlimited mileage	**pentru un număr nelimitat de kilometri** _pentroo oon noomer neleemeetat deh kilometree_
with insurance	**cu asigurare** _coo aseegoorareh_
Are there any discounts?	**Oferiți și reduceri?** _ofereetsy shee redoochehry_

YOU MAY HEAR…

drept înainte _drept uhnaeenteh_	straight ahead
stânga _stuhngah_	left
dreapta _dreh-aptah_	right
după colț _dooper colts_	around the corner
vis-à-vis _veez-a-vee_	opposite
înapoi; în spate _uhnapoy; uhn spateh_	behind
lângă _luhnger_	next to
după _duper_	after
nord/sud _nord, sood_	north/south
est/vest _est/vest_	east/west
la semafor _la semafor_	at the traffic light
la intersecție _la intersectsyeh_	at the intersection

Places to Stay

Can you recommend a hotel?	**Puteți să-mi recomandați un hotel?** _pootetsy sermy recomandatsy oon hotel_
I made a reservation.	**Am o rezervare.** _am o rezervareh_
My name is…	**Mă numesc…** _mer noomesc…_
Do you have a room…?	**Aveți o cameră…?** _avetsy oh camerer …_
for one/two	**pentru o persoană/două persoane** _pentroo o perswaner/do-wer perswaneh_
with a bathroom	**cu baie** _coo bayeh_
with air conditioning	**cu aer condiționat** _coo a-er condeetsee-onat_

For...	**Pentru...** _Pentroo..._
Tonight	**O noapte** _O nwapteh_
two nights	**două nopți** _do-wer nopts^y_
one week	**o săptămână** _o serptermuhner_
How much?	**Cât costă?** _cuht coster_
Is there anything cheaper?	**Aveți ceva mai ieftin?** _avets^ycheva migh yefteen_
When's check-out?	**Când trebuie eliberată camera?**
	Cuhnd trebooye eleebehrater camera
Can I leave this in the safe?	**Pot să las asta în seif?** _Pot ser las asta uhn seif_
Can I leave my bags?	**Pot să îmi las bagajele?** _Pot ser uhm^y las bagazheleh_
The bill please.	**Nota de plată, vă rog!** _nota deh plater ver rog_
Can I have a receipt?	**Puteți să-mi dați, vă rog, o chitanță?** _pootets^y sermy dats^y_
	ver rog o keetantser
I'll pay in cash/	**Voi plăti cu numerar/card de credit.** _Voi plertee coo_
by credit card.	_noomerar/card deh credeet_

Communications

Where's an	**Unde se află pe aici un Internet-Cafe?** _oondeh seh afler_
internet cafe?	_pe aeechy uhn eenternet cafe_
Does it have wireless	**Are Internet wireless?** _are eenternet wireless_
internet?	
What is the WiFi	**Care este parola pentru WiFi?**
password?	_care yesteh parolah pentroo Wee-Fee_
Is the WiFi free?	**Este gratuit WiFi-ul?** _yesteh gratooeet Wee-Fee-ool_
Do you have bluetooth?	**Aveți Bluetooth?** _avets^y Bluetooth_
Can you show me how to	**Îmi puteți arăta cum să pornesc/opresc computerul?**
turn on/off the computer?	_uhm^y pootets^y arerta coom ser pornesc/opresc compyooterool_
Can I...?	**Pot să...** _pot ser..._
access the internet	**accesez Internetul** _akchesez eenternetool_
check my e-mail	**verific e-mail-ul** _vereefeec ee-maylool_
print	**imprim** _eempreem_
plug in/charge my	**conectez/încarc laptopul/iPhone-ul/iPad-**
laptop/iPhone/	**ul/BlackBerry-ul?** _conectez/uhncarc laptopool,_
iPad/BlackBerry?	_iPhoneool/iPadool/BlackBerryool_
access Skype?	**accesez Skype-ul?** _akchesez Skype-ool_
How much per half	**Cât costă o jumătate de oră/o oră de folosire?**
hour/hour?	_cuht coster o joomratateh deh orer/o orer deh foloseere_

How do I...?	**Cum să (mă)...?** *coom ser (mer)* ...
connect/disconnect	**conectez/deconectez** *conectez/deconectez*
log on/off	**conectez/deconectez** *conectez/deconectez*
type this symbol	**tastez acest simbol** *tastez achest seembol*
What's your e-mail?	**Care este e-mail-ul dumneavoastră?**
	careh yesteh ee-maylool doomneh-avwastrer
My e-mail is...	**E-mail-ul meu este...** *ee-maylool me⁰⁰ yesteh*...
Do you have a scanner?	**Aveţi un scaner?** *avetsʸ oon scanner*

Social Media

Are you on Facebook/Twitter?	**Ai cont pe Facebook/Twitter?** *Ay cont peh Facebook/Twitter*
What's your user name?	**Care este numele tău de utilizator?** *Careh yesteh noomeleh teroo deh ooteeleezator*
I'll add you as a friend.	**Te voi adăuga ca prieten.** *Teh voi aderoogah ca pree-ehten*
I'll follow you on Twitter.	**Te voi urmări pe Twitter.** *Teh voi oormeree peh Twitter*
Are you following...?	**Umăreşti...?** *Oormereshtʸ*...

Conversation

Hello!/Hi!	**Bună!** *booner*
How are you?	**Ce mai faceţi?** *cheh migh fachetsʸ*
Fine, thanks.	**Mulţumesc bine.** *mooltsoomesc beeneh*
Excuse me!	**Pardon, vă rog!** *pardon ver rog*
Do you speak English?	**Vorbiţi englezeşte?** *Vorbeetsʸ englezeshteh*
What's your name?	**Cum vă numiţi?** *coom ver noomeetsʸ*
My name is...	**Mă numesc...** *mer noomesc*...
Nice to meet you.	**Încântat de cunoştinţă.** *uhncuhntat deh coonoshteentser*
Where are you from?	**De unde veniţi?** *deh oondeh veneetsʸ*
I'm from the U.K./U.S.	**Vin din Marea Britanie/Statele Unite.** *veen deen Mareh-ah Breetanyeh/Stateleh Ooneeteh*
What do you do for a living?	**Cu ce vă ocupaţi?** *coo cheh ver ocoopatsʸ*
I work for...	**Lucrez pentru...** *Loocrez pentroo* ...
I'm a student.	**Sunt student.** *soont stoodent*
I'm retired.	**Sunt pensionar.** *Soont pensee-onar*
Do you like...?	**Doriţi...?** *doreetsʸ* ...

| Goodbye. | **La revedere.** *la revedereh* |
| See you later. | **Pe curând.** *peh coaruhnd* |

Romance

Would you like to go out for a drink/dinner?	**Vrei să ieşim să bem ceva/să luăm cina?** *vrey ser yesheem ser bem cheva/ser lwerm cheenah*
What are your plans for tonight/tomorrow?	**Ce planuri ai pentru diseară/mâine?** *cheh planoor^y igh pentroo deeseh-arer/muhyneh*
Can I have your (phone) number?	**Îmi dai numărul tău de telefon?** *Uhm^y digh noomer-rool ter^{oo} deh telefon*
Can I join you?	**Pot să te însoţesc?** *pot ser teh uhnsotsesc*
Can I buy you a drink?	**Ce doriţi să beţi?** *cheh doreets^y ser bets^y*
I love you.	**Te iubesc.** *teh yoobesc*

Accepting & Rejecting

I'd love to.	**Cu plăcere.** *coo plerchereh*
Where should we meet?	**Unde ne întâlnim?** *oondeh neh uhntuhlneem*
I'll meet you at the bar/your hotel.	**Ne întâlnim la bar/la hotelul tău.** *Neh uhntuhlneem la bar/la hoteelool ter^{oo}*
I'll come by at…	**O să vin la…** *Oh ser veen la…*
I'm busy.	**Sunt ocupat.** *soont ocoopat*
I'm not interested.	**Nu mă interesează.** *noo mer eenteresazer*
Leave me alone.	**Lăsaţi-mă în pace.** *lersatsee-mer uhn pacheh*
Stop bothering me!	**Nu mă mai deranja!** *Noo mer migh deranzhah*

Food & Drink

Eating Out

| Can you recommend a good restaurant/bar? | **Îmi puteţi recomanda un restaurant/bar bun?** *uhm^y pootets^y recomanda oon resta^{oo}rant/bar boon* |
| Is there a traditional/an inexpensive restaurant nearby? | **Există vreun restaurant tradiţional/nu prea scump prin apropiere?** *egzeester vreh-oon resta^{oo}rant traditsional/noo preh-a scoomp preen apropee-ereh* |

A table for…, please.	**Putem avea o masă…?** *pootem aveh-a o maser*	
Can we sit…?	**Putem sta…?** *pootem sta*	
here/there	**aici/acolo?** *a-eechy/acolo*	
outside	**afară** *afarer*	
in a non-smoking area	**într-o zonă pentru nefumători** *uhntroh zoner pentroo nefoomertory*	
I'm waiting for someone.	**Aştept pe cineva.** *Ashtept peh cheneva.*	
Where are the toilets?	**Unde este toaleta?** *oondeh yesteh twaleta*	
The menu, please.	**Meniul, vă rog.** *menee-ool ver rog*	
What do you recommend?	**Ce ne recomandaţi?** *cheh neh recomandatsy*	
I'd like…	**Aş vrea…** *ash vreh-a*	
Some more…, please.	**Mai vreau puţin…, vă rog.** *migh vreh-a⁰⁰ pootseen,…ver rog*	
Enjoy your meal!	**Poftă bună!** *Pofter booner*	
The check [bill], please	**Nota de plată, vă rog.** *Notah deh plater, ver rog*	
Is service included?	**Serviciul este inclus?** *serveechyool yesteh eencloos*	
Can I pay by credit card/have a receipt?	**Pot plăti cu această carte de credit?** *pot plertee coo achaster carteh deh credeet*	

YOU MAY SEE…

MENIU FIX	set menu
LISTĂ DE VINURI	wine list
MÂNCĂRURI PENTRU VEGETARIENI	vegetarian dishes
SPECIALITĂŢI ALE ZILEI	specials of the day
PREŢ	price
SERVICIUL ESTE INCLUS	service included

Breakfast

slănină *slerneener*	bacon
pâine *puhyneh*	bread
unt *oont*	butter
brânză *bruhnzer*	cheese
ouă *o-wer*	eggs
şuncă şi ouă *shooncer shee o-wer*	ham and eggs

gem/jeleu *jem/jele°°*	jam/jelly
chifle *keefleh*	roll
pâine prăjită *puhyneh prerzheeter*	toast
cârnaţi *cuhrnatsy*	sausage
iaurt *yaoort*	yogurt

Appetizers

cabanos prăjit *cabanos prerjeet*	fried pieces of sausage
cârnaţi cu usturoi *cuhrnatsy coo oostooroy*	garlic sausage
mezeluri *mezeloory*	assortment of cold meats
muşchi filet *mooshky feeleh*	processed pork sirloin
pastramă *pastramer*	smoked mutton
paté de ficat *pateh deh feecat*	liver paté
salată de vinete *salater deh veeneteh*	aubergine salad
sardele *sardeleh*	sardines
şuncă *shooncer*	ham

Meat

carne de vacă *carneh deh vacer*	beef
pulpă de miel *poolper de myehl*	leg of lamb
pui *pooy*	chicken
raţă *ratser*	duck
carne de porc *carneh deh porc*	pork
carne de viţel *carneh deh veetsel*	veal
caltaboş cu sânge *caltabosh coo suhnjeh*	black pudding
cap de porc *cap deh porc*	pig's head
căprioară *cerpreewarer*	venison

Fish & Seafood

biban *beeban*	river perch
caviar *cavyar*	caviar
crab *crab*	crab
crap *crap*	carp
creveţi *crevetsy*	shrimps
homar *homar*	lobster
macrou *macro°°*	mackerel
sardele *sardeleh*	sardines

sturion *stooryon*		sturgeon
știucă *shtyoocer*		pike
țipar *tseepar*		eel

Vegetables

fasole (boabe) *fasoleh (bwabeh)*	beans
varză *varzer*	cabbage
ciuperci *chooperchy*	mushrooms
ceapă *chaper*	onions
cartofi *cartofy*	potatoes
roșii *rosheey*	tomatoes

Sauces & Condiments

sare *sareh*	salt
piper *peeper*	pepper
muștar *mooshtar*	mustard
ketchup *ketchoop*	ketchup

Fruit & Dessert

mere *mereh*	apples
banane *bananeh*	bananas
lămâi *lermuhy*	lemons
portocale *portocaleh*	oranges
prune *prooneh*	plums
căpșune *cerpshooneh*	strawberries
bezele *bezeleh*	small meringues
înghetață *uhngetsater*	ice cream
ștrudel cu mere *shtroodel coo mereh*	apple strudel
tort *tort*	large layer cake

Drinks

The wine list/drink menu, please.	**Puteți să-mi dați lista de vinuri, vă rog?** *pootetsy sermy datsy leesta deh veenoory ver rog*
What do you recommend?	**Ce îmi recomandați?** *cheh uhmy recomandatsy*
I'd like a bottle/glass of red/white wine.	**Aș vrea o sticlă/un pahar de vin roșu/alb.** *ash vreh-a o steecler deh veen roshoo/alb*
The house wine, please.	**Vinul casei, vă rog.** *Veenool casey, ver rog*

Another bottle/ glass, please.	**Mai aduceţi-mi o sticlă/un pahar de..., vă rog.** *migh adoochetseemʸ o steecler/oon pahar deh...ver rog*
I'd like a local beer.	**Aş vrea o bere locală.** *ash vreh-a o bereh loc(aler*
What would you like to drink?	**Ce doriţi să beţi?** *cheh doreetsʸ ser betsʸ*
Cheers!	**Noroc!** *noroc*
A coffee/tea, please.	**O cafea/un ceai, vă rog.** *o cafeh-a/oon chaʸ ver rog*
Black.	**Neagră.** *neh-agrer*
With...	**Cu...** *coo...*
milk	**lapte** *lapteh*
sugar	**zahăr** *zaherr*
artificial sweetener	**îndulcitor artificial** *undoolchitor arteefeecyal*
A..., please.	**..., vă rog.** *oon..., ver rog.*
juice	**un suc** *oon sooc*
soda	**un sifon** *oon seefon*
sparkling/still water	**O apă gazoasă/plată** *oh aper gazwaser/plater*

Leisure Time

Sightseeing

Where's the tourist information office?	**Unde se află oficiul de turism?** *oondeh seh afler ofee-chee-ool deh tooreesm*
What are the main sights?	**Care sunt obiectivele turistice importante?** *careh soont obyectee-veleh tooreesteecheh eemportanteh*
Do you offer tours in English?	**Oferiţi excursii în limba engleză?** *Ofereetsʸ excoorseeʸ uhn leembah englezer*
Can I have a map/guide?	**Îmi puteţi da o hartă/un ghid?** *Uhmʸ pootetsʸ dah oh harter/oon geed*

YOU MAY SEE...

deschis/închis *deskees/uhnkees*	open/closed
leşire *yeshire*	exit

Shopping

Where's the market/mall?	**Unde-i o piață** *oondeh^y o pyatser*
I'm just looking.	**Mă uit doar.** *mer ooyt dwar*
Can you help me?	**Puteti să mă ajutati?** *pootets^y ser mer azhootats^y*
I'm being helped.	**Sunt ajutat.** *Soont azhootat*
How much?	**Cât costă?** *cuht coster*
That one, please.	**acela, vă rog** *achela ver rog*
That's all.	**Asta-i tot.** *asta^y tot*
Where can I pay?	**Unde pot să plătesc?** *Oonde pot ser plertesc*
I'll pay in cash/	**O să plătesc cu această carte de credit?**
by credit card.	*o ser plertehsc coo achaster carteh deh credeet*
A receipt, please.	**Puteti să-mi dati, vă rog, o chitantă?** *pootets^y serm^y dats^y ver rog o keetantser*

Sport & Leisure

When's the game?	**Când este jocul?** *Cuhnd yesteh zhocool*
Where's...?	**Unde este...?** *oondeh yesteh...*
the beach	**plajă** *plazher*
the park	**parcul** *parcool*
the pool	**piscină** *pees-cheener*
Is it safe to swim here?	**Se poate înota în siguranță aici?** *Seh pwateh uhnota seegoorantser a-eech^y*
Can I hire clubs?	**Pot să închiriez crose de golf?** *Pot ser uhnkeeree-ehz croseh deh golf*
How much per hour/day?	**Cât costă o oră/zi de folosire?** *cuht coster o orer/zee deh foloseere*
How far is it to...?	**Este departe până la...?** *yesteh departeh puhner la*
Show me on the map, please.	**Puteti să-mi arătați pe hartă.** *pootets^y serm^y arertats^y peh harter*

Going Out

What's there to do at night?	**Ce se poate face noaptea?** *Cheh seh pwateh facheh nwapteh-a?*
Do you have a program of events?	**Aveți un program al evenimentelor?** *Avets^y oon program al eveneementelor*

What's playing tonight?	**Ce rulează în seara asta?**
	Cheh rooleh-azer uhn seh-ara asta
Where's…?	**Unde este… _oon_deh ehsteh…**
the downtown area	**zona centrală** *zona cen_tra_ler*
the bar	**barul** *_ba_rool*
the dance club	**discoteca** *deesco_te_ca*

Baby Essentials

Do you have…?	**Aveți…?** *avetsy…*
a baby bottle	**un biberon** *oon beeberon*
baby food	**alimente pentru copii** *aleementeh pentroo copeey*
baby wipes	**şerveţele pentru copii** *shervetseleh pentroo copeey*
a car seat	**un scaun auto pentru copii**
	oon scaoon a-ootoh pentroo copeey
a children's menu/ portion	**un meniu/o porţie pentru copii**
	oon meneeoo/o portsee-eh pentroo copeey
a child's seat/ highchair	**un scaun de masă pentru copii**
	oon scaoon deh maser pentroo copee
a crib/cot	**un pătuţ** *oon pertoots*
diapers [nappies]	**scutece de unică folosinţă** *scootecheh deh ooneecer*
	foloseentser
formula	**lapte praf** *lapteh praf*
a pacifier [dummy]	**o suzetă** *o soozeter*
a playpen	**un ţarc pentru copii** *oon tsarc pentroo copeey*
a stroller [pushchair]	**un cărucior** *oon cer-roochor*
Can I breastfeed the baby here?	**Pot alăpta bebeluşul aici?**
	Pot alerpta bebelooshool a-eechy
Where can I breastfeed/change the baby?	**Unde aş putea alăpta/schimba bebeluşul?**
	_Oon_de ash pootee-a alerpta/skeemba bebelooshool

For Eating Out, see page 204.

Disabled Travelers

Is there…?	**Este/Există…?** *_yes_teh/eg_zees_ter*
access for the disabled	**Există acces pentru persoane invalide?**
	eg_zees_ter ac_ches_ pen_tro_o pers_wa_neh eenva_lee_deh

a wheelchair ramp	**o rampă pentru scaune cu rotile**
	o ramper pentroo scaooneh coo roteeleh
a disabled- accessible toilet	**o toaletă pentru persoane cu handicap** *o twaleter pentroo pehrswaneh coo handeecap*
I need…	**Am nevoie de …** *am nevoyeh deh*
assistance	**ajutor** *azhootor*
an elevator [a lift]	**liftul** *leeftool*
a ground-floor room	**o cameră la parter** *o camerer la partehr*

Health & Emergencies

Emergencies

Help!	**Ajutor!** *ajootor*
Go away!	**Pleacă de aici!** *pleh-acer deh a-eechy*
Stop, thief!	**Stop, hoţul!** *stop hotsool*
Get a doctor!	**Chemaţi un doctor!** *kematsy oon doctor*
Fire!	**Foc!** *foc*
I'm lost.	**M-am rătăcit.** *mam rertercheet*
Can you help me?	**Puteţi să mă ajutaţi?** *pootetsy ser mer azhootatsy*
Police!	**Poliţia!** *poleetsee-a*
Call the police!	**Chemaţi poliţia!** *kematsy poleetsee-a*
Where's the police station?	**Unde este un post de poliţie?** *oondeh yesteh oon post deh poleetsee-eh?*
My child is missing.	**Copilul meu s-a pierdut.** *copeelool meoo sa pyerdoot*

YOU MAY HEAR…

Completaţi acest formular.
completatsy achest formoolar

Fill out this form.

Documentul de identitate, vă rog.
docoomentool deh eedenteetateh, ver rog

Your ID, please.

Când/Unde s-a întâmplat?
Cuhnd/Oonde sa uhtermplat

When/Where did it happen?

Ce înfăţişare a avut? *Cheh uhnfertseshare a avoot*

What does he/she look like?

In an emergency in all European Union countries, you can dial: **112**

Health

I'm sick.	**Sunt bolnav.** *soont bolnav*
I need an English-speaking doctor.	**Unde pot găsi un doctor care vorbeşte englezeşte?** *oondeh pot gersee oon doctor careh vorbeshteh englezeshteh*
It hurts here.	**Mă doare aici.** *mer dwareh a-eechy*
Where's the pharmacy?	**Unde se află o farmacie (non stop) prin apropiere?** *oondeh seh afler o farmachee-eh preen preen apropee-ereh*
I'm (…months) pregnant.	**Sunt gravidă (în luna…).** *soont graveeder (…uhn loona)*
I'm on…	**Iau…** *Yaoo*
I'm allergic to antibiotics/penicillin.	**Sunt alergic m/alergică f la antibiotice/penicilină.** *soont alerjeec/alerjeecer la anoomeeteh anteebee-oteecheh/peneecheeleener*

Dictionary

adaptor **adaptor** *nt*
and **şi**
antiseptic cream **cremă f antiseptică**
aspirin **aspirină** *f*
baby **copil** *m*
bad **rău**
bag **sac** *m*; **pungă** *f*
Band-Aid® **pansamente** *ntpl*
bandage **bandaj** *nt*
beige **bej**
bird **pasăre** *f*
black **negru**
blue **albastru**
bottle-opener **deschizător** *nt* **de sticle**

boy **băiat** *m*
boyfriend **prieten** *m*
bra **sutien** *nt*
brown **maro**
camera **aparat de fotografiat**
can opener **deschizător** *n* **de conserve** *t*
castle **castel** *nt*
cigarette **ţigară** *f*
cold **rece; frig**
condom **preservativ** *m*
corkscrew **tirbuşon** *nt*
cup **ceaşcă** *f*
diabetic **diabetic**
dog **câine** *m*

doll **păpușă** f

fork **furculiță** f

girl **fată** f

girlfriend **prietenă** f

glass **pahar** nt

good **bun**

gray **gri**

green **verde**

hair spray **fixativ** nt **de păr**

hairbrush **perie** f **de păr**

husband **soț** m

ice **gheață** f

injection **injecție** f

insect repellent **spray** nt **contra insectelor**

jeans **blugi** mpl

knife **cuțit** nt

large **mare**

lighter **brichetă** f

lotion **loțiune** f

matches **chibrit** nt,

medium (meat) **bine făcut, potrivit**

museum **muzeu** nt

my **al meu**

napkin **șervețel** nt

nurse **soră (medicală)** f

or **sau**

orange (fruit) **portocală** f

orange (colour) **portocaliu**

park **parc** nt

pen **stilou** nt

pink **roz**

plate **farfurie** f

purple **roșu-închis, purpuriu**

rain **ploaie** f

raincoat **haină** f **de ploaie**

razor **aparat** nt **de ras**

razor blades **lamă** f **de ras**

red **roșu; wine vin** nt **roșu**

salty **sărat**

sandals **sandale** fpl

sanitary napkin/towel **tampon** nt **extern**

scissors **foarfece** nt; **foarfecă** f

shampoo **șampon** nt

shoe **pantof** m

small **mic**

sneaker **pantofi** mpl **de tenis**

snow **zăpadă** f

soap **săpun** nt

sock **șosetă** f

spoon **lingură** f

stamp (postage) **timbru** nt

suitcase **valiză** f

sun **soare** m

sun-tan cream **cremă** f **de bronzat**

sunglasses **ochelari** ntpl **de soare**

sweater **pulover** nt

swimsuit **costum** nt **de înot**

T-shirt **cămașă** f

tampon **tampon** nt **intern**

tissue (handkerchief) **batistă de hârtie** f

toilet paper **hârtie** f **igienică**

toothbrush **perie** f **de dinți**

toothpaste **pastă de dinți** f

tough (meat) **(carne) tare**

toy **jucărie** f

underpants **chiloți** mpl

white **alb**

wife **soție** f

with **cu**

without **fără**

yellow **galben**

Russian

Essentials

Hello.	**Здравствуйте.** _zdrahst_·vooy·tee
Goodbye.	**До свидания.** dah svee·_dah_·nee·yah
Yes.	**Да.** dah
No.	**Нет.** nyet
Okay.	**Хорошо.** khah·rah·_shoh_
Excuse me! (to get attention)	**Простите!** prah·_stee_·tee
Excuse me. (to get past)	**Разрешите.** rahz·ree·_shih_·tee
I'd like…	**Я хотел _m_/хотела _f_ бы…** yah khah·_tyehl_/khah·_tyeh_·lah bih…
How much?	**Сколько?** _skol'_·kah
Where is…?	**Где…?** gdyeh…
Please.	**Пожалуйста.** pah·_zhahl_·stah
Thank you!	**Спасибо!** spah·_see_·bah
You're welcome.	**Пожалуйста.** pah·_zhahl_·stah
Speak more slowly, please.	**Говорите медленнее, пожалуйста.** gah·vah·_ree_·tee _myed_·leen·nee·yeh pah·_zhahl_·stah
I don't understand.	**Я не понимаю.** yah nee pah·nee·_mah_·yoo
Do you speak English?	**Вы говорите по-английски?** vih gah·vah·_ree_·tee pah ahn·_gleey_·skee
I don't speak Russian.	**Я не говорю по-русски.** yah nyeh gah·vah·_ryoo_ pah·_roos_·kee
Where is the restroom [toilet]	**Где туалет?** gdyeh too·ah·_lyet_
Help!	**Помогите!** pah·mah·_gee_·tee

Numbers

0	**ноль** nol'
1	**один** ah·_deen_
2	**два** dvah
3	**три** tree
4	**четыре** chee·_tih_·ree
5	**пять** pyaht'
6	**шесть** shest'

7	**семь** *syem'*
8	**восемь** <u>*voh*</u>*•seem'*
9	**девять** <u>*dyeh*</u>*•veet'*
10	**десять** <u>*dyeh*</u>*•seet'*
11	**одиннадцать** *ah•*<u>*dee*</u>*•nah•tsaht'*
12	**двенадцать** *dvee•*<u>*nah*</u>*•tsaht'*
13	**тринадцать** *tree•*<u>*nah*</u>*•tsaht'*
14	**четырнадцать** *chee•*<u>*tihr*</u>*•nah•tsaht'*
15	**пятнадцать** *peet•*<u>*nah*</u>*•tsaht'*
16	**шестнадцать** *shihs•*<u>*nah*</u>*•tsaht'*
17	**семнадцать** *seem•*<u>*nah*</u>*•tsaht'*
18	**восемнадцать** *vah•seem•*<u>*nah*</u>*•tsaht'*
19	**девятнадцать** *dee•veet•*<u>*nah*</u>*•tsaht'*
20	**двадцать** <u>*dvah*</u>*•tsaht'*
21	**двадцать один** <u>*dvah*</u>*•tsaht' ah•*<u>*deen*</u>
22	**двадцать два** <u>*dvah*</u>*•tsaht' dvah*
30	**тридцать** <u>*tree*</u>*•tsaht'*
31	**тридцать один** <u>*tree*</u>*•tsaht' ah•*<u>*deen*</u>
40	**сорок** <u>*soh*</u>*•rahk*
50	**пятьдесят** *peet'•dee•*<u>*syaht*</u>
60	**шестьдесят** *sheez'•dee•*<u>*syaht*</u>
70	**семьдесят** <u>*syem'*</u>*•dee•seet*
80	**восемьдесят** <u>*voh*</u>*•seem'•dee•seet*
90	**девяносто** *dee•vee•*<u>*nos*</u>*•tah*
100	**сто** *stoh*
101	**сто один** *stoh ah•*<u>*deen*</u>
200	**двести** <u>*dvyes*</u>*•tee*
500	**пятьсот** *peet•*<u>*sot*</u>

You'll find the pronunciation of the Russian letters and words written in gray after each sentence to guide you. Simply pronounce these as if they were English, noting that any underlines and bolds indicate an additional emphasis or stress or a lengthening of a vowel sound. As you hear the language being spoken, you will quickly become accustomed to the local pronunciation and dialect.

1,000	**тысяча** _tih_•see•chah
10,000	**десять тысяч** _dyeh_•seet' _tih_•seech
1,000,000	**миллион** mee•lee•_on_

Time

What time is it?	**Который час?** kah•_toh_•riy chahs
It's noon [midday].	**Сейчас полдень.** see•_chahs pol_•deen'
At midnight.	**В полночь.** f _pol_•nahch
From nine o'clock	**С девяти до пяти часов.** s dee•vyah•_tee_ dah
to five o'clock.	pyah•_tee_ chah•_sof_
Twenty after [past] four.	**Двадцать минут пятого.** _dvah_•tsaht' mee•_noot_ pyah•tah•vah
A quarter to nine.	**Без четверти девять.** byes _chet_•veer•tee _dyeh_•veet'
5:30 a.m./p.m.	**Пять тридцать утра/вечера.** pyaht' _tree_•tsaht' oot•_rah_/ _vyeh_•chee•rah

Days

Monday	**понедельник** pah•nee•_dyel_'•neek
Tuesday	**вторник** _ftohr_•neek
Wednesday	**среда** sree•_dah_
Thursday	**четверг** cheet•_vyerk_
Friday	**пятница** _pyaht_•nee•tsah
Saturday	**суббота** soo•_boh_•tah
Sunday	**воскресенье** vahs•kree•_syen_'•yeh

Dates

yesterday	**вчера** fchee•_rah_
today	**сегодня** see•_vod_•nyah
tomorrow	**завтра** _zahf_•trah
day	**день** dyen'
week	**неделя** nee•_dyeh_•lyah
month	**месяц** _myeh_•seets
year	**год** got

Months

January	**январь** yeen•_vahr_'
February	**февраль** feev•_rahl_'
March	**март** mahrt

April	**апрель** *ahp·ryel'*
May	**май** *mie*
June	**июнь** *ee·yoon'*
July	**июль** *ee·yool'*
August	**август** *ahf·goost*
September	**сентябрь** *seen·tyahbr'*
October	**октябрь** *ahk·tyahbr'*
November	**ноябрь** *nah·yahbr'*
December	**декабрь** *dee·kahbr'*

Arrival & Departure

I'm here on vacation [holiday]/business.	**Я здесь в отпуске/по делам.** *yah zdyehs' v ot·poos·kee/pah dee·lahm*
I'm going to…	**Я еду в…** *yah yeh·doo v…*
I'm staying at the…Hotel	**Я живу в гостинице…** *yah zhih·voo v gahs·tee·nee·tseh…*

Money

Where's…?	**Где…?** *gdyeh…*
the ATM	**банкомат** *bahn·kah·maht*
the bank	**банк** *bahnk*
the currency exchange office	**обмен валюты** *ahb·myen vah·lyoo·tih*
What time does the bank open/close?	**Во сколько открывается/закрывается банк?** *va skol'·kah aht·krih·vah·ee·tsah/zah·krih·vah·ee·tsah bahnk*
I'd like to change dollars/pounds into rubles.	**Я хотел *m*/хотела *f* бы обменять доллары/фунты на рубли.** *yah khah·tyel/khah·tyeh·lah bih ahb·mee·nyaht' dol·lah·rih/foon·tih nah roob·lee*

YOU MAY SEE…

The monetary unit is the ruble (**рубль** *roobl'*), which is divided into 100 kopecks (**копеек** *kah·pyeh·yek*).
Coins: 1, 5, 10, 50 **kopecks**; 1, 2, 5 **rubles**
Notes: 10, 50, 100, 500, 1000 **rubles**

I want to cash some traveler's checks.	**Я хочу обменять дорожные чеки.** *yah khah•choo ahb•mee•nyaht' dah•rozh•nih•ee cheh•kee*

For Numbers, see page 215.

Getting Around

How do I get to town?	**Как мне добраться до города?** *kahk mnyeh dah•brah•tsah dah goh•rah•dah*
Where's…?	**Где…?** *gdyeh…*
the airport	**аэропорт** *ah•eh•rah•port*
the train [railway] station	**вокзал** *vahg•zahl*
the bus station	**автовокзал** *ahf•tah•vahg•zahl*
the metro [underground] station	**станция метро** *stahn•tsih•yah mee•troh*
How far is it?	**Как далеко это отсюда?** *kahk dah•lee•koh eh•tah aht•syoo•dah*
Where can I buy tickets?	**Где можно купить билеты?** *gdyeh mozh•nah koo•peet' bee•lyeh•tih*
A one-way [single]/ return-trip ticket.	**Билет в один конец/туда и обратно.** *bee•lyet v ah•deen kah•nyets/too•dah ee ahb•raht•nah*
How much?	**Сколько?** *skol'•kah*
Are there any discounts?	**Есть какая-нибудь скидка?** *yehst' kah•kah•yah•nee•boot' skeet•kah*
Which gate/line?	**Какой выход/путь?** *kah•koy vih•khaht/poot'*
Which platform?	**Какая платформа?** *kah•kah•yah plaht•for•mah*
Where can I get a taxi?	**Где можно взять такси?** *gdyeh mozh•nah vzyat' tahk•see*
Please take me to this address.	**Пожалуйста, отвезите меня по этому адресу.** *pah•zhahl•stah aht•vee•zee•tee mee•nyah pah eh•tah•moo ahd•ree•soo*
Where can I rent a car?	**Где можно взять машину напрокат?** *gdyeh mozh•nah vzyat' mah•shih•noo nah•prah•kaht*
Could I have a map?	**Можно мне карту?** *mozh•nah mnyeh kahr•too*

Tickets

When's…to Moscow?	**Когда…в Москву?** kahg·*dah*…v mahs·*kvoo*
the (first) bus	**(первый) автобус** (*pyer*·viy) ahf·*toh*·boos
the (next) flight	**(следующий) рейс** (*slyeh*·doo·yoo·shcheey) reys
the (last) train	**(последний) поезд** (pahs·*lyed*·neey) *poh*·eest
Where can I buy tickets?	**Где можно купить билеты?** gdyeh *mozh*·nah koo·*peet'* bee·*lyeh*·tih
One ticket/Two tickets, please.	**Один билет/Два билета, пожалуйста.** ah·*deen* bee·*lyet*/dvah bee·*lyeh*·tah pah·*zhahl*·stah
For today/tomorrow.	**На сегодня/завтра.** nah seh·*vod*·nyah/*zahf*·trah
A first/economy class ticket.	**Билет на первый/туристический класс.** bee·*lyet* nah *pyer*·viy/too·rees·*tee*·chees·keey klahss
A…ticket.	**Билет…** bee·*lyeht*
one-way	**в один конец** v ah·*deen* kah·*nyets*
return trip	**туда и обратно** too·*dah* ee ahb·*raht*·noh
business class	**бизнес-класс** biz·nes klahss
How much?	**Сколько?** *skol'*·kah
Is there a discount for…?	**Есть скидка…?** yest' *skeet*·kah…
children	**на детей** nah dee·*tyey*
students	**студентам** stoo·*dyen*·tahm
senior citizens	**пенсионерам** peen·see·ah·*nyeh*·rahm
tourists	**туристам** too·*rees*·tahm
I have an e-ticket.	**У меня электронный билет.** oo mee·*nyah* ee·leek·*tron*·niy bee·*lyet*
Can I buy a ticket on the bus/train?	**Я могу купить билет в автобусе/поезде?** yah mah·*goo* koo·*peet'* bee·*lyet* v ahf·*toh*·boo·see/ *poh*·eez·dee
Do I have to stamp the ticket before boarding?	**Нужно ли перед посадкой компостировать билет?** *noozh*·nah lee peret pah·*saht*·koy kam·pas·*tee*·ro·vat' bee·*lyet*
How long is this ticket valid?	**Как долго действителен билет?** kahk *dol*·go dey·*stvee*·tee·lyen bee·*lyet*
Can I return on the same ticket?	**Могу я вернуться по этому билету?** mah·*goo* yah vyer·*noo*·tsah poh *yeh*·tah·moo bee·*lye*·too
I'd like to…my reservation.	**Я хотел m/хотела f бы…свой предварительный заказ.** yah khah·*tyel*/khah·*tyeh*·lah bih…svoy preed·vah·*ree*·teel'·niy zah·*kahz*

cancel	**отменить** *aht·mee·neet'*
change	**изменить** *eez·mee·neet'*
confirm	**подтвердить** *paht·tveer·deet'*

For Time, see page 217.

Car Hire

Where can I rent a car?	**Где можно взять машину напрокат?** *gdyeh mozh·nah vzyaht' mah·shih·noo nah·prah·kaht*
I'd like to rent [hire]…	**Я хотел *m*/хотела *f* бы взять напрокат…** *yah khah·tyel/khah·tyeh·lah bih vzyaht' nah·prah·kaht…*
a cheap/small car	**недорогую/небольшую машину** *nih·do·ro·goo·yoo/ nye·bol'·shoo·yoo mah·shih·noo*
a 2-/4-door car	**двух/четырёх дверную машину** *dvookh/chee·tih·ryokh dvyer·noo·yoo mah·shih·noo*
an automatic/ manual car	**машину с автоматической/ручной трансмиссией** *mah·shih·noo s ahf·tah·mah·tee·chees·koy/rooch·noy trahns·mee·see·yey*

YOU MAY HEAR…

прямо *pryah·mah*	straight ahead
слева *slyeh·vah*	on the left
справа *sprah·vah*	on the right
на углу/за углом *nah oo·gloo/zah oo·glohm*	on/around the corner
напротив *nah·proh·teef*	opposite
позади *pah·zah·dee*	behind
рядом с *ryah·dahm s*	next to
после *pos·lee*	after
север/юг *syeh·veer/yook*	north/south
восток/запад *vahs·tok/zah·paht*	east/west
у светофора *oo svee·tah·foh·rah*	at the traffic light
на перекрестке *nah pee·ree·kryost·kee*	at the intersection

a car with air-conditioning	**машину с кондиционером** mah-_shih_-noo s kahn-dee-tsih-ah-_nyeh_-rahm
a car with a car seat	**машину с детским сидением** mah-_shih_-noo s dyets-keem see-_dyen'_-yem
How much...?	**Сколько...?** _skol'_-kah . . .
per day/week	**в день/неделю** v dyen'/nee-_dyeh_-lyoo
per kilometer	**за километр** zah kee-lah-_myetr_
for unlimited mileage	**за неограниченный пробег** zah nee-ahg-rah-_nee_-cheen-niy prah-_byek_
with insurance	**со страховкой** sah strah-_khof_-kie
Are there any special weekend rates?	**Есть особый тариф по выходным?** yest' ah-_soh_-biy tah-_reef_ pah vih-khahd-_nihm_

Places to Stay

Can you recommend a hotel?	**Можете порекомендовать гостиницу?** _moh_-zhih-tee pah-ree-kah-meen-dah-_vaht'_ gahs-_tee_-nee-tsoo
I have a reservation.	**У меня заказ.** oo mee-_nyah_ zah-_kahs_
My name is...	**Меня зовут...** mee-_nyah_ zah-_voot_...
Do you have a room...?	**У вас есть номер...?** oo vahs yest' _noh_-meer...
for one/two	**на одного/двоих** nah ahd-nah-_voh_/dvah-_eekh_
with a bathroom	**с ванной** s _vahn_-nie
with air-conditioning	**с кондиционером** s kahn-dee-tzih-ah-_nyeh_-rahm
For tonight.	**На эти сутки.** nah _eh_-tee _soot_-kee
For two nights.	**На два дня.** nah dvah dnyah
For one week.	**На неделю.** nah nee-_dyeh_-lyoo
How much?	**Сколько?** _skol'_-kah
Do you have anything cheaper?	**Есть что-нибудь подешевле?** yest' _shtoh_-nee-_boot'_ pah-dee-_shev_-lee
When's check-out?	**Во сколько надо освободить номер?** vah _skol'_-kah _nah_-dah ah-svah-bah-_deet'_ _noh_-_meer_
Can I leave this in the safe?	**Можно оставить это в сейфе?** _mozh_-nah ah-_stah_-veet' _eh_-tah f _sey_-fee
Can I leave my bags?	**Можно я оставлю сумки?** _mozh_-nah yah ah-_stahv_-lyoo _soom_-kee
Can I have the bill/a receipt?	**Можно счёт/чек?** _mozh_-nah shchot/chehk

I'll pay in cash/by credit card.	**Я заплачу наличными/по кредитной карточке.** *yah zah•plah•<u>choo</u> nah•<u>leech</u>•nih•mee/pah kree•<u>deet</u>•noy <u>kahr</u>•tahch•kee*

Communications

Where's an internet cafe?	**Где находится интернет-кафе?** *gdyeh nah•<u>khoh</u>•dee•tsah een•ter•<u>net</u> kah•<u>feh</u>*
Does it have wireless internet?	**Есть беспроводной Интернет?** *yest' bees•prah•vahd•<u>noy</u> een•ter•<u>net</u>*
What is the WiFi password?	**Какой пароль от WiFi?** *kah•<u>koy</u> pah•rol' ot WiFi*
Is the WiFi free?	**WiFi бесплатный?** *WiFi behs•<u>plaht</u>•niy*
Do you have bluetooth?	**У Вас есть bluetooth?** *oo vas yest' bluetooth*
How do I turn the computer on/off?	**Как мне включить/выключить компьютер?** *kahk mnyeh fklyoo•<u>cheet</u>'/vih•klyoo•cheet' kahm•<u>pyoo</u>•ter*
Can I...?	**Я смогу...?** *yah smah•<u>goo</u>...*
access the internet here	**войти в Интернет здесь** *vie•<u>tee</u> v een•ter•<u>net</u> zdyes'*
check e-mail	**проверить электронную почту** *prah•<u>vyeh</u>•reet' ee•leek•<u>tron</u>•noo•yoo <u>poch</u>•too*
print	**распечатать** *rahs•pee•<u>chah</u>•taht'*
plug in/charge my laptop/iPhone/iPad/BlackBerry?	**подключить/зарядить ноутбук/iPhone/iPad/BlackBerry?** *pod•klyoo•<u>cheet</u>'/zah•rya•<u>deet</u>' notebook/iPhone/iPad/BlackBerry*
access Skype?	**войти в Skype?** *voy•<u>tee</u> v Skype*
How much per hour/half hour?	**Сколько за час/полчаса?** *<u>skol</u>'•kah zah chahs/pol•chah•<u>sah</u>*
How do I...?	**Как мне...?** *kahk mnyeh...*
connect/disconnect	**подключиться/отключиться** *paht•klyoo•<u>chee</u>•tsah/aht•klyoo•<u>chee</u>•tsah*
log on/off	**войти/выйти** *vie•<u>tee</u>/<u>viy</u>•tee*
type this symbol	**напечатать этот символ** *nah•pee•<u>chah</u>•taht' <u>eh</u>•taht <u>seem</u>•vahl*
What's your e-mail?	**Какой у вас адрес электронной почты?** *kah•<u>koy</u> oo vahs <u>ahd</u>•rees ee•leek•<u>tron</u>•nie <u>poch</u>•tih*

| My e-mail is… | **Мой адрес электронной почты…** *moy ahd·rees ee·leek·tron·nie poch·tih…* |
| Do you have a scanner? | **У Вас есть сканер?** *oo vas est' skah·nehr* |

Social Media

Are you on Facebook/Twitter?	**Вы есть в Facebook/Twitter?** *vih est' v Facebook/Twitter*
What's your user name?	**Какое у Вас имя пользователя?** *kah·koh·eh oo vas ee·mya pol'·zo·vah·tyeh·lya*
I'll add you as a friend.	**Я добавлю Вас в друзья.** *yah doh·bahv·lyoo vas v drooz'·ya*
I'll follow you on Twitter.	**Я присоединюсь к Вам в Twitter.** *yah pree·soh·eh·dee·nyus' k vam v Twitter*
Are you following…?	**Вы присоединились…?** *vih pree·soh·eh·dee·nee·lees'*
I'll put the pictures on Facebook/Twitter.	**Я выложу фотографии на Facebook/Twitter.** *yah vih·lah·zhoo·fo·to·grah·fee·ee na Facebook/Twitter*
I'll tag you in the pictures.	**Я отмечу Вас на фотографиях.** *yah ot·meh·choo vas na foh·to·grah·fee·yakh*

Conversation

Hello./Hi!	**Здравствуйте./Привет!** *zdrah·stvooy·tee/pree·vyet*
How are you?	**Как дела?** *kahk dee·lah*
Fine, thanks.	**Спасибо, хорошо.** *spah·see·bahkhah·rah·shoh*
Excuse me!	**Извините!** *eez·vee·nee·tee*
Do you speak English?	**Вы говорите по-английски?** *vih gah·vah·ree·tee pah ahn·gleey·skee*
What's your name?	**Как Вас зовут?** *kahk vahz zah·voot*
My name is…	**Меня зовут…** *mee·nyah zah·voot…*
Pleased to meet you.	**Очень приятно.** *oh·cheen' pree·yaht·nah*
Where are you from?	**Откуда вы приехали?** *aht·koo·dah vih pree·yeh·khah·lee*
I'm from the U.S./U.K.	**Я из США/Великобритании.** *yah ees seh sheh ah/ vee·lee·kah·bree·tah·nee·ee*
What do you do?	**Ваша профессия?** *vah·shah prah·fyeh·see·yah*
I work for…	**Я работаю в…** *yah rah·boh·tah·yoo v…*
I'm a student.	**Я студент.** *yah stoo·dyehnt*
I'm retired.	**Я на пенсии.** *yah nah pyehn·see·ee*
Do you like…?	**Вы любите…?** *vih lyoo·bee·tee…*

| Goodbye. | **До свидания.** *dah svee-dah-nee-yah* |
| See you later. | **Увидимся.** *oo-vee-deem-syah* |

Romance

Would you like to go out for a drink/meal?	**Не хотите выпить/поесть где-нибудь?** *nee khah-tee-tee vih-peet'/pah-yest' gdyeh-nee-boot'*
What are your plans for tonight/tomorrow?	**Какие у вас планы на сегодняшний вечер/завтра?** *kah-kee-yeh oo vahs plah-nih nah see-vod-neesh-neey vyeh-cheer/zahf-trah*
Can I have your number?	**Можно Ваш номер телефона?** *mozh-nah vahsh noh-meer tee-lee-foh-nah*
Can I join you?	**Можно к Вам присоединиться?** *mozh-nah k vahm pree-sah-ee-dee-nee-tsah*
Let me buy you a drink.	**Позвольте вам предложить что-нибудь выпить.** *pahz-vol'-tee vahm preed-lah-zheet' shtoh-nee-boot' vih-peet'*
I like you.	**Вы мне нравитесь.** *vih mnyeh nrah-vee-tees'*
I love you.	**Я Вас люблю.** *yah vahs lyoob-lyoo*

Accepting & Rejecting

Thank you! I'd love to.	**Спасибо! Я с удовольствием.** *spah-see-bah yah s oo-dah-vol'-stvee-yem*
Where shall we meet?	**Где встретимся?** *gdyeh fstryeh-teem-syah*
I'll meet you at the bar/your hotel.	**Встретимся в баре/вашем отеле.** *fstryeh-teem-syah v bah-ryeh/vah-shem ah-teh-lee*
I'll come by at . . .	**Я зайду в . . .** *yah zayh-doo v . . .*
Thank you, but I'm busy.	**Спасибо, но я занят *m*/занята *f*.** *spah-see-bah noh yah zah-nyaht/zah-nyah-tah*
I'm not interested.	**Меня это не интересует.** *mee-nyah eh-tah nee een-tee-ree-soo-eet*
Leave me alone.	**Оставьте меня в покое.** *ah-stahf'-tee mee-nyah f pah-koh-yeh*
Stop bothering me!	**Перестаньте мне надоедать!** *pee-ree-stahn'-tee mnyeh nah-dah-ee-daht'*

Food & Drink

Eating Out

Can you recommend a good restaurant/bar?	**Можете посоветовать хороший ресторан/бар?** *moh·zhih·tee pah·sah·vyeh·tah·vaht' khah·roh·shiy ree·stah·rahn/bahr*
Is there a traditional Russian/an inexpensive restaurant near here?	**Здесь есть традиционный русский/недорогой ресторан поблизости?** *zdyes' yest' trah·dee·tsih·on·niy roos·keey/nee·dah·rah·goy ree·stah·rahn pah·blee·zahs·tee*
A table for…, please.	**Столик на…, пожалуйста.** *stoh·leek nah… pah·zhahl·stah*
Could we sit…?	**Можно нам сесть…?** *mozh·nah nahm syehst'…*
here/there	**здесь/там** *zdyehs'/tahm*
outside	**на улице** *nah oo·lee·tseh*
in a non-smoking area	**где не курят** *gdyeh nee koo·ryaht*
I'm waiting for someone.	**Я кое-кого жду.** *yah koh·ee kah·voh zhdoo*
Where are the toilets?	**Где туалет?** *gdyeh too·ah·lyeht*
A menu, please.	**Меню, пожалуйста.** *mee·nyoo pah·zhahl·stah*
What do you recommend?	**Что вы посоветуете?** *shtoh vih pah·sah·vyeh·too·ee·tee*
I'd like…	**Я хотел** *m***/хотела** *f* **бы…** *yah khah·tyel/khah·tyeh·lah bih…*
Some more…, please.	**Можно ещё…, пожалуйста.** *mozh·nah ee·shchoh… pah·zhahl·stah*
Enjoy your meal!	**Приятного аппетита!** *pree·yaht·nah·vah ah·pee·tee·tah*
The check [bill], please.	**Счёт, пожалуйста.** *shchoht pah·zhahl·stah*

YOU MAY SEE...

НАЦЕНКА *nah·tsen·kah*	cover charge
КОМПЛЕКСНЫЙ МЕНЮ *kom·plyeks·niy меню*	fixed-price menu
МЕНЮ ДНЯ *mee·nyoo dnyah*	menu of the day
ОБСЛУЖИВАНИЕ (НЕ) ВКЛЮЧЕНО *ahp·sloo·zhih·vah·nee·yeh (nee) fklyoo·chee·noh*	service (not) included
БЛЮДО ДНЯ *blyoo·dah dnyah*	specials

Is service included?	**Счёт включает обслуживание?** *shchot fklyoo·chah·eet ahp·sloo·zhih·vah·nee·yeh*
Can I pay by credit card?	**Можно платить кредитной карточкой?** *mozh·nah plah·teet' kree·deet·noy kahr·tahch·kie*
Can I have a receipt?	**Можно чек?** *mozh·nah chek*
Thank you!	**Спасибо!** *spah·see·bah*

Breakfast

вареное яйцо *vah·ryoh·nah·yeh yie·tsoh*	bacon
хлеб *khlyep*	bread
масло *mahs·lah*	butter
сыр *sihr*	cheese
яичница *yah·eesh·nee·tsah*	fried eggs
яичница-болтунья *yah·eesh·nee·tsah bahl·toon'·yah*	scrambled eggs
яичница с ветчиной *yah·eesh·nee·tsah s veet·chee·noy*	ham and eggs
джем *dzhem*	jam
булочка *boo·lahch·kah*	rolls
тост *tost*	toast
йогурт *yoh·goort*	yogurt

Appetizers

ассорти мясное *ah·sahr·tee myahs·noh·yeh*	assorted meat
ассорти рыбное *ah·sahr·tee rihb·nah·yeh*	assorted fish
икра *eek·rah*	caviar
ветчина *veet·chee·nah*	ham
сельдь *syel't'*	herring
грибы *gree·bih*	mushrooms
хачапури *khah·chah·poo·ree*	hot pancake filled with cheese (Georgian dish)
паштет *pahsh·tyet*	paté (mostly liver)
пирог *pee·rok*	pie
колбаса *kahl·bah·sah*	sausage
креветки *kree·vyet·kee*	shrimp [prawns]
кильки *keel'·kee*	spiced herring
осетрина *ah·seet·ree·nah*	sturgeon

Meat

beef	**говядина**	gah-<u>vyah</u>-dee-nah
lamb	**молодая баранина**	mah-lah-<u>dah</u>-yah bah-<u>rah</u>-nee-nah
chicken	**курица**	<u>koo</u>-ree-tsah
duck	**утка**	<u>oot</u>-kah
pork	**свинина**	svee-<u>nee</u>-nah
veal	**телятина**	tee-<u>lyah</u>-tee-na
liver	**печёнка**	pee-<u>chon</u>-kah
rabbit	**кролик**	<u>kroh</u>-leek
beef stroganoff	**бефстроганов**	beef-<u>stroh</u>-gah-nahf

YOU MAY HEAR...

с кровью s <u>krov'</u>-yoo		(rare)
средне прожаренный <u>sryed</u>-nee prah-<u>zhah</u>-ree-niy	medium
хорошо прожаренный khah-rah-<u>shoh</u>		
prah-<u>zhah</u>-ree-niy		well-done

Fish & Seafood

carp	**карп**	kahrp
crab	**краб**	krahp
herring	**сельдь**	syel't'
lobster	**омар**	ah-<u>mahr</u>
mackerel	**макрель**	mahk-<u>ryel'</u>
oysters	**устрицы**	<u>oos</u>-tree-tsih
shrimp [prawns]	**креветки**	kree-<u>vyet</u>-kee
salmon	**сёмга**	<u>syom</u>-gah
sprats	**шпроты**	<u>shproh</u>-tih
trout	**форель**	fah-<u>ryel'</u>
tuna	**тунец**	too-<u>nyets</u>
sturgeon...	**осетрина...**	ah-seet-<u>ree</u>-nah...

Vegetables

фасоль fah-<u>sol'</u>	beans
капуста kah-<u>poos</u>-tah	cabbage

грибы *greeb•ih*	mushrooms
лук *look*	onion
горох *gah•rokh*	peas
картофель *kahr•toh•feel'*	potato
помидор *pah•mee•dor*	tomato
свёкла *svyok•lah*	beet
морковь *mahr•kof'*	carrots
цветная капуста *tsveet•nah•yah kah•poos•tah*	cauliflower

Sauces & Condiments

соль *sol'*	Salt
перец *pyeh•reets*	Pepper
горчица *gahr•chee•tsah*	Mustard
кетчуп *Keht•choop*	Ketchup

Fruit & Dessert

яблоко в тесте *yahb•lah•kah f tyes•tee*	apple baked in pastry
…мороженое *…mah•roh•zhih•nah•yeh*	…ice cream
шоколадное *shah•kah•lad•nah•yeh*	chocolate
фруктовое *frook•toh•vah•yeh*	fruit
ванильное *vah•neel'•nah•yeh*	vanilla
рисовый пудинг *ree•sah•viy poo•deenk*	rice pudding
оладьи с яблоками *ah•lahd'•yee s yahb•lah•kah•mee*	small apple pancakes

Drinks

May I see the wine list/drink menu?	**Можно посмотреть карту вин/меню напитков?** *mozh•nah pah•smah•tryet' kahr•too veen/mee•nyoo nah•peet•kahf*
What do you recommend?	**Что вы порекомендуете?** *shtoh vih pah•ree•kah•meen•doo•ee•tee*
I'd like a bottle/glass of red/white wine.	**Я хотел *m*/хотела *f* бы бутылку/бокал красного/белого вина.** *yah khah•tyel/khah•tyeh•lah bih boo•tihl•koo/bah•kahl krahs•nah•vah/byeh•lah•vah vee•nah*
The house wine, please.	**Вино ресторана, пожалуйста.** *vee•noh ree•stah•rah•nah pah•zhahl•stah*

Another bottle/ glass, please.	Ещё одну бутылку/один бокал, пожалуйста. *yee-shchoh ahd-noo boo-tihl-koo/ ah-deen bah-kahl pah-zhahl-stah*
I'd like a local beer.	Я хотел *m*/хотела *f* бы местного пива. *yah khah-tyel/khah-tyeh-lah bih myes-nah-vah pee-vah*
Let me buy you a drink.	Позвольте вам предложить что-нибудь выпить. *pahz-vol'-tee vahm preed-lah-zhiht' shtoh-nee-boot' vih-peet'*
Cheers!	За ваше здоровье! *za vah-sheh zdah-rov'-yeh*
A coffee/tea, please.	Кофе/Чай, пожалуйста. *koh-fye/chie pah-zhahl-stah*
Black.	Чёрный. *chor-niy*
With...	С... *s...*
milk	молоком *mah-lah-kom*
sugar	сахаром *sah-khah-rahm*
artificial sweetener	заменителем сахара *zah-mee-nee-tee-lyem sah-khah-rah*
..., please.	..., пожалуйста. *...pah-zhahl-stah*
Juice	Сок *sok*
Soda	Содовую *soh-dah-voo-yoo*
Sparkling/Still water	Воду с газом/без газа *voh-doo z gah-zahm/beez gah-zah*
Is the tap water safe to drink?	Безопасно ли пить воду из крана? *bee-zah-pahs-nah lee peet' voh-doo ees krah-nah*

Leisure Time

Sightseeing

Where's the tourist information office?	Где турбюро? *gdyeh toor-byoo-roh*
What are the main points of interest?	Какие главные достопримечательности? *kah-kee-yeh glahv-nih-yeh dah-stah-pree-mee-chah-teel'-nahs-tee*
Do you have tours in English?	У вас есть экскурсии на английском? *oo vahs yehst' ehks-koor-see-ee nah ahn-gleey-skahm*
Can I have a map/guide?	Можно мне карту/путеводитель? *mozh-nah mnyeh kahr-too/poo-tee-vah-dee-teel*

YOU MAY SEE…

ОТКРЫТО/ЗАКРЫТО aht‑*krih*‑tah/zah‑*krih*‑toh	open/closed
ВЫХОД *vih*‑khaht	exit

Shopping

Where is the shop/mall?	**Где магазин/торговый центр?** gdyeh mah‑gah‑*zeen*/tahr‑*goh*‑viy tsehntr
I'm just looking.	**Я просто смотрю.** yah *proh*‑stah smath‑*ryoo*
Can you help me?	**Можете мне помочь?** *moh*‑zhih‑tee mnyeh pah‑*mohch*
I'm being helped.	**Меня уже обслуживают.** mee‑*nyah* oo‑zheh ahp‑*sloo*‑zhih‑vah‑yoot
How much?	**Сколько?** *skol'*‑kah
That one.	**Вон то.** vohn toh
That's all, thanks.	**Это всё, спасибо.** *eh*‑tah fsyoh spah‑*see*‑bah
Where do I pay?	**Куда платить?** koo‑*dah* plah‑*teet'*
I'll pay in cash/by credit card.	**Я заплачу наличными/по кредитной карточке.** yah zah‑plah‑*choo* nah‑*leech*‑nih‑mee/pah kree‑*deet*‑noy *kahr*‑tahch‑kee
A receipt, please.	**Чек, пожалуйста.** chehk pah‑*zhahl*‑stah

Sport & Leisure

When's the game?	**Во сколько игра?** vah *skohl'*‑kah eeg‑*rah*
Where's…?	**Где…?** gdyeh…
the beach	**пляж** plyahsh
the park	**парк** pahrk
the pool	**бассейн** bah‑*syehyn*
Is it safe to swim/dive here?	**Здесь не опасно плавать/нырять?** zdyehs' nee ah‑*pahs*‑nah *plah*‑vaht'/nih‑*ryaht'*
Can I hire golf clubs?	**Я могу взять напрокат клюшки для гольфа?** yah mah‑*goo* vzyaht' nah‑prah‑*kaht* klyoosh‑kee dlyah *gohl'*‑fah
How much per hour?	**Сколько стоит в час?** *skohl'*‑kah *stoh*‑eet f chahs
How far is it to…?	**Далеко до…отсюда?** dah‑lee‑*koh* dah… aht‑*syoo*‑dah
Can you show me on the map?	**Можете показать мне на карте?** *moh*‑zhih‑tyeh pah‑kah‑*zaht'* mnyeh nah *kahr*‑tyeh

Going Out

What is there to do in the evenings?	**Что здесь можно делать по вечерам?** shtoh zdyehs' mozh·nah dyeh·laht pah vee·chee·rahm
Do you have a program of events?	**У Вас есть программа мероприятий?** oo vahs yehst' prah·grah·mah mee·rah·pree·yah·teey
What's playing at the movies [cinema] tonight?	**Что идёт в кинотеатре сегодня вечером?** shtoh ee·dyot f kee·nah·tee·aht·ree see·vohd·nyah vyeh·chee·rahm
Where's...?	**Где...?** gdyeh...
the downtown area	**центр города** tsehntr goh·rah·dah
the bar	**бар** bahr
the dance club	**дискотека** dees·kah·tyeh·kah
Is there a cover charge?	**Нужно платить за вход?** noozh·nah plah·teet' zah fkhot

Baby Essentials

Do you have...?	**У Вас есть...?** oo vahs yest'...
a baby bottle	**детская бутылочка** dyets·kah·yah boo·tih·lahch·kah
baby food	**детское питание** deht·skoh·ye pee·tah·nee·yeh
baby wipes	**гигиенические салфетки** gee·gee·ee·nee·chees·kee·yeh sahl·fyet·kee
a car seat	**детское сиденье** dyets·kah·yeh see·dyen'·yeh
a children's menu/portion	**меню/порции для детей** mee·nyoo/por·tsih·ee dlyah dee·tyey
a child's seat/highchair	**детский/высокий стульчик** dyets·keey/vih·soh·keey stool'·cheek
a crib/cot	**колыбель/детская кроватка** kah·lih·byel'/dyets·kah·yah krah·vaht·kah
diapers [nappies]	**подгузники** pahd·gooz·nee·kee
formula	**молочная смесь** mah·loch·nah·yah smyes'
a pacifier [dummy]	**соска** sos·kah
a playpen	**манеж** mah·nyesh
a stroller [pushchair]	**прогулочная коляска** prah·goo·lahch·nah·yah kah·lyas·kah
Can I breastfeed the baby here?	**Я могу здесь покормить грудью ребёнка?** yah mah·goo zdyes' pah·kahr·meet' grood'·yoo ree·byon·kah
Where can I breastfeed/change the baby?	**Где можно покормить/переодеть ребёнка?** gdyeh mozh·nah pah·kahr·meet'/pee·ree·ah·dyet' ree·byon·kah

For Eating Out, see page 226.

Disabled Travelers

Is there…?	**Есть…?** *yest'…*
access for the disabled	**условия для инвалидов** *oos-loh-vee-yah dlyah een-vah-lee-dahf*
a wheelchair ramp	**пандус для инвалидного кресла** *pahn-doos dlyah een-vah-leed-nah-vah kryes-lah*
a disabled-accessible toilet	**туалет с условиями для инвалидов** *too-ah-lyet s oos-loh-vee-yah-mee dlyah een-vah-lee-dahf*
I need assistance.	**Мне нужна помощь.** *mnyeh noozh-nah poh-mahshch*
I need an elevator [lift].	**Мне нужен лифт.** *mnyeh noo-zhehn left*
I need a ground-floor room.	**Мне нужен номер на первом этаже.** *mnyeh noo-zhehn noh-meer nah pyer-vahm eh-tah-zheh*

Health & Emergencies

Emergencies

Help!	**Помогите!** *pah-mah-gee-tee*
Go away!	**Идите отсюда!** *ee-dee-tee aht-syoo-dah*
Stop, thief!	**Держите вора!** *deer-zhih-tee voh-rah*
Get a doctor!	**Вызовите врача!** *vih-zah-vee-tee vrah-chah*
Fire!	**Пожар!** *pah-zhahr*
I'm lost.	**Я заблудился** *m* **/заблудилась** *f.* *yah zah-bloo-deel-syah/ zah-bloo-dee-lahs'*
Help me, please.	**Помогите мне, пожалуйста.** *pah-mah-gee-tee mnyeh pah-zhahl-stah*
Call the police!	**Вызовите милицию!** *vih-zah-vee-tee mee-lee-tsih-yoo*
My child is missing.	**У меня пропал ребёнок.** *oo mee-nyah prah-pahl ree-byoh-nahk*
Where's the police station?	**Где отделение милиции?** *gdyeh aht-dee-lyeh-nee-yeh mee-lee-tsih-ee*

In an emergency, dial: **02** for the police
01 for the fire brigade
03 for the ambulance

YOU MAY HEAR...

Заполните бланк. zah·*pol*·nee·tyeh blahnk
Please fill out this form.

Ваши документы, пожалуйста. *vah*·shih dah·koo·*myen*·tih pah·*zhahl*·stah
Your identification, please.

Где/Когда это произошло? gdyeh/kahg·*dah eh*·tah prah·ee·zah·*shloh*
When/Where did it happen?

Как он/она выглядит? kahk on/ah·*nah vih*·glyah·deet
What does he/she look like?

Health

I'm sick [ill].	**Я заболел *m* /заболела *f*.** yah zah·bah·*lyel*/zah·bah·*lyeh*·lah
I need an English-speaking doctor.	**Мне нужен англоговорящий врач.** mnyeh *noo*·zhen *ahn*·glah·gah·vah·*ryah*·shcheey vrahch
It hurts here.	**Мне больно вот здесь.** mnyeh *bohl'*·nah voht zdyehs'
I have a stomachache.	**У меня болит живот.** oo mee·*nyah* bah·*leet* zhih·*voht*
I'm (...months) pregnant.	**Я беременна (на...месяце).** ya beh·*reh*·meh·nah (nah...*meh*·sya·tse)
I'm on...	**Я принимаю...** yah pree·nee·*mah*·yoo...
I'm allergic to antibiotics/penicillin.	**У меня аллергия на антибиотики/пенициллин.** oo mee·*nyah* ah·leer·*gee*·yah nah ahn·tee·bee·*oh*·tee·kee/pee·nee·tsih·*leen*

234

Dictionary

acetaminophen **парацетамол**
adapter **адаптер**
antiseptic *n* **антисептик**
aspirin **аспирин**
baby **ребёнок**
backpack **рюкзак**
bad **плохой**
bikini **бикини**
bird **птица**

bottle opener **открывалка**
boy **мальчик**
boyfriend **друг**
bra **бюстгальтер**
camera **фотоаппарат**
can opener **консервный нож**
castle **замок**
cigarette **сигарета**
cold *adj* **холодный** *n* (flu) **простуда**

comb **расчёска**
condom **презерватив**
corkscrew **штопор**
cup **чашка**
dangerous *adj* **опасный**
deodorant **дезодорант**
diabetic *n* **диабетик**
doll **кукла**
fork **вилка**
girl **девочка**
girlfriend **подруга**
glass **стакан**
good **хороший**
gray **серый**
hairbrush **щётка для волос**
hairspray **лак для волос**
horse **лошадь**
hot *adj* **горячий**
husband **муж**
icy **гололёд**
injection **укол**
jeans **джинсы**
knife **нож**
large **большой**
lighter (cigarette) **зажигалка**
love *v* **любить**
matches **спички**
museum **музей**
my **мой**
napkin **салфетка**
nurse **сестра**
or **или**
paracetamol *[BE]* **парацетамол**
park **парк**
pen **ручка**
plate **тарелка**

rain *v* **идёт дождь**
raincoat **плащ**
razor **бритва**
sandals **сандалии**
sanitary napkins **гигиенические салфетки**
sauna **сауна**
scissors **ножницы**
shampoo **шампунь**
shoes **туфли**
small (in size) **маленький**
sneakers **теннисные туфли**
snow **снег**
soap **мыло**
socks **носки**
spoon **ложка**
stamp **марка**
sunglasses **солнечные очки**
sweater **пуловер**
sweatshirt **байка**
swimsuit **купальник**
T-shirt **майка**
tampon **тампон**
terrible **ужасный**
tie **галстук**
tissue **бумажная салфетка**
toilet paper **туалетная бумага**
toothbrush **зубная щётка**
toothpaste **зубная паста**
toy **игрушка**
vegetarian **вегетарианец**
wife **жена**
with **с**
without **без**
yellow **жёлтый**
zoo **зоопарк**

Slovenian

Essentials

Hello/Hi.	**Živjo!** *Zheevyo!*
Good morning.	**Dobro jutro.** *dobro yootro*
Good afternoon.	**Dober dan.** *dohberr vecherh*
Good night.	**Lahko noč.** *laa-hko nohch*
Good-bye.	**Na svidenje.** *na sveedenye*
Yes/No/Okay (Ok).	**Ja/Ne/V redu.** *ya/ne/Ver rehdoo*
Excuse me! (to get attention)	**Oprosti/Oprostite.** *Ohprostee/Ohprosteeteh.*
Excuse me. (to get past)	**Samo malo, prosim.** *Sahmoh mahloh, prohsim.*
I'm sorry.	**Oprosti/Oprostite.** *Ohprostee/Ohprosteeteh.*
I'd like…	**Rad** *m* /**Rada** *f* **bi** *rat/raada bih*
How much?	**Koliko?** *kohliko*
And/or.	**in/ali** *in/aalih*
Please.	**Prosim.** *prohsim*
Thank you.	**Hvala.** *hvaala*
You're welcome.	**Izvoli/Izvolite.** *Izvohlih/Izvohleeteh.*
I'm going to…	**Nameravam…** *Nahmehraavahm…*
My name is…	**Ime mi je…** *imeh mi yeh…*
Please speak slowly.	**Prosim, govorite počasi.** *Prohsim, govoreete pohchahsee.*
Can you repeat that?	**Ali lahko ponovite?** *Aalih laa-hkoh pohnohveeteh?*
I don't understand.	**Ne razumem.** *ne razoomem*
Do you speak English?	**Govorite angleško?** *govoreete anglehshko*
I don't speak Slovenian.	**Govorim malo slovensko.** *govoreem maalo slovehnsko*
Where's the restroom [toilet]?	**Kje je stranišče?** *kyeh ye stranshche*
Help!	**Na pomoč!** *na pomohch*

Numbers

0	**nič** *neech*
1	**ena** *ena*
2	**dva** *dva*
3	**tri** *tree*
4	**štiri** *shteeri*

You'll find the pronunciation of the Slovenian letters and words written in gray after each sentence to guide you. Simply pronounce these as if they were English, noting that we give both the informal (inf) and polite (pl) version for 'you'. Chose the one that is appropriate. As you hear the language being spoken, you will quickly become accustomed to the local pronunciation and dialect.

5	**pet**	*peht*
6	**šest**	*shehst*
7	**sedem**	*sehderm*
8	**osem**	*ohserm*
9	**devet**	*deveht*
10	**deset**	*deseht*
11	**enajst**	*enaayst*
12	**dvanajst**	*dvanaayst*
13	**trinajst**	*trinaayst*
14	**štirinajst**	*shtirinaayst*
15	**petnajst**	*petnaayst*
16	**šestnajst**	*shestnaayst*
17	**sedemnajst**	*sedermnaayst*
18	**osemnajst**	*ohsermnaayst*
19	**devetnajst**	*devetnaayst*
20	**dvajset**	*dvaayset*
21	**enaindvajset**	*dvaayset ena*
30	**trideset**	*treedeset*
40	**štirideset**	*shteerideset*
50	**petdeset**	*pehtdeset*
60	**šestdeset**	*shehstdeset*
70	**sedemdeset**	*sehdermdeset*
80	**osemdeset**	*ohsermdeset*
90	**devetdeset**	*devehtdeset*
100	**sto**	*stoh*
101	**sto ena**	*stoh ehna*
200	**dvesto**	*dvestoh*
500	**petsto**	*petstoh*

1,000	**tisoč** *teesoch*
10,000	**deset tisoč** *deseht teesoch*
1,000,000	**milijon** *ehn milyohn*

Time

What time is it?	**Koliko je ura?** *Kohliko yeh oorah?*
It's midday.	**Je poldne.** *Ye powdne*
Five past three.	**Ura je tri in pet minut.** *Oorah yeh tree in peht meenoot*
A quarter to ten.	**Ura je petnajst do desetih.**
	Oorah yeh petnaayst doh deseteech
5:30 a.m./p.m.	**5:30 zjutraj/popoldne** *peht in treedeset zyutraay/pohpowdneh*

Days

Monday	**ponedeljek** *ponedehlyek*
Tuesday	**torek** *torek*
Wednesday	**sreda** *srehda*
Thursday	**četrtek** *cheterrtek*
Friday	**petek** *pehtek*
Saturday	**sobota** *sobohta*
Sunday	**nedelja** *nedehlya*

Dates

yesterday	**včeraj** *vcheraay*
today	**danes** *dahnes*
tomorrow	**jutri** *yootree*
day	**dan** *dahn*
week	**teden** *tehdehn*
month	**mesec** *mesets*
year	**leto** *lehtoh*
Happy New Year!	**Srečno novo leto!** *Srechnoh nohvoh lehtoh!*
Happy Birthday!	**Vse najboljše za rojstni dan!**
	Vseh naaybolysheh zah roystnee dahn!

Months

January	**januar** *yaanooar*
February	**februar** *fehbrooar*
March	**marec** *maarets*

April	**april** *apreew*
May	**maj** *maay*
June	**junij** *yooniy*
July	**julij** *yooliy*
August	**avgust** *awgoost*
September	**september** *septemberr*
October	**oktober** *oktohberr*
November	**november** *novemberr*
December	**december** *detsemberr*

Arrival & Departure

I'm here on holiday (vacation)/on business.	**Tu sem na počitnicah/poslovno.** *too serm napocheetnctsa-h/poslowno*
I'm going to…	**Grem v…** *Grehm ver…*
I'm staying at the…Hotel.	**Nastanil** *m***/Nastanila** *f* **se bom v hotelu…** *Nahstaaniw/Nahstahneelah seh bom ver hohtehluh…*

Money

Where's…?	**Kje je…?** *kyeh ye…*
the ATM	**bankomat** *bahnkohmaat*
the bank	**banka** *bahnkah*
the currency exchange office	**menjalnica** *mehnyaalnitsah*
When does the bank open/close?	**Ob kateri uri se banka odpre/zapre?** *Ob kahtehrih oorih seh bahnkah odpreh/zapreh?*
I'd like to change dollars/ pounds sterling into euros.	**Rad bi zamenjal** *m***/Rada bi zamenjala** *f* **dolarje/ funte šterlinge v evre.** *Rat bih zahmehnyaw m/ Raada bih zahmehnyahlah f dohlaryeh/foonteh shterlingeh/ ewreh ver ewreh*
I'd like to cash traveler's cheques.	**Rad bi unovčil** *m***/Rada bi unovčila** *f* **potovalne čeke.** *Rat bih oonowcheew Raadaa bih oonowcheelah pohtohvaalneh chehkeh*
Can I pay in cash?	**Ali lahko plačam z gotovino?** *Aalih laa-hkoh plaachahm z gohtohveenoh?*
Can I pay by (credit) card?	**Ali lahko plačam s kreditno kartico?** *Aalih laa-hkoh plaachahm s kredeetnoh karteetsoh?*

For Numbers, see page 237.

YOU MAY SEE...

The Slovenian currency is the **euro**, **€**, which is divided into 100 **cents**.
Coins: 1, 2, 5, 10, 20 and 50 **cents**; €1, 2
Bills: €5, 10, 20, 50, 100, 200 and 500

Getting Around

How do I get to town?	**Kako priti do mesta?** *Kahkoh prihtih doh mestah?*	
Where's...?	**Kje je...?** *kyeh ye...*	
the airport	**letališče**	
the train station	**železniška postaja** *zhelehznishkah pohstahyah*	
the bus station	**avtobusna postaja** *awtohboosnah pohstayah*	
the subway [underground] station	**postaja metroja** *pohstahyah metrohyah*	
Is it far from here?	**Ali je to daleč od tukaj?** *Aalih ye toh dahlech od tookaay?*	
Where do I buy a ticket?	**Kje lahko kupim vozovnico?** *Kyeh laa-hkoh koopihm vohzownitsoh?*	
A one-way/return-trip ticket to...	**Enosmerna/povratna vozovnica do...** *Enohsmernah/pohvratnah vohzownitsah doh...*	
How much?	**Koliko?** *Kohliko?*	
Which gate/line?	**Katera vrata/proga?** *Kahtehrah vrahtah/prohgah?*	
Which platform?	**Kateri peron?** *Kahtehrih pehrohn?*	
Where can I get a taxi?	**Kje lahko dobim taksi?** *Kyeh laa-hkoh dohbeem taaksee?*	
Take me to this address.	**Zapeljite me, prosim, na ta naslov.** *Zahpeljeeteh meh, prohsim, nah tah nahslow?*	
To...Airport, please.	**Na letališče...prosim.** *Nah lehtahleeshcheh...prohseem?*	
I'm in a rush.	**Mudi se mi.** *muhdih seh mee*	
Can I have a map?	**Ali lahko dobim zemljevid?** *Aalih laa-hkoh dohbeem zehmlyehveed?*	

Tickets

When's...to Koper?	**Kdaj odhaja...za Koper?** *Kdaay odhaayah...zah Kohpehr?*	
the (first) bus	**(prvi) avtobus** *(perrvih) awtohboos*	
the (next) flight	**(naslednje) letalo** *(nahslednyeh) lehtaaloh*	
the (last) train	**(zadnji) vlak** *(zahdnyih) vlahk*	

One/Two ticket(s) please.	**Eno vozovnico/Dve vozovnici, prosim.** *Enoh vohzowneetsoh/Dveh vohzowneetsih prohsim*
For today/tomorrow.	**za danes/jutri** *zah dahnes/yootree*
A…ticket.	**…vozovnico.** *…vohzowneetsoh*
one-way	**enosmerno** *enohsmernoh*
return trip	**povratno** *pohvratnoh*
first class	**za prvi razred** *zah perrvee raazred*
I have an e-ticket.	**Imam elektronsko vozovnico.** *Ihmaam ehlektronskoh vohzowneetsoh*
How long is the trip?	**Koliko časa traja pot?** *Kohliko chaasah traaya poht?*
Is it a direct train?	**Ali je to neposredni vlak?** *Aalih yeh toh nehpohsrednih vlaak?*
Is this the bus to…?	**Ali je to avtobus za…?** *Aalih ye toh aawtohboos zah…?*
Can you tell me when to get off?	**Mi lahko poveste, kdaj moram izstopiti?** *mi la-hkoh prohsim povehste kdaay mohram eestopiti*
I'd like to…	**Rad bi** *m*/**Rada bi** *f***…** *rat (raada) bih*
my reservation.	**rezervacijo.** *rezervaatsiyo*
cancel	**odpovedal(a)** *otpovedaw (otpovehdala)*
change	**zamenjal(a)** *zamehnyaw (zamehnyala)*
confirm	**potrdil(a)** *poterrdiw (poterrdeela)*

For Time, see page 239.

Car Hire

Where's the car hire?	**Kje je izposojevalnica avtomobilov?** *Kyeh ye izpohsoyevalnitsa awtomobeelow?*
I'd like…	
a cheap/small car	**poceni/majhen avto** *potsehnih/maayhen awtoh*
an automatic/ a manual	**avtomatski menjalnik** *awtohmahtskee menyaalnik*
air conditioning	**klimatizacija** *klihmahtihzaatsiya*
a car seat	**otroški sedež** *otroshkih sedezh*
How much…?	**Koliko stane…?** *Kohliko staaneh…?*
per day/week	**na dan/teden** *nah dahn/tehdehn*
Are there any discounts?	**Ali so kakšni popusti?** *Aalih soh kaakshnih pohpoostih?*

YOU MAY HEAR...

naravnost *nahraavnost*	straight ahead
na levi *nah lehvih*	left
na desni *nah desnih*	right
za vogalom *zah vohgaalohm*	around the corner
nasproti *nasprohtih*	opposite
zadaj *zahdaay*	behind
zraven *zrahven*	next to
za *zah*	after
severno/južno *sehvernoh/joozhnoh*	north/south
vzhodno/zahodno *verzhodnoh/zahodnoh*	east/west
ob semaforju *ob sehmafohryuh*	at the traffic light
na križišču *nah kreezheeshchuh*	at the intersection

Places to Stay

Can you recommend a hotel?	**Mi lahko priporočiš/priporočite hotel?** *Mee laa-hkoh preeporocheesh/preeporocheeteh hohtehl?*
I made a reservation.	**Imam rezervacijo.** *Ihmaam rezervaatsiyoh.*
My name is...	**Ime mi je...** *Ihmeh mee ye...*
Do you have a room...?	**Ali imate...sobo?** *Aalih ihmaateh...sohboh?*
for one/two	**enoposteljno/dvoposteljno** *ehnopostelynoh/dvopostelynoh*
with a bathroom	**s kopalnico** *s kohpahlnitsoh*
with air-conditioning	**s klimatizacijo** *s klihmahtizaatsiyoh*
For...	**za...** *zah...*
tonight	**nocoj** *notsoy*
two nights	**dve noči** *dveh nochee*
one week	**en teden** *ehn tehdehn*
How much?	**Koliko to stane?** *Kohliko toh stahneh?*
Is there anything cheaper?	**Ali imate kaj cenejšega?** *Aalih ihmaateh kaay tseneyshegah?*
When's checkout?	**Kdaj se moram odjaviti?** *Kdaay seh mohrahm odyaavihtih?*
Can I leave this in the safe?	**Ali lahko to shranim v sef?** *Aalih laa-hkoh toh shraanim v sef?*

Can I leave my bags?	**Ali lahko pustim tu svojo prtljago?** *Aalih laa-hkoh puhsteem too svoyoh perrtljaagoh?*
Can I have my bill/ a receipt?	**Ali lahko dobim račun?** *Aalih laa-hkoh dohbeem rachoon?*
I'll pay in cash/by credit card.	**Plačal** *m*/**Plačala** *f* **bom z gotovino/s kartico.** *Plaachaw / Plaachahlah bom z gohtohveenoh/s karteetso*

Communications

Where's an internet cafe?	**Kje je internetna kavarna?** *Kyeh ye internetnah kahvarnah?*
Can I access the internet/check my email?	**uporabim internet/preverim e-pošto?** *uhporaabihm internet/prehvehrihm e-poshtoh?*
How much per half hour/ hour?	**Koliko stane pol ure/ena ura?** *Kohliko staaneh pohl uhreh/ ehna uhrah?*
How do I connect/log on?	**Kako se povezati/prijaviti?** *Kahkoh seh pohvehzahtih/ priyaavihtih?*
A phone card, please.	**Telefonsko kartico, prosim.** *Telefonskoh karteetsoh, prohsim.*
Can I have your phone number?	**Te** *(inf)*/**Vas** *(pl)* **lahko prosim za telefonsko številko?** *Teh/Vahs laa-hkoh prohsim zah telefonskoh shteveelkoh?*
Here's my number/ email.	**Moja številka/moj elektronski naslov.** *moyah shteveelkah/moy elektronskih nahslohv*
Call me.	**Pokliči** *m*/**Pokličite** *f* **me.** *Pokleechih/Pokleechiteh meh*
Text me.	**Piši/Pišite mi.** *Peeshih/Peeshiteh mee.*
I'll text you.	**Pisal** *m*/**Pisala** *f* **ti** *(inf)*/**vam** *(pl)* **bom.** *Peesahw / Peesahlah tee /vahm bohm*
Email me.	**Pošlji** *m*/**Pošljite** *f* **mi e-pošto.** *Poshl'ih/Poshl'iteh mee e-poshtoh.*
Hello. This is…	**Dober dan, sem…** *Dohber dahn, sehm…*
Can I speak to…?	**Ali lahko govorim z…?** *Aalih laa-hkoh govoreem z…?*
Can you repeat that?	**Ali lahko ponoviš/ponovite?** *Aalih laa-hkoh pohnohveesh/pohnohveeteh?*
I'll call back later.	**Poklical** *m*/**Poklicala** *f* **te bom nazaj.** *Pohkleetsaw /Pokleetsahlah teh bom nahzaay*
Bye.	**Adijo.** *Ahdeeyoh.*
Where's the post office?	**Kje je pošta?** *Kyeh ye poshtah?*
I'd like to send this to…	**Rad bi to poslal** *m*/**a bi to poslala** *f*… *Raad bee toh pohslaawm/Raada bih toh pohslaala…*

Can I...?	**Ali lahko...** *Aalih laa-hkoh*
access the internet	**uporabim internet** *uhpohraabihm internet*
check my email	**preverim elektronsko pošto** *prehvehrihm elektronskoh poshtoh*
print	**nahteesnehm** *nahteesnehm*
plug in/charge my laptop/iPhone/iPad/ BlackBerry?	**priključim/napolnim svoj prenosnik/iPhone/ iPad/BlackBerry?** *priklyoochim/nahpohlnihm svoy prehnosnik/iPhone/iPad/BlackBerry?*
access Skype?	**se prijavim na Skype?** *seh priyaavihm nah Skype?*
What is the WiFi password?	**Kakšno je geslo za WiFi?** *Kahkshnoh ye gesloh zah WiFi?*
Is the WiFi free?	**Ali je WiFi brezplačen?** *Aalih ye WiFi brezplaachehn?*
Do you have bluetooth?	**Ali imate Bluetooth?** *Aalih ihmaateh Bluetooth?*
Do you have a scanner?	**Ali imate optični bralnik?** *Aalih ihmaateh optichnih brahlnik?*

Social Media

Are you on Facebook/ Twitter?	**Ali si na Facebooku/Twitterju?** *Aalih see nah Facebookuh/ Twitteryuh?*
What's your username?	**Kakšno je tvoje uporabniško ime?** *Kakshnoh ye tvohyeh uhporaabnishkoh ihmee?*
I'll add you as a friend.	**Dodal *m*/Dodala *f* te bom med prijatelje.** *Dohdaaw /Dohdaalah teh bom med prihyaatelyeh.*
I'll follow you on Twitter.	**Opazoval *m*/Opazovala *f* te bom na Twitterju.** *Ohpahzohvaaw/Ohpahzohvaalah teh bom nah Twitteryuh.*
Are you following...?	**Ali slediš/sledite...?** *Aalih sleedhish...?*
I'll put the pictures on Facebook/Twitter.	**Naložil *m*/Naložila *f* bom slike na Facebook/ Twitter.** *Nalohzhiw/Nahlohzheelah bom sleekeh nah Facebook/Twitter*
I'll tag you in the pictures.	**Označil *m*/Označila *f* te bom na slikah.** *Oznaachiw/Oznaachilah teh bom nah sleekah*

Conversation

Hello!/Hi!	**Živjo!** *Zheevyo!*
Good morning.	**Dobro jutro.** *dobro yootro*
Good afternoon.	**Dober dan.** *dohberr vechehr*
Good night.	**Lahko noč.** *laa-hko nohch*
How are you?	**Kako ste?** *kakoh ste*

Fine thanks.	**Dobro, hvala.** *dobro hvaala*
Excuse me!	**Oprostite!** *Oprohsteeteh!*
Do you speak English?	**Govorite angleško?** *govoreeteanglehshko*
What's your name?	**Kako vam je ime?** *kakoh vam ye imeh*
My name is...	**Ime mi je...** *imeh mi yeh...*
Nice to meet you.	**Me veseli.** *Meh vehsehlee*
Where are you from?	**Od kod ste?** *ot koht ste*
I'm from the U.K./U.S.	**Združenih držav/Velike Britanije.** *Zdroozhenich derrzhaaw/Vehlihkeh Britaaniyeh*
What do you do for a living?	**Kaj ste/si po poklicu?** *Kay sthee/see poh pokleetsuh?*
I work for...	**Delam za...** *Dehlahm zah...*
I'm a student.	**Sem študent** *m* **/študentka** *f*. *Sehm shtuhdent/shtuhdentkah*
I'm retired.	**Sem upokojenec** *m*/**upokojenka** *f*. *Sehm uhpokoyehnets/uhpokoyehnkah*

Romance

Would you like to go out for a drink/dinner?	**Ali bi šel** *m* **/šla** *f* **na kosilo/pijačo?** *Aalih bee shew /shlah nah kohseeloh/pihyaachoh?*
What are your plans for tonight/tomorrow?	**Kakšne načrte imaš za zvečer/jutri?** *Kaakshneh nahcherteh ihmaash zah zvecher/yootree?*
Can I have your (phone) number?	**Mi daš svojo telefonsko številko?** *Mee dash svoyoh telefonskoh shteveelkoh?*
Can I join you?	**Se ti lahko pridružim?** *Seh tee laa-hkoh prihdroozhim?*
Can I buy you a drink?	**Ti lahko kupim pijačo?** *Tee laa-hkoh koopim pihyaachoh?*
I love you.	**Rad te imam.** *Raad teh ihmaam*

Accepting & Rejecting

I'd love to.	**Z veseljem.** *Z vehsehlyehm*
Where should we meet?	**Kje se dobiva?** *Kyeh seh dohbeevah?*
I'll meet you at the bar/ your hotel.	**v baru/v tvojem hotelu.** *Dohbeevah v baaruh/v tvoyehm hohtehluh*
I'll come by at...	**Prišel** *m*/**Prišla** *f* **bom ob...** *Prihshew m/Prihshlah f bom ob...*
I'm busy.	**Sem zaposlen** *m*/**zaposlena** *f*. *Sehm zapohslehn/zapohslenah*
I'm not interested.	**Me ne zanima.** *Meh neh zahneemah*

Leave me alone. **Pusti me pri miru.** *Poostih meh prih meeruh*
Stop bothering me! **Nehaj težiti!** *Ne-haay tezheetih!*

Food & Drink

Eating Out

Can you recommend a good restaurant/bar?	**Mi lahko priporočite…?** *Mee laa-hkoh prihporochiteh…?* **dobro restavracijo/bar?** *dobroh restahvratsiyoh/bar?*
Is there a traditional/ an inexpensive restaurant nearby?	**Ali je v bližini kakšna tradicionalna/cenovno ugodna restavracija?** *Aalih ye v blizheenih kahkshnah traditsionahlnah/tsenovnoh uhgodnah restahvratsiyah?*
A table for…, please.	**Prosim mizo za…** *Prohsim meezoh zah…*
Can we sit…?	**Ali se lahko usedeva *(dual)*/usedemo *(plural)*…?** *Aalih seh laa-hkoh uhsehdehvah (dual)/uhsehdehmoh (plural)…?*
here/there	**(tu/tam) sem/tja** *serm/tyah*
outside	**(na zewnątrz) zunaj** *zoonaay*
in a non-smoking area	**v prostoru za nekadilce** *v prostoruh zah nehkadeeltseh*
I'm waiting for someone.	**Nekoga čakam.** *Nehkohgah chaakahm*
Where are the toilets?	**Kje je stranišče?** *Kyeh ye strahnishcheh?*
The menu, please.	**Jedilnik prosim.** *Yedeelnik prohsim*
What do you recommend?	**Kaj priporočate?** *Kaay prihpohrochahteh?*
I'd like…	**… prosim.** *…prohsim*
Some more…, please.	**Prosim več…** *Prohsim vech…*
Enjoy your meal!	**Dober tek!** *Dohber tek!*
The check [bill], please.	**Račun, prosim.** *Rahchoon prohsim*
Is service included?	**Ali je postrežba všteta v ceno?** *Aalih ye postrezhbah vshtehtah v tsenoh?*
Can I pay by credit card/have a receipt?	**Ali lahko plačam s kreditno kartico/dobim račun?** *Aalih laa-hkoh plaachahm s kredeetnoh kartitsoh/dohbeem rachoon?*

Breakfast

kruh/maslo *kru-h/maslo*	bread/butter
sir *seer*	cheese
jajce/šunka *yaaytse/shoonka*	egg/ham

marmelada *marmelaada*	jam
žemlje *zhehmlye*	rolls
omleta *ohmlehtah*	omelet
prepečenec *prehpechehnets*	toast
klobasa *klohbaasah*	sausage
jogurt *yogoort*	yogurt

Appetizers

goveja juha *goveya yoo-ha*	clear beef broth
hladetina *hladehtina*	aspic
narezek *narehzek*	assorted cold cuts
pršut *perrshoot*	dry-cured Italian ham
šunka *shoonka*	ham
vložene gobice *wlozhene gohbitse*	pickled mushrooms

Meat

govedina/ovčetina *govehdina/owchehtina*	beef/lamb
svinjina/teletina *svin^yina/teleteena*	pork/veal
čevapčiči *chevaapchichi*	minced meat, grilled in rolled pieces
dunajski zrezek *doonayski zrehzek*	breaded veal escalope
golaž *gohlazh*	gulash
meso na žaru *mesoh na zhaaru*	assorted grilled meat
pečenka *pechehnka*	beef, pork or veal roast
polnjene paprike *pownyene paaprike*	stuffed green peppers
svinjska *sveen^yska*	roasted pork
telečja krača *telehchya kraacha*	veal shank
zelje s klobaso *zehlye s klobaaso*	sauerkraut with sausage

YOU MAY SEE...

vstopnina	cover charge
stalna cena	fixed price
(dnevni) meni	menu (of the day)
postrežba je/ni všteta	service (not) included
posebna ponudba	specials

YOU MAY HEAR...

malo pečeno *maalo pecheno*	rare
srednje pečeno *srehdnye pecheno*	medium
dobro pečeno *dobro pecheno*	well-done

Fish & Seafood

jastog *yaastok*	lobster
jegulja *yegoolya*	eel
lignji *leegnʸi*	deep fried squid
morski list *morski leest*	sole
postrvi *posterrvi*	trout
škampi *shkaampi*	scampi
školjke *shkohRke*	mussels
zobatec *zobaatets*	dentex

Vegetables

fižol *fizhow*	beans
zelje *zehlʸe*	cabbage
kisla kumarica *keesla koomaritsa*	gherkin
leča *lehcha*	lentils
goba *gohba*	mushroom
čebula *cheboola*	onion
krompir *krompeer*	potatoes
paradižnik *paradeezhnik*	tomato
ocvrti jajčevci *otsverrti yaaychewtsi*	deep-fried eggplant
omleta s sirom *omlehta s seerom*	cheese omelet
omleta s šunko *omlehta s shoonko*	ham omelet
ocvrti sir *ochvrthee seer*	breaded fried cheese

Sauces & Condiments

sol *sohl*	Salt
poper *pohper*	Pepper
gorčica *gorcheetsah*	Mustard
kečap *kechap*	Ketchup

Fruit & Dessert

jabolko/banana *yaabowko/banaana*	apple/banana
torta *tohrta*	gateau
sladoled *sladoleht*	ice-cream
limona/pomaranča *limohna/pomaraancha*	lemon/orange
sliva/jagode *sleeva/yaagode*	plum/strawberries
jabolčni zavitek *yaabowchni zaveetek*	thin layers of pastry filled with apple slices and raisins
palačinke *palacheenke*	crepes with jam or nut fillings
potica *poteetsa*	walnut roll

Drinks

The wine list/drink menu, please.	**Vinsko karto/meni pijač, prosim.** *Veenskoh kartoh/ mehnee peeyaach, prohsim*
What do you recommend?	**Kaj priporočate?** *Kaay prihpohrohchahteh?*
I'd like a bottle/glass of red/white wine.	**Steklenico/kozarec črnega/belega vina, prosim.** *Steklehneetsoh/kohzaarets cherrnegah/ behlehgah veenah, prohsim*
The house wine, please.	**Domače vino, prosim.** *Dohmaacheh veenoh, prohsim.*
Another bottle/glass, please.	**Še eno steklenico/en kozarec, prosim.** *Sheh enoh steklehneetsoh/ehn kohzahrets, prohsim*
I'd like a local beer.	**Lokalno pivo, prosim.** *Lohkaalnoh peevoh, prohsim*
Can I buy you a drink?	**Ali ti lahko kupim pijačo?** *Aalih tee la-hkoh koopim pihyaachoh?*
Cheers!	**Na zdravje!** *Nah zdravyeh!*
A coffee/tea, please.	**Kavo/čaj, prosim.** *Kaavoh/chaay, prohsim*
Black.(Czarna.)	**Ruski.** *Rooskih*
With...	**z** *z*
milk	**mlekom** *mlehkom*
sugar	**sladkorjem** *slahdkoryehm*
artificial sweetener	**sladilom** *slahdeelohm*
A..., please.	**Prosim...** *Prohsim...*
juice	**sok** *sohk*
soda [soft drink]	**gazirano pijačo** *gahzeerahnoh pihyaachoh*
(sparkling/still) water	**gazirano/negazirano vodo** *gahzeerahnoh/nehgahzeerahnoh vohdoh*

Leisure Time

Sightseeing

Where's the tourist information office?	**Kje je turistična agencija?** *kyeh ye tooreestichnaagentseeya*
What are the main sights?	**Katere so glavne znamenitosti?** *Kahtehreh soh glaavneh znahmehneetohstih?*
Do you offer tours in English?	**Ali nudite vodene izlete v angleščini?** *Aalih noodihteh vohdehneh izlehteh v angleshchihnih?*
Can I have a map/guide?	**Ali lahko dobim zemljevid/vodič?** *Aalih laa-hkoh dohbeem zemlyehveed/vodeech?*

YOU MAY SEE...

odprto/zaprto *odperrtoh/zaperrtoh*	open/closed
vhod/izhod *vhohd/izhohd*	entrance/exit

Shopping

Where's the market/mall?	**Kje je tržnica/nakupovalni center?** *Kyeh yeh terrzhnitsah/nahkuhpohvaalni tsenterr?*
I'm just looking.	**Samo gledam.** *Sahmoh glehdahm*
Can you help me?	**Mi lahko pomagate?** *Mee laa-hkoh pohmaagahteh?*
I'm being helped.	**Naročil m/Naročila f sem že.** *Nahrochiw/Nahrocheelah sehm zhe*
How much?	**Koliko to stane?** *Kohliko toh staaneh?*
That one, please.	**Tole prosim.** *Tohleh prohsim*
I'd like...	**Rad m/Rada f bi...** *Rat m/Raada f bih...*
That's all.	**To je vse.** *Toh ye vseh*
Where can I pay?	**Kje lahko plačam?** *Kyeh laa-hkoh plaacham?*
I'll pay in cash/by credit card.	**Plačal m/Plačala f bom z gotovino.** *Plaachaw/Plaachahlah bom z gohtohveenoh*
A receipt, please.	**Račun, prosim.** *Rachoon, prohsim*

Sport & Leisure

When's the game?	**Kdaj je tekma?** *Kdaay ye tekmah?*
Where's...?	**Kje je...?** *Kyeh yeh...?*

the beach	**plaža** *plaazha*	
the park	**park** *park*	
the pool	**bazen** *bahzehn*	
Is it safe to swim here?	**Je tukaj varno plavati?** *Yeh tuhkaay vaarno plaavahtih?*	
Can I hire clubs?	**Ali si lahko izposodim palice?** *Aalih see laa-hkoh izposohdim pahlitseh?*	
How much per hour/day?	**Koliko stane ena ura/en dan?** *Kohliko staaneh enah oorah/ ehn daan?*	
How far is it to…?	**Kako daleč je do…?** *Kahkoh daalech yeh doh…?*	
Show me on the map, please.	**Pokaži mi na zemljevidu, prosim.** *Pohkaazhih mee nah zemlyeveeduh, prohsim*	

Going Out

What's there to do at night?	**Kaj lahko počneš tukaj ponoči?** *Kaay laa-hkoh pochnesh tookaay ponochih?*
Do you have a program of events?	**Ali imate razpored prireditev?** *Aalih ihmaateh razpohrehd prihredeetehv?*
What's playing tonight?	**Kdo igra nocoj?** *Kdoh igrah notsoy?*
Where's…?	**Kje je…?** *Kyeh yeh…?*
the downtown area	**staro mestno jedro** *staaroh mestnoh jedroh*
the bar	**bar** *bar*
the dance club	**plesni klub** *plesnih kloob*
Is this area safe at night?	**Ali je ta četrt varna ponoči?** *Aalih ye tah cheterrt varnah pohnochih?*

Baby Essentials

Do you have…?	**Ali imate…?** *Aalih ihmaateh…?*
a baby bottle	**otroško steklenico** *otroshkoh stekleneetsoh*
baby food	**otroško hrano** *otroshkoh hraanoh*
baby wipes	**vlažilne robčke** *vlazheelhne robchkeh*
a car seat	**otroški sedež** *otroshkih sehdezh*
a children'smenu/ portion	**otroški meni/otroške porcije** *otroshkih menee/otroshkeh portseeyeh*
a child's seat/ highchair	**otroški/visoki stol** *otroshkih/vihsohkih stow*
a crib/cot	**zibelko/otroško posteljo** *zeebelkoh/otroshkoh postelyoh*

diapers [nappies]	**plenice za enkratno uporabo** *plehneetseh zah ehnkrahtnoh uhporaaboh*
formula	**formulo za dojenčke** *formuhloh zah doyenchkeh*
a pacifier [dummy]	**dudo** *doodoh*
a playpen	**stajico** *sthaayichoh*
a stroller [pushchair]	**otroški voziček** *otroshkih vohzeechek*
Can I breastfeed the baby here?	**Ali lahko tukaj dojim?** *Aalih laa-hkoh tookaay doyeem?*
Where can I breastfeed/ change the baby?	**Kje lahko nahranim/previjem otroka?** *Kyeh laa-hkoh nahraanihm/prehveeyem otrohkah?*

For Eating Out, see page 248.

Disabled Travelers

Is there…?	**Ali je tukaj…?** *Aalih ye tookay…?*
access for the disabled	**dostop za invalide** *dohstop zah invahleedeh*
a wheelchair ramp	**klančina za invalidske vozičke** *klahncheenah zah invahleedskeh vohzeechkeh*
a disabled-accessible toilet	**stranišče za invalide** *strahnishcheh zah invahleedeh*
I need…	**Potrebujem…** *Potrebooyem…*
assistance	**pomoč** *pomohch*
an elevator [a lift]	**dvigalo** *dvihgaaloh*
a ground-floor room	**sobo v pritličju** *sohboh v pritleechyuh*
Please speak louder.	**Prosim, govorite glasneje.** *Prohsim, govoreeteh glasnehyeh*

Health & Emergencies

Emergencies

Help!	**Na pomoč!** *na pomohch*
Go away!	**Pojdite stran!** *Poydihteh straan!*
Stop, thief!	**Primite tatu!** *Preemite tatoo*
Get a doctor!	**Pokličite zdravnika!** *pokleechite zdrawneeka*
Fire!	**Požar!** *Pozhar!*
I'm lost.	**Zgubil *m*/Zgubila *f* sem se.** *zgubeew/zgubeela serm se*

Can you help me?	**Mi lahko pomagate?** *Mee laa-hkoh pohmaagahteh?*
Call the police!	**Pokličite policijo!** *Pokleechihteh pohlihtseeyoh!*
Where's the police station?	**Kje je policijska postaja?** *Kyeh yeh pohlihtseeyskah postaayah?*
My child is missing.	**Moj otrok se je izgubil.** *Moy otrohk seh ye izgoobil*

In an emergency, dial: **112**

YOU MAY HEAR...

Prosim, izpolnite obrazec. *Prohsim, izpohlnihteh obraazets.*	Fill out this form.
Osebno izkaznico, prosim. *Osehbnoh izkaaznitsoh, prohsim.*	Your ID, please.
Kdaj/Kje se je to zgodilo? *Kdaay/Kyee seh ye toh zgodeeloh?*	When/Where did it happen?
Kako on/ona izgleda? *Kahkoh ohn/ohnah izglehdah?*	What does he/she look like?

Health

I'm sick.	**Bolan (bolna) sem** *bolaan (bowna) serm*
I need an English-speaking doctor.	**Potrebujem angleško govorečega zdravnika.** *Potrebooyehm ahngleshkoh govorechegah zdravneekah*
It hurts here.	**Tukaj me boli.** *Tookaay meh bohleh.*
Where's the pharmacy?	**Kje je lekarna?** *Kyeh ye lehkaarnah?*
I'm (...months) pregnant	**Sem noseča./Sem v...mesecu nosečnosti.** *Sehm nosechah/Sehm v...mehsetsuh nosechnostih*
I'm on...	**Jemljem...** *Yehmlyehm...*
I'm allergic to antibiotics/penicillin.	**Alergijo imam na antibiotike/penicilin.** *Alergeeyoh ihmaam nah ahntihbiyotihkeh/penitsileen*

adaptor **adapter**
aid worker **humanitarni delavec**
and **(i) in**
antiseptic cream **antiseptična krema**
aspirin **aspirin**
baby **dojenček**
a backpack **nahrbtnik**
bad **slab**
bag **torba**
Band-Aid [plasters] **obliži**
bandages **ovoji**
battleground **bojišče**
bee **čebela**
beige **bež**
bikini **bikini**
bird **ptica, ptič**
black **črna**
bland (food) **neokusna (hrana)**
blue **modra**
bottle opener **odpirač za steklenice**
bowl **skleda**
boy **fant**
boyfriend **fant**
bra **modrc**
brown **rjava**
camera **fotoaparat**
can opener **odpirač za konzerve**
cat **mačka**
castle **grad**
charger **polnilnik**
cigarettes **cigarete**
cold **hladno; prehlad**
comb (n) **glavnik**
computer **računalnik**

condoms **kondomi**
contact lens solution **tekočina za
    kontaktne leče**
corkscrew **odpirač za vino**
cup **skodelica**
dangerous **nevarno**
deodorant **dezodorant**
diabetic **diabetik**
dog **pes**
doll **lutka**
fly n **muha**
fork **vilice**
girl **dekle**
girlfriend **dekle**
glass **steklo**
good **dobro**
gray **siva**
great **imeniten**
green **zelena**
a hairbrush **krtača za lase**
hairspray **lak za lase**
horse **konj**
hot **vroče**
husband **mož**
ibuprofen **ibuprofen**
ice **led**
icy **ledeno**
injection **injekcija**
I'd like… **Rad** m/**Rada** f **bi…**
insect repellent **sredstvo proti mrčesu**
jeans **kavbojke**
(steak) knife **nož (za steak)**
lactose intolerant **ne prenaša laktoze**
large **velik**

lighter **vžigalnik**

lion **lev**

lotion [moisturizing cream] **balzam** [vlažilna krema]

love **ljubezen**

market **trg**

matches **vžigalice**

medium **srednje**

museum muzej **moozey**

my **moje**

a nail file **pilica za nohte**

napkin **robec**

nurse **medicinska sestra**

or **ali**

orange **oranžna**

park **park**

partner **partner** m **partnerica** f

pen **pero**

pink **rožnata**

plate **krožnik**

purple **vijoličasta**

pyjamas **pižama**

rain **dež**

a raincoat **dežni plašč**

a (disposable) **razor breetew**

razor blades **britvice**

red **rdeča**

safari **safari**

salty **slano**

sandals **sandali**

sanitary napkins [pads] **damski vložki**

scissors **škarje**

shoes **čevlji**

ski slopes **smučišča**

small **majhno**

sneakers **superge**

snow **sneg**

soap **milo**

socks **nogavice**

spicy **pekoče**

spider **pajek**

spoon **žlica**

a sweater **pulover**

stamp(s) **znamka/znamke**

suitcase **kovček**

sun **sonce**

sunglasses **sončna očala**

sunscreen **krema za sončenje**

supermarket **supermarket**

a sweatshirt **mikica**

a swimsuit **kopalke**

a T-shirt **majica s kratkimi rokavi**

tampons **tamponi**

terrible adj **grozno**

tie **vezati**

tissues **robčki**

toilet paper **toaletni papir**

toothbrush **zobna ščetka**

toothpaste **zobna pasta**

tough (meat) **trdo (meso)**

toy **igrača**

underwear **spodnje perilo**

vegetarian **vegetarijanec** m/ **vegetarijanka** f

vegan **vegahne** m/**vegankah** f

white **bela**

with **z/s**

wife **žena**

without **brez**

yellow **rumena**

your **vaše**

zoo **živalski vrt**